BUILDING BUSINESS WITH CRM

RICHARD KNUDSON

Using Processes in Microsoft Dynamics CRM 2011

Building Business with CRM

Published by

We Speak You Learn, LLC
2928 Straus Lane Ste 200
Colorado Springs, CO 80907

www.crmbizbook.com

Limit of Liability/Disclaimer of Warranty: The author and publisher have taken care in the preparation of this book, but make no expressed or implied warranty of any kind and assume no responsibility for errors or omissions. No liability is assumed for incidental or consequential damages in connection with or arising out of the use of the information or programs contained herein. The advice and strategies contained herein may not be suitable for every situation. This work is sold with the understanding that the publisher is not engaged in rendering legal, accounting, or other professional services. If professional assistance is required, the services of a competent professional person should be sought. Neither the publisher nor the author shall be liable for damages arising herefrom. The fact that an organization or Website is referred to in this work as a citation and/or a potential source of further information does not mean that the author or the publisher endorses the information the organization or Website may provide or recommendations it may make. Further, readers should be aware that Internet Websites listed in this work may have changed or no longer exist between when this work was written and when it is read.

ISBN-13: 978-0-9815118-4-9

ISBN-10: 0-9815118-4-8

This book is dedicated to my wife Mary, son Jack and daughter Bridget. This is appropriate, since without their dedication to me, it never would have been written.

--Richard Knudson

About the Author

Richard Knudson, a thought-leader in the CRM industry, was recently recognized by Microsoft with its Microsoft® Most Valuable Professional (MVP) Award for Dynamics CRM. He is the author of a popular blog, The Dynamics CRM Trick Bag, which like his career is dedicated to helping organizations build business value on the Dynamics CRM platform. As Director of the CRM practice at Wheaton, IL based Magenium Solutions, he assists clients from a wide range of industries in designing, customizing and deploying Dynamics CRM. A few areas of special interest to him include sales and marketing applications of CRM, and extending the Dynamics CRM platform with information from complementary sources such as SharePoint and social media applications.

And not surprisingly, given the topics covered in this book, he's passionate about helping businesses improve their sales, marketing, service and other processes using tools such as Dynamics CRM workflow and dialog processes. Dr. Samuel Johnson said, *"A man is seldom more innocently occupied than when he is engaged in making money"*, and the fundamental truth captured by that quote provides much of the motivation for this book.

Originally from Seattle, he moved to Chicago to attend grad school at the University of Chicago, and now lives in Winnetka, IL with his family. Richard is an avid skier and a White Sox fan, and you can read and comment on his blog at www.DynamicsCRMTrickBag.com.

Richard Knudson, Richard.knudson@hotmail.com

- http://twitter.com/RichardKnudson
- http://www.linkedin.com/in/richardknudson
- http://www.youtube.com/user/RichardKnudson

Credits

Editor
Julie Yack

Assistant Editor
Joy Garscadden

Cover Design
Joe Stammen

Thank you to the following folks that helped us review and validate our content. Without you this book would not have been possible.

Robert Boyers, Philippe Brissaud, Daniel Cai, Jason Cosman, Dylan Haskins , Gareth Howells, Chet Kloss, Jamie Miley, Sheila Shahpari, Mark Smith, Tanguy Touzard, Jerry Weinstock, David Yack

Acknowledgments

This book took a lot longer to write than I'd anticipated, so if you are among the dozens of colleagues, Trick Bag readers, friends and family members who have been growing increasingly skeptical each time I've responded "About another month" to the question "How long until it's done?" I thank you for your patience!

I also want to thank the friendly and efficient staff at the Panera restaurant on Waukegan Road in Glenview IL. I wrote much of the book there, taking copious advantage of the fresh coffee and excellent bandwidth, and while I bought something every time I went there and eventually spent a lot of money, I suspect my *rate* of spending, measured in dollars per minute spent on site, was among the lowest of any of their customers over the period.

My wife Mary has been patient beyond reason, and I hope she can get used to me being around the house again on the weekends. My daughter Bridget became an accomplished sports fan as I was writing this book, and watching White Sox, Bears and Bulls games with her was one of my few and most enjoyable extra-curricular activities. Thanks Missy! My son Jack graduates from high school in 2012 and I am in awe over how much he studies. He probably does five hours of homework for every hour I did in high school. Besides his grades, the good news is that any of the late nights I spent working on the book were also late nights he was studying, so we overlapped a lot more than we would have otherwise. As kids do when they go off to college, he'll be moving out next year, and when I think about him leaving I have to quick think about something else or I get very sad. Both he and his sister hate it when I get all mushy and emotional, so I figured I'd tell them both here how much Mary and I love them, since it's the only place they're less likely to see it than if I wrote it on my Facebook page.

Introduction

To some extent this is an updated version of a previous book I wrote, *Building Workflows in Dynamics CRM 4.0*, but in many ways it's a brand new book. For one thing, the present book's title – *Building Business with CRM* – reflects an important difference between Dynamics CRM 4.0 and the current version of the product: in addition to *workflows*, Dynamics CRM 2011 introduces the new concept of *dialog* processes. Dialogs are guided, step-by-step processes that gather information from a user and do something with the gathered information, much like the familiar wizard experience. I won't go into details now on the differences between workflows and dialogs – that's what the rest of the book is for! – but the addition of a brand new and important feature area is just one reason there's so much more in this book than my previous one.

So, the title of the book has two meanings:

First, I use the term *business process* in the conventional way business people do: to refer to the various processes we use to automate tasks, make outcomes more predictable and repeatable, reduce manual or unnecessarily repetitive work, and the like.

Second, I use it in the Dynamics CRM 2011-specific sense: *workflows* and *dialogs* are the two specific types of *processes* you can build in Dynamics CRM 2011 to automate your organization's business processes.

Semantics aside, I believe that the business process functionality in Dynamics CRM is one of the most important reasons to implement the product, and my goal for this book is to help you understand it.

I start by providing an overview of the Dynamics CRM 2011 business process architecture, and contrast workflows and dialogs. I provide several examples of what you can do with each type of process, and give you a guide to what will be covered in the rest of the book.

Next is a comprehensive treatment of Dynamics CRM 2011 workflows. I cover workflows here at a basic level, and include lots of examples to illustrate the most important concepts. Then the next section applies a similar approach to dialogs: comprehensive, plenty of examples, but not overly complex.

We go on to cover both workflows and dialogs, and add more complex topics. Also, while this is not a book on the more general topic of customizing Dynamics CRM, I do include a few topics and examples in that are outside the strict "workflows and dialogs" scope. For example, the "round-robin" lead assignment workflow I present requires the creation of a custom entity and a custom one-to-many relationship. And in order to understand the appropriateness of workflows for certain tasks it is important to contrast them with alternative approaches, such as whether to use a workflow or a Jscript function to set default values or update fields on Dynamics CRM forms.

Finally, don't be scared off the "Advanced Topics" title later on! By the time you get there you'll have the required ammunition, and in any event the topics aren't really all *that* advanced. This is really just a collection of topics that

    a. are important enough that I wanted to include them;

    b. didn't really fit anywhere else; and

    c. in many cases really *are* somewhat more advanced.

Sample Processes, Exercises and Customizations

The topic of solutions – both managed and unmanaged – is an important one, and from the standpoint of people like myself who make a living assisting organizations in customizing the Dynamics CRM platform one of the most important new feature areas in the current version of the product. While a detailed treatment of building and working with solutions is beyond the scope of this book, I have included some later in the book that introduces the topic and provides what I consider the essential *business process-specific* information you need on the topic.

The reason I mention this here is that the example processes and customizations I cover in the book are all included in a Dynamics CRM 2011 managed solution. As a purchaser of the book you are entitled to use this solution, just head over to the book site to get your download, www.crmbizbook.com .

Typographic Conventions

Here's a guide to the various typographic conventions I use in the book:

Convention	Meaning
Step by Step	Brief introduction to step by step exercise
1. Step 1 2. Step 2	Multiple steps in step by step exercises
Bold-faced type	Indicates the name of a user-interface construct in Dynamics CRM, or the name of a window or dialog. Examples: 1. On the site map, click **Settings**, and then click **Administration**. 2. On the **Administration** page, click **Users**.
Bold-faced italicized type	Indicates something you should type if you're following along with one of the step by step exercises. Examples: Type ***Lead Assignment*** in the **Name** field, and then click **OK**.
	Notes, Tips, Gotchas, New Features These will be items I've found to be a combination of interesting, useful, or problematic...and that were not obvious! I'll also use these to call out important new functionality in Dynamics CRM 2011.

Who is this book for?

The ability to write and maintain workflow and dialog processes should be considered a required skill for Dynamics CRM power-users, system administrators, and customizers, and this book is primarily intended for people in those roles. While some of the content may be difficult for less technical readers, I've tried throughout the book to focus on how the tools can be used to solve real business problems, so if you're a reasonably tech-savvy business manager you should also get plenty out of the content.

How to use this book?

Read it cover to cover or simply skip and jump to the areas you need more details on, there is no single correct way to use this book. You could use it online or carry around the printed book to each of your client visits. Write on the pages, fold the corners and make notes of your own ideas. If you end up building something cool, drop us a note and tell us about it.

Contents overview

Chapter 1 – Introduction – This chapter discusses the importance of business processes in a general sense, and compares and contrasts them across several dimensions: how they vary by business function, across industries, and how they change over time. It also describes some of the most common use-case scenarios for Dynamics CRM business processes, and provides an overview of the characteristic processes applied to the most common record types, such as leads, accounts, contacts, opportunities and cases.

Chapter 2 – Business Process Fundamentals – This chapter explains the fundamentals of building business processes in Dynamics CRM. Topics include creating a new workflow process, workflow properties, automatic and on-demand processes, and the basics of how to use the workflow designer. Also covered are the **actions** that can be performed by workflow processes and how to monitor running processes.

Chapter 3 – Dynamic Values and Business Process Logic - This chapter includes a thorough discussion of dynamic values, a foundation skill required to be productive in designing processes. It also provides detailed coverage of the logical constructs available in business processes: conditional branching and wait conditions.

Chapter 4 – Introducing Dialog Processes – This chapter introduces dialog processes, starting with a comparison of workflow and dialog processes. It covers dialog properties and the basic dialog constructs including pages, prompts and responses. It introduces the actions available in dialog processes that are not available in workflows, discusses the most common kinds of conditional branching in dialogs, and introduces the important dialog-specific ability to query CRM data.

Chapter 5 –Data Advanced Topics in Dialog Processes – This chapter covers three important topics that allow you to create powerful and flexible dialog processes: calling child processes with **Link Child Dialog**, using variables in dialog processes, and the ability to call a dialog with a URL.

Chapter 6 – Security, Troubleshooting and Advanced Topics – This chapter contains a comprehensive coverage of security and Dynamics CRM business processes. It also explains how business processes function as solution components, with a special focus on what you need to do to move processes from one Dynamics CRM organization to another.

Chapter 7 – Business Process Tips, Tricks and Traps – This chapter is a *potpourri*: things I thought you should know but didn't fit anywhere else, troubleshooting tips, interesting facts about business processes that are useful to know, and some commonly encountered traps you should be on the lookout for.

Where do I get the Samples, Exercises and Solutions?

There's no need to re-make the examples in the book unless that's what you really like to do! You can download the samples, solutions and any other supporting files for the book from the book website at www.crmbizbook.com. Make sure to get on the e-mail list to get update notices if we make any changes to the downloads.

What about stuff we screwed up...You know Errata

In the process of writing, everyone sure wanted to make sure it was 100% accurate, but since nobody is perfect, we are sure you might find a few typos or other things that aren't correct. We would love to hear your feedback and will do our best to incorporate it into the next printing of the book. You can look at our website, www.crmbizbook.com for any last minute changes. Feel free to email us as well, info@thecrmbook.com if you find a typo.

Table of Contents

Chapter 1 - Introduction

Why are Business Processes Important?

Before we dive into the specifics of automating business processes using the tools available in Microsoft Dynamics CRM 2011, let's think about business processes in a more general way. As with so many other concepts, when it comes to a definition, Wikipedia is the best place to start.

From Wikipedia[1], we learn that

> A **business process** or **business method** is a collection of related, structured activities or _tasks_[2] that produce a specific service or product (serve a particular goal) for a particular customer or customers. It often can be visualized with a _flowchart_[3] as a sequence of activities.

That's a pretty serviceable definition. It's so general, in fact, that it's hard to imagine _business_ without this notion of business process. And of course there's nothing new about it; what's an HR manual other than the codification of rules, regulations and processes?

The Business Process Value Proposition

And just as Wikipedia is a good place to start for general concept definitions, philosopher Adam Smith is always a good source for fundamental truths regarding business and economics. Read a little more in the Wikipedia article and you can read his famous description of a specific business process, from _The Wealth of Nations_ (1776):

> One man draws out the wire, another straightens it, a third cuts it, a fourth points it, a fifth grinds it at the top for receiving the head: to make the head requires two or three distinct operations: to put it on is a particular business, to whiten the pins is another ... and the important business of making a pin is, in this manner, divided into about eighteen distinct operations, which in some manufactories are all performed by distinct hands, though in others the same man will sometime perform two or three of them.

---

[1] http://en.wikipedia.org/wiki/Business_process
[2] http://en.wikipedia.org/wiki/Task_(project_management)
[3] http://en.wikipedia.org/wiki/Flowchart

However, Smith went a lot further than providing a charmingly specific description of the pin-making process. His *real* contribution was in identifying the productivity improvements made possible by dividing labor into smaller tasks within a larger process. Using the pin example, he asserted that the 18-step process he described allowed ten workers to produce 48,000 pins per day, or 4,800 per worker. He claimed that, working entirely alone, each worker could "...scarce, perhaps, with his utmost industry, make one pin in a day, and certainly could not make twenty."

So the division of labor allowed by well-defined business processes yields productivity improvements, in Smith's pin example, of at least 24,000 percent! Now even allowing for some exaggeration in the pin example (no hard data were presented in The Wealth of Nations), Smith seems to have been the first to articulate the fundamental role of business *processes* in the creation of business *value*.

Wal-Mart provides a more modern example of the potential value of business processes: it's not so much that the things you can buy there can't be found anywhere else; rather it's the efficiency of their processes – purchasing, real estate, supply chain management, store layout, employee training – that gave them the edge over competitors.

So, we know that business process has the potential to create value. Before we dive into the how-to, let's look at some of the ways we can compare and contrast processes.

Comparing Business Processes by Function

Sales processes and methodologies will be familiar to many sales professionals. For example, an organization might adapt the well-known *Solution Selling* process to its specific requirements, with stated goals like the following:

- Faster lead follow up
- Consistent processes for assigning leads and opportunities
- Improved pipeline velocity
- Better pre- and post-sales reporting and analytics
- A more consistent customer experience
- Improved ability of management to control pricing and discounting

Other important goals of sales process improvement might be implicit, un-stated, or de-emphasized:

- Lessen dependence on super-star sales people
- Improve the productivity of average producers or new hires

- Decrease the cost of sales as a percentage of revenue

Of course sales processes aren't the only ones that can be automated. Customer service, service scheduling and management, case and contract management, time tracking and billing, marketing, production processes, vendor management, event management...virtually any area of business can be improved by the implementation of repeatable processes. So within an organization, there will typically be several different functional areas that might have (or need) well-defined business processes. Some of these may be natively available in Dynamics CRM, others would be custom.

And sometimes, these processes can seemingly be at cross purposes. For example, operations and sales processes often appear to have a different flavor: operations want to get it done *right*, sales wants to get it done *fast*! Of course this is a generalization, but one with a kernel of truth, I think. I'll develop this in more detail below, and then later in the book we'll see some examples of how automated processes in Dynamics CRM 2011 can help mitigate the possible tension arising from differences like these.

Comparing Business Processes by Industry

Another way to think about the importance of business processes is to compare different industries. For example, the core production processes of pin manufacturers (Threads magazine has an excellent reference on the subject, by the way[4]), probably don't have any more in common with those of an IT consulting firm than they do with jet plane manufacturing[5].

And while specific details of sales processes will of course be different across industries, a fundamental similarity might apply. For example, a glance at the Prime Resource Group's customer list[6] indicates that organizations in a wide range of industries apparently all benefit from the sales process lessons in the classic book, *Mastering the Complex Sale*[7].

Business Processes Changing over Time

Certainly the last few years have provided plenty of data points on the topic of how business processes can change over time. Several examples can be found in banking and financial services. The mortgage lending sales process, for one, changed drastically following the September 2008 crisis, but there are plenty of less dramatic examples as well.

---

[4] http://www.threadsmagazine.com/item/3830/a-pin-for-every-purpose
[5] http://hondajet.honda.com/designinnovations/allcompositefuselage.aspx
[6] http://www.primemarketingstrategy.com/prime-resource-customers.htm
[7] http://www.primeresourcestore.com/product_p/bkmcsse.htm

I have first-hand experience with one that illustrates the combined impact of several trends. A client of mine is a bank, and in the process of deploying Dynamics CRM 2011. Perhaps more than in many industries, cross-departmental referrals are an important source of leads for bankers: John owns a company that banks with Acme Banccorp., and his relationship manager in commercial banking might refer him to mortgage lending after learning he's looking to buy a house. Now these kinds of referrals are easy to implement and track in a CRM, but there's a relatively new catch: data security and privacy rules might restrict the information one department is allowed to share with another. We're all familiar with being required to respect *opt-outs* in email marketing, but here's an example that might require an *opt-in* requirement for internal referrals.

Another dramatic example comes from the health care industry, in the form of the Health Insurance Portability and Accountability Act. Among other things, HIPAA illustrates the impact *regulation* can have on business process, with the required national standards for health care transactions, and identifiers for the various participants, such as insurance providers, plans, employers.

For a dramatic example of HIPAA's impact, visit the NPPES web site This is the official web site of the National Plan & Provider Enumeration System (NPPES), which was developed by the Centers for Medicare & Medicaid Services (CMS). The CMS, in turn, was charged to develop NPPES by the Department of Health and Human Services, which got the original requirement from Congress when HIPAA was passed in 1996.

One very tangible outcome is the National Provider Identifier (NPI), a ten-digit ID required for health care providers. To see HIPAA in action, follow these steps to search the NPI registry:

1. Navigate to the NPI registry, and click the Organizational Provider link

2. Enter your search criteria, such as zip code, or city, or state.
3. Click the Search button.

Apart from the obvious market research potential (the Norton Sound Health Corporation seems to have a lock on the Nome health care market, which could present an excellent opportunity to an enterprising competitor), think of the implications from a business process standpoint of having an accurate national database of health care providers, each identified with a unique ID. Kick-started by regulation, such a database could enable the creation of powerful cross-organizational business processes, streamline insurance claims processing, reduce fraud, eliminate redundant data entry, and who knows what else.

Another interesting example of how dramatically business processes can change over time – and at the other end of the spectrum from the regulation-imposed HIPAA example – can be seen in the rise of social media, especially in the rapid adoption of social media for business and marketing uses:

- **LinkedIn**, launched in 2003, is the oldest of the mainstream social sites and for a long time has been the most popular social option for professionals.
- **Facebook** targeted the younger set for several years after its 2004 launch, but to me it looks like Facebook is on the verge of passing LinkedIn even with the professional networking crowd.
- **Twitter**, the youngest of the big three, was widely derided as an exercise in e-narcissism after its 2006 launch, but that early ill-informed criticism obviously didn't do much to slow down the micro-blogging network's explosive growth.

In 2011, the business rush to social has become a tsunami. Facebook will likely pass Yahoo as the number one provider of web display ads this year with a little over $2 billion (U.S) compared to Yahoo's predicted $1.62 billion[8]. And *social CRM* might be defined in any number of ways, but its acknowledgement of a single fundamental truth seems unarguable: our *customers* are on social media networks, so our *customer relationship management* apps better come to grips with them as well.

Salesforce.com introduced Chatter in 2010, providing users with a Salesforce-specific wall, the ability to follow and post on records and so forth. In the November 2011 service update, Microsoft introduced the Activity Feeds feature in the form of a managed solution available for both on-premise and Online Dynamics CRM deployments. Activity Feeds provides CRM users with a CRM-specific wall, the ability to follow and post on records and so forth. So, yes, there's a lot of similarity between Chatter and Activity Feeds. And while neither is really social CRM, *per se*, both are indicators of things to come. There are already several social CRM add-ons available from companies such as Sonoma Partners (Vibe), Neudesic (Pulse) and some others. Microsoft will continue to innovate on the social front, and my guess is within a year we'll see options available in the core feature set (or a managed solution!) that extend CRM's data reach into the social sphere.

---

[8] http://www.pronetadvertising.com/articles/facebook-display-ads-on-the-rise-may-overcome-yahoo.html

Automated and Interactive Processes

When it comes to implementing business processes with the assistance of software applications, it's useful to distinguish between automated and interactive processes. At one end of the spectrum, you can characterize an **automated process** as one that is based on a set of rules and executes automatically, as one or more software applications run and communicate with each other.

One of the most familiar examples of an automated process is the auto-responder: a web site visitor provides some personal information on a form, and in return receives an automated email reply, with a white paper attached or the requested trial software key included. Obviously, the more narrowly you define a process, the easier it is to completely automate it. Even a seemingly simple auto-responder process can become complex, depending on the tools you're working with, your business requirements and other factors.

Processes that need a little help in the form of human interaction can be characterized as **interactive processes**. The frequently encountered "wizard" UI is an example of this, as are online surveys, routing and approval processes, the Dynamics CRM lead qualification process (see below) and so forth.

Most business processes feature both automated and interactive components. The next time you see the movie War Games, perhaps you will have a new appreciation for the challenges involved in designing a completely automated process, or "taking the people out of the loop" in the immortal words of Dabney Coleman's Dr. McKittrick.

Business Processes in Dynamics CRM 2011: Dialogs and Workflows

Let's proceed from our conceptual discussion and move on to the main topic covered in this book: how business processes can be implemented using the tools in Dynamics CRM 2011. I want to start with a quote from the Dynamics CRM 2011 SDK, from the topic titled **Processes in Microsoft Dynamics CRM (Formerly Workflows)**:

*Business processes are an integral part of any enterprise software application. A business process can be of two types: **automated** processes that rely solely on communication among applications based on a set of rules, and **interactive** processes that also rely on people to initiate and run the process, and to make the appropriate decisions during the running of the process.*

In Microsoft Dynamics CRM 2011 and Microsoft Dynamics CRM Online, a process enables you to create and manage your automated and interactive business processes.

Notice the distinction between automated and interactive processes. That's why I closed out the previous section with this distinction, which is central to the kinds of business processes you can build with the tools available in Dynamics CRM 2011.

Semantically, *business process* is a general concept, and refers collectively to the two specific types of business processes you can implement in Dynamics CRM 2011: a *workflow* process is entirely automated, and a *dialog* process is interactive. The following table summarizes the differences between the two kinds of processes.

Dialogs	Workflows
Present a wizard-like UI, and always require user input to start and run to completion	**Always run in the background, and do not support user input**
Always run synchronously	Always run asynchronously
Cannot be triggered automatically; must be started by a user	Can be started by a user ("on-demand"), or triggered automatically
Can query CRM data	Cannot query CRM data
Can call child dialogs and pass information to them	Can call child workflows but cannot pass information
Can only be run on one record at a time	Can be run on multiple records

If you are familiar with workflows from Dynamics CRM 4.0, you'll notice that *workflows* are essentially the same in 2011 as in 4.0: they can be triggered automatically or run on demand, but they never expose a UI or pause for input. Dialogs are different: they can never be triggered automatically, and always require user input to complete. To see the difference, let's compare running a *workflow* to running a *dialog*.

As an example, let's compare an on-demand workflow that makes a copy of a selected goal record with a dialog that does essentially the same thing. Goal records have a relatively complex form with lots of required fields, so being able to automate the process of creating new records can save you a lot of time. These are examples of what I refer to as "utility" processes, and we will examine them in detail later in the book. The following figure shows the data grid for the Goal entity, with a single goal record selected.

Notice that both the **Run Workflow** and **Start Dialog** buttons are available in the Process section of the Goals ribbon. If you click **Run Workflow**, the **Look Up Record** dialog opens. If there are any activated workflow processes for the goal record type available to run on-demand, they will be available for selection, as the following figure illustrates for this example:

With a workflow selected, you can click OK and then confirm you want to run it:

After clicking OK, the workflow runs in the background, with no further user input.

Running a dialog process is different. Referring back to Figure 1, if you click the **Start Dialog** button, you will see a similar first step, but here the **Look Up Record** dialog allows you to select any on-demand dialog processes activated for the current record type:

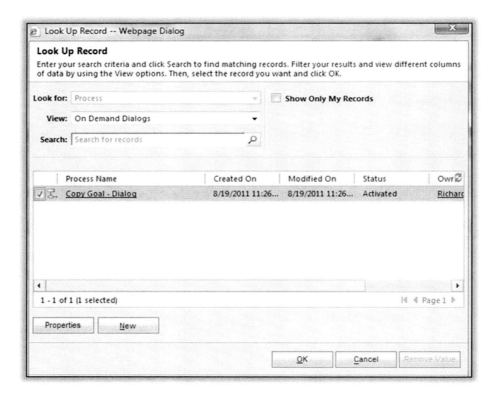

Select the dialog process and click **OK**, and the custom user interface of the dialog process takes over. In this example, the dialog displays a single page, with several prompts, to which the user supplies responses by selecting an option from an option set, entering a value and so forth:

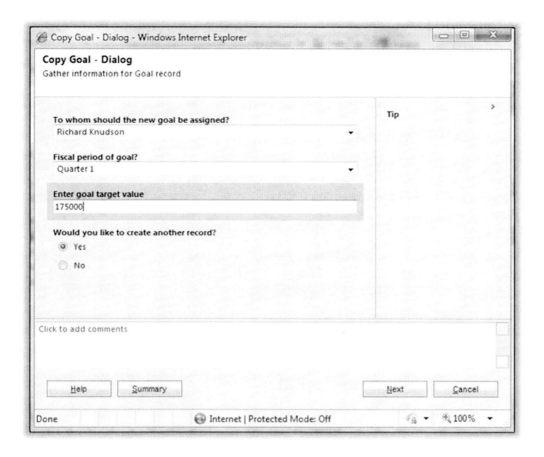

So, workflow processes can be triggered automatically by an event, or they can be run on-demand. In either case, once a workflow is started, it always runs through to completion without any further user input. Dialog processes, on the other hand, must be started by a user, and always require user input to complete.

Business Processes and Utility Process

In this context the term *business process* probably makes you think of lead qualification, sales process, case routing and the like. These kinds of processes are what the Wikipedia definition of business process has in mind, and a large part of this book is devoted to showing you how to create both automatic (workflow) and interactive (dialog) processes like that within Dynamics CRM 2011.

In one sense the term *business process* is a little too narrow, however, since you can use workflows and dialogs to automate lots of activities that might not meet the Wikipedia definition in a strict sense. For example, I frequently use workflows and dialogs as a substitute for repetitive data entry in Dynamics CRM. Here are a few scenarios for which these tools can be valuable time-saving devices:

- Many record types support a bulk-edit function: select several records in a data grid, click **Edit** on the ribbon and perform bulk updates of field values. But some record types don't allow bulk edits. For example, you cannot bulk edit user records, so if you ever need to change the e-mail access settings from Outlook to the E-Mail Router for hundreds of users, you will be happy to know you can do that with a workflow rather than record by record!

- Another thing workflows can do that bulk edit cannot is to apply logic when updating data. Suppose your organization assigns customer records to territories. This can be performed automatically by a workflow, exploiting the capability of workflows to combine conditional logic with record updates. But if you ever need to *change* territory definitions, the fact that you can apply the new territory assignment logic effectively as a "batch process" will come in handy. For example, suppose the following two Visio diagrams represent your current (Old) and desired (New) territory assignment rules:

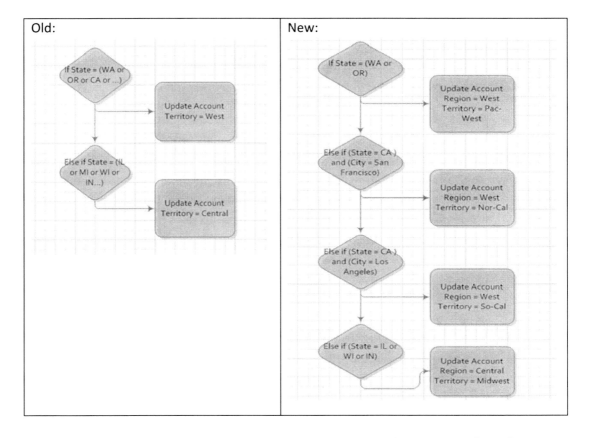

A workflow can run automatically when an account is created or certain values change, and perform the new territory assignment logic. But you can also use the same workflow, exposing it for what's referred to as "on-demand" use, to fix up all of the account records assigned to territories according to the old logic.

- If you've ever wished you could copy a record in Dynamics CRM, you've probably noticed that keyboard shortcuts like **Ctrl+C** and **Ctrl+V** are not available in the application! Luckily, both workflows and dialogs can be used to create a new record and fill its fields with the corresponding values from an existing record. A workflow can "copy" a single record at a time, but since a dialog pauses for user input, you can have it prompt the user if they'd like to make another copy, repeating the process as necessary.

These are all examples of what I refer to as *utility processes*. They aren't necessarily business processes in the conventional sense…but if you know how to use Dynamics CRM 2011 workflows and dialogs to automate them it can sure save you a lot of time!

Organizational, Departmental and Personal Processes

In an organizational context, one very important aspect of business process automation is *who* a process should run for. To explain this concept, I find it useful to contrast organizational, departmental, and personal processes. Here's an example to illustrate:

- Suppose an organization has a single customer service or call-center department, and may want the same case-routing process applied whenever a case is created, regardless of who in the organization creates it. Let's refer to this as an **organizational process**.
- The same organization has several different sales departments, however. For example, a bank might have mortgage lending, commercial, retail banking, and so forth. Each of these different departments may have a unique sales process, and in Dynamics CRM terms that means when an opportunity record is created, it very much matters who it was created by! Each of these departments may want an automated sales/pipeline process, but each wants its own unique **departmental process**.
- And even in the most regimented, process-driven organization, there still may be some scope for individual initiative. Even if sending out "happy birthday" emails is not automated at the organizational or departmental levels, an individual sales representative might want to do it herself, or at least be reminded when birthdays or other milestones are approaching. Let's call this an **individual process**. (The Dynamics CRM security model can be used to restrict the records an individual process can be applied to; security will be covered in detail later in the book.)

The business process toolset in Dynamics CRM 2011 supports all of these scenarios, plus a lot more. This last distinction – organizational, departmental and personal processes – provides a nice segue into the more specific implementation topics included in the rest of the book. As you will see, the important topic of business process *security* – who can create workflows and dialogs, and when they are created, which users can run them – is what this distinction has to do with, and it is critically important to successfully implementing business processes in Dynamics CRM 2011.

Dynamics CRM Entities and Business Processes

One good way to get some intuition about Dynamics CRM business processes is to think about the different kinds of records (or "entities" in CRM geek-speak) you will write them for, and how the characteristics of those entities influence the kinds of workflows you might create. In the rest of this section I provide overviews of the most frequently encountered entities, and several examples of the characteristic workflows and dialogs you will build for them.

Leads

In Dynamics CRM, the lead record type is conventionally used to store information about *prospective* customers. A lead can contain information about a person, about an organization, about a sales opportunity...or any combination of those three things. Here are a couple of the most important determinants of "when something should be a lead record":

- Leads are often used for situations when you need more or better information, aren't sure there's a fit and so forth.
- Leads are not intended as "permanent" records: leads generally go through a qualification process, at the end of which they are either *qualified* (and converted to "customer" records), or *disqualified*.

For the purposes of this discussion, the main point is that lead records are "process-centric": there's a goal (qualify the lead, or disqualify it), and a process to help achieve that goal. And when we use a term like "qualify" in this context, we mean something specific, such as clicking the **Qualify** button on the lead form, which will open a dialog like the following one:

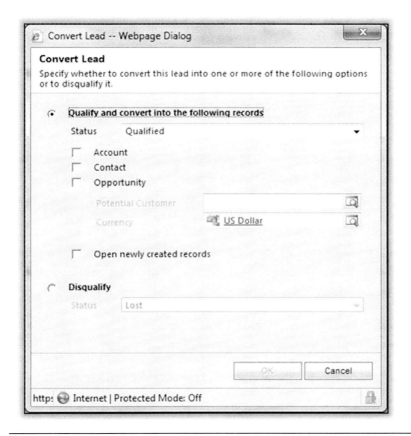

As you can see from the figure, when you qualify a lead, you can convert it to an account, or a contact, or both. You can also convert it to an opportunity, but if you do, you must also convert it to an account or a contact, or both. And if you do, you better remember to select the **Open newly created records** checkbox or you'll never remember which records you created!

As you can see, the default lead conversion process is flexible, and with flexibility comes complexity. Many organizations don't need that much flexibility, and don't want that much complexity. Here are two requests I encounter frequently:

- Whenever we convert a lead, we always convert it to a contact record. Can't you make all those other check-boxes go away?
- When we convert leads we sometimes create opportunities, but if we do we always want the opportunity attached to an account record. Can't you make the contact check-box go away?

Workflows can be used to accommodate these requests, and in Dynamics CRM 2011, a custom dialog process can even be exposed from a custom button on the ribbon to replace the standard **Qualify** button.

Accounts, Contacts

The account and contact record types in Dynamics CRM are referred to collectively as the "customer" record types. Unlike leads, account and contact records should generally be thought of as permanent fixtures of your CRM database.

While they are similar in that both are considered customer records, they are different in an obvious way: an account is an organization, and a contact is a person. Often these are used to model the relationship between an employer and an employee, but this is not a requirement.

Also, while they are referred to as customer records, these records can certainly be used to store information about organizations and people besides the ones you sell things to! For example, in addition to using accounts to store information about customers, many organizations also use them to store information about vendors, suppliers, resellers, competitors, and so forth.

Account and contact records tend to be the most static records, in the sense that they remain in the same state (a CRM status value of **Active**) longer than most other records.

Typical business processes we encounter for these customer records will include things like:

- **Automatically updating fields**. When a record is created, update certain field values automatically, based on the values of other ones. For example, when a new account record is saved, a workflow might update the territory value automatically, based on the value of the zip code.
- **Automatically assigning records.** If an account record has a certain value for the industry field, or has annual revenue above a certain level, a workflow might assign the record to the appropriate sales rep or sales manager.
- **Sending emails.** Workflows can send emails to account or contact records, and when you send an email with a workflow you can use an email template. Given the frequency of e-mail communication with our customers, anything we can do to automate it is potentially useful, and this is definitely true when it comes to business processes and emails!

Opportunities

In Dynamics CRM, the Opportunity entity represents a potential sale and will often have a sales process. Opportunities are always attached to a customer (account or contact) record, and have status values of **Open**, **Won**, or **Lost**. Opportunity records are among the most process-centric record types in Dynamics CRM, with the desired outcome generally being a closed sale. Here are a few of the business objectives you can accomplish by applying workflow and dialog processes to opportunities in Dynamics CRM 2011:

- Create opportunity records with dialog processes.
- Apply naming conventions to opportunity records.
- Implement a specific sales process with an automatic workflow.
- Create copies of opportunity records with either workflow or dialog processes.
- Automatically create activity records or send e-mails when an opportunity reaches a stage in a sales process.
- Enforce business rules by automatically closing out past-due opportunities.

Cases

The Case entity is used to keep track of customer incidents, issues... and, well *cases*. Just like opportunities, cases must always be attached to an account or contact record. Case records have status values of **Active** or **Resolved**. The goal of most customer service organizations is to *resolve* a case – so although we think of cases as being "reactive", as compared to the "proactive" sales nature of opportunities, they're similar to opportunities in the sense of being very process-centric, generally with a well-defined end-point. Some typical business processes for cases include the following:

- Conditionally route cases to specific queues.
- Implement escalation processes to enforce service level agreements.
- Notify customers of case creation, case number.
- Automatically create a case record for a customer, based on information entered onto a web site or portal page.

Activities

Dynamics CRM has a number of different record types all classified as activities. The simplest way to see this is to click **New Activity** on the File menu, as you see here:

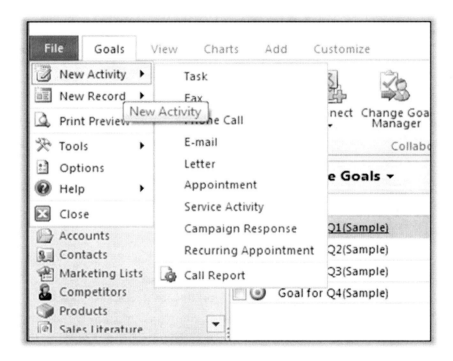

Dynamics CRM workflows can both *create* activity records, and can be made to run automatically when an activity record is *created*. Both are important scenarios and you will see many examples in the rest of the book. Here are some common workflow scenarios involving activity records:

- Activities such as emails, phone calls and appointments often make up the actual *work* of a business process. So, workflows for opportunities and cases will often create and assign those activities.

- A workflow might create an activity record, assign it to a user or route it to a queue, and then wait until the activity is completed. In Dynamics CRM terms, an activity is "completed" when its **Activity Status** is equal to **Completed**, so that's a condition your workflows will often check for.

- Another equally common scenario is for the workflow to both create *and* complete an activity. Probably the most frequent example of this is with email. Dynamics CRM workflows can automatically send emails; for example, to notify a user of an important event, or to send an "auto-responder" email to a web site visitor who filled out a form requesting information. On the other hand, it's also possible for a workflow to *create an e-mail record but not send it*. This can be useful because it allows a user to customize or personalize an email before it is sent.

Summary

Before diving down into detail, I wanted to start with some intuition. My goals aren't as grandiose as to put forth a General Theory of Workflows...but on the other hand, I would like to give you a good feel for what you can do, and the business problems you can solve with workflows.

Think of it as the *Zen* of Dynamics CRM business process, and try to see things from the perspective of the record types you will be writing workflows and dialogs *for*:

- **Account** and **Contact** records want to be with you for a long time. They need good owners and good data.

- **Lead** records want to be converted to accounts or contacts (or both, not to mention opportunities). They need a good process to help them in their conversion, and the easier the process is to perform, the better.

- **Opportunities** ache to be closed as won. They often need a process to get them there, and although they do not necessarily care about being closed by a specific date, they don't want to sit there and languish.

- **Cases** long to be resolved. Similar to opportunities, they often need a well-defined process to help them get there. More so than opportunities, cases want to be resolved by a specific date and often should be escalated if they aren't. Cases often use routing and queues as part of their processes.

- Workflows can also be written for any custom entities you create. And since the characteristics of custom entities are only limited by your imagination (and your business requirements), the same can be said of the processes you might want to apply to them, in the form of Dynamics CRM 2011 workflows and dialog processes.

I struggled a little bit with how to divide the coverage between workflow and dialog processes. Since 90% or more of the fundamental skills required for business process competency – properties, actions, dynamic values, conditional logic – are exactly the same for workflow and dialog processes, an argument could be made to cover them together, illustrating each of them with example processes of both types. I decided against that approach, however, because I wanted to have a comprehensive treatment of dialog processes in one place. My thinking was that if you already know the basics of workflow processes – which after all haven't changed too dramatically from the previous version – this approach would be better.

With that, here's the plan for the rest of the book:

- Chapter 2 – Business Process Fundamentals and Workflows – starts with a discussion of business process properties, covering both workflow and dialog processes. The rest of Chapter 2 focuses specifically on workflow processes: first introducing the workflow design environment and then with a comprehensive treatment of the actions that can be performed by workflows.
- Chapter 3 – Dynamic Values and Business Process Logic -covers the topics of dynamic values and flow of control. While both chapters 2 and 3 cover the topics and present examples in the specific context of *workflow* processes, most of the topics are equally applicable to dialog processes. When important, I will point out differences.
- In Chapter 4 - Introducing Dialog Processes I introduce dialog processes, covering the basic Page and Prompt/Response constructs, the actions that can be performed by dialogs, how data types work and the basics of querying CRM data.
- Chapter 5 – Advanced Topics in Dialog Processes – extends the discussion to dynamic queries, recursive dialogs, using variables, and calling dialog processes with URLs. The theme of both chapters 4 and 5 is essentially "all the stuff you can do with dialogs that you cannot do with workflows". So while the topics in chapters 2 and 3, although covered in a workflow context, generally apply to both types of processes, the topics in chapters 4 and 5 are in most cases specific to dialogs.
- Chapter 6 - Security, Troubleshooting and Advanced Topics - covers security issues, troubleshooting and other advanced topics.
- Chapter 7 – Business Process Tips, Tricks and Traps – applies all of the earlier topics to creating workflows and dialogs for all kinds of tricky situations you're likely to encounter out there.

Chapter 2 - Business Process Fundamentals and Workflows

Creating a Workflow Process

A Dynamics CRM user with any of the default security roles can create a business process of either the Workflow or Dialog category. Let's start with the following step by step procedure to create an automatic workflow to assign leads. For now we will simply create and configure the most basic of the properties of the workflow; a little later in the chapter we will return to it and add the lead assignment logic.

Step by Step: Create a Workflow Process

1. On the site map (left navigation) click **Settings**, and then click **Processes** in the **Process Center** section, it's near the bottom.
2. Above the processes data grid, click **New**.
3. In the New Process dialog, provide the following values:
   a. Provide an appropriate name for the new process (in this example, *Lead Assignment*)
   b. Select **Lead** in the **Entity** drop-down,
   c. In the **Type** field, select the **New blank process** option.

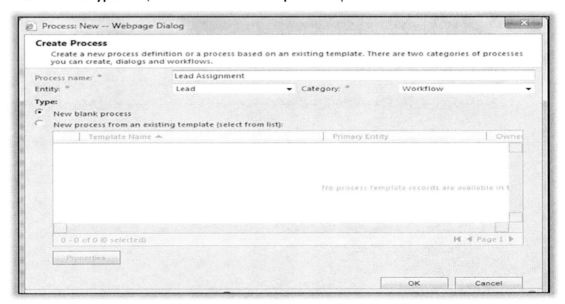

4. Then click **OK**. The workflow designer opens.
5. In the **Options for Automatic Processes** section:
   a. Select **Organization** in the Scope field
   b. Select the **Record is created** option in the **Start when** section.

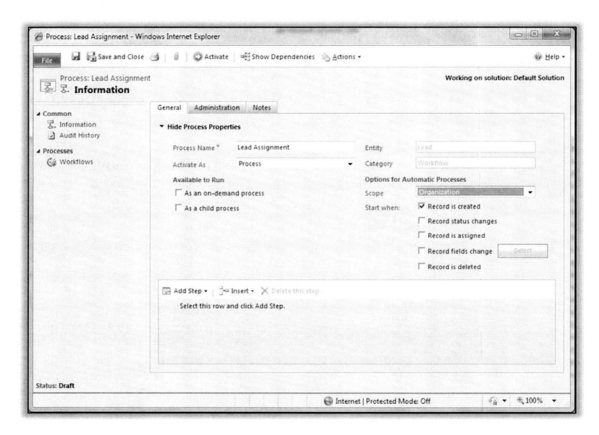

6. Click on **Hide Process Properties** to free up more space in the workflow designer. This is a toggle switch, so you can minimize or maximize the **Properties** section as necessary.

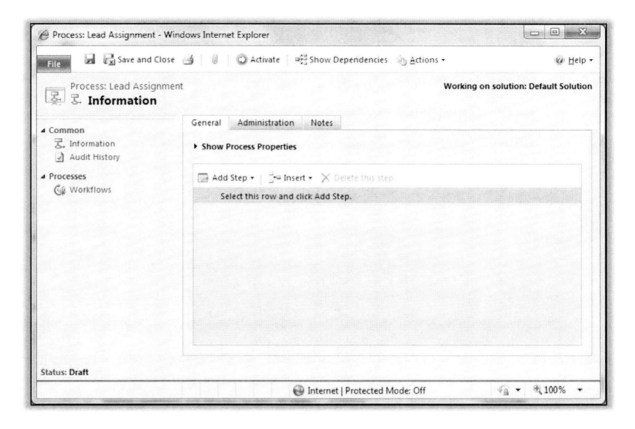

7. Click the **Administration** tab. Dynamics CRM business processes are user-owned entities, so the user creating the workflow is by default the **Owner**. Use the **Description** field to document the purpose of the workflow. Optionally, select the **Automatically delete completed workflow jobs** option.

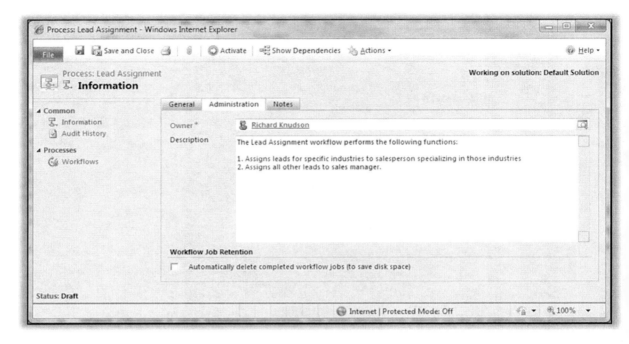

8. Click the **Notes** tab. As a best practice, consider adding Notes to document changes made to a business process. Or click the **Attach a File** button on the ribbon to add a Visio diagram describing the workflow process.

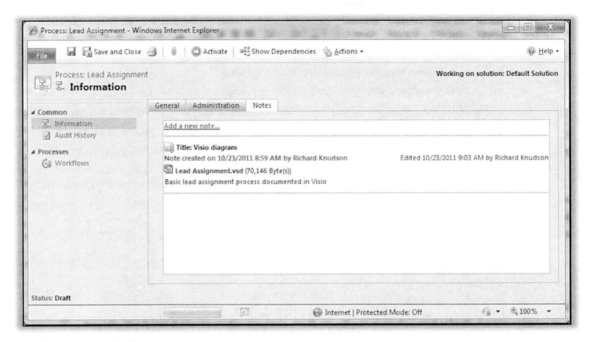

9. Click **Save and Close**.

In the next section we will discuss workflow process properties in more detail. But first I want to explain a couple of points raised by the Administration and Notes tabs we just saw.

Workflow Administration Properties

Workflows and dialogs are user-owned entities but, unlike other user owned entities they cannot be assigned to teams. This has important implications for a more detailed discussion of workflow security, which we will have later in the book.

Also, the option to automatically delete completed workflow jobs warrants further discussion. Workflows run as **system jobs.** This is a special record type used to track asynchronous processes such as bulk record deletions, bulk email, automatic checks for duplicate records...and workflows. You can see this by creating an advanced find query for system jobs and filtering for **system job type** value of **workflows**. (This is discussed in more detail later in the book.) Normally, a workflow runs and finishes with a status of **completed**. However, the workflow designer also allows you to stop a workflow with a status of canceled. This can be a useful troubleshooting technique, and will be discussed in more detail later in the book. Regarding the **Automatically delete completed workflow jobs** option, the main point is that if this option is selected, all system jobs for that workflow with a status value of completed will be deleted automatically. Workflow jobs with a status of **canceled** will not be deleted, so if you select this option you can still use the troubleshooting technique just mentioned.

Use Visio Diagrams to Design Business Processes

Another recommendation, if you don't have another visual tool you prefer, is to develop some basic Visio skills and use the application to document the workflow and dialog processes you need to implement in Dynamics CRM. Generally speaking, if a process is not well-defined enough to diagram it in Visio, it's not well-defined enough to implement in Dynamics CRM!

For example, the following figure shows a simple Visio diagram for the simple Lead Assignment workflow we will complete in the next section.

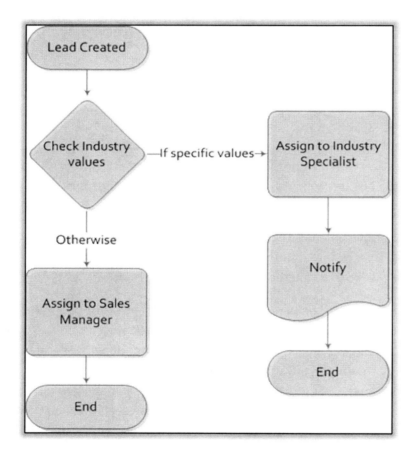

For most of the examples in this book, I've used Visio 2010, and when I create a new Visio diagram, I usually base it on the template, **Basic Flowchart (US Units)**.

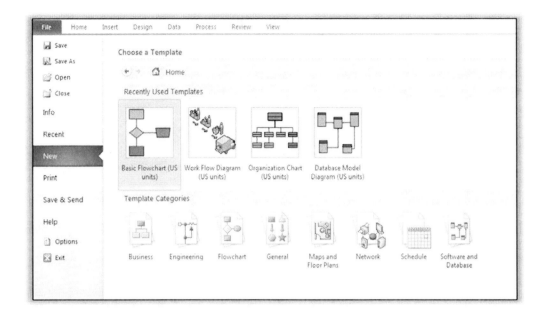

Workflow Properties

When creating a new business process, the first thing you need to do is specify its properties. Properties specify the basic behavior of a process, such as for whom it runs for and for which events trigger it. Workflow processes properties are described in the following table. The entity and category options cannot be changed once the process is saved.

Property	Possible Values	Description
Process Name	Text field	The name of the workflow
Entity	Dynamics CRM entities	The primary entity for which the workflow is designed (selected in New Process dialog; read only in designer)
Category	<ul><li>Workflow</li><li>Dialog</li></ul>	(selected in New Process dialog; read only in designer)
Options for Automatic Processes:		
Scope	<ul><li>Organization</li><li>Parent-Child Business Unit</li><li>Business Unit</li><li>User</li></ul>	Only applies to automatic workflows: answers the question, "for which users will this workflow run?" This is discussed in detail in the next section and later in the book in the section on workflow security.
Start When	<ul><li>Record is created</li><li>Record status changes</li></ul>	Only applies to automatic workflows: answers the question, "which events will trigger this

	• Record is assigned • Record fields change • Record is deleted	process?" Your business logic will determine which events should trigger a process; several examples are presented in the next section.
Available to Run:		
As an on-demand process	Yes or No checkbox	Can the workflow be run manually?
As a child process	Yes or No checkbox	Can the workflow be called from another workflow?
Activate as	• Process • Template	Select Process to activate as a workflow Select Template to activate as a template from which you can create other workflows

Name, Primary Entity, and Type

Name

Choose a name that is short and descriptive. If you are going to be creating many workflows for your organization it's best to come up with naming conventions before starting out. One important thing to keep in mind is that workflow names are not required to be unique. But it will obviously be very confusing to have multiple workflows doing different things for the same entity...all with the same name! So however you define your workflow naming conventions, we recommend you start with a rule saying "no two workflows shall have the same name" (unfortunately, you cannot use Dynamics CRM built-in duplicate checking to create a duplicate detection rule on the Workflow entity, so you will need to enforce a rule like this manually).

Also, you should be aware that the default view for processes is **My Processes**, which means that you might not even be aware of a process with the same name if it's owned by another user. So you should get in the habit of checking the **All Processes** view, or consider customizing the Process entity to make the **All Processes** view the default public view.

Primary Entity

One of the most basic facts about Dynamics CRM workflows is that they are always associated with a primary entity. So when you create a new workflow, one of the required properties you need to set is the entity – Account, Contact, Opportunity, Case, or any custom entity – for which the workflow is designed. This cannot be changed once the workflow is saved.

Activate As: Process or Process Template

Dynamics CRM processes can either be created "from scratch", or from a pre-existing process template. Process templates are often helpful if you need to create many workflows with a similar structure, especially if the structure is complex or the workflow is large. Rather than create a complex process ten times with just a few differences, you can create a template, and then create the ten workflows based on the template. Then you only need to implement the differences between the workflows, and save yourself some time.

After you save a process, you cannot change its primary entity or the category. However, you can change the **Activate As** option. This means that if you create a process and only later decide it would make a good template for other processes, you can always turn it into a process template.

Options for Automatic Processes

Notice that in the previous example, the **Scope** value was set to **Organization**, and **Start when** was set to **Record is created**. These are both in the **Options for Automatic Processes** section, since both of these settings only apply to processes that run automatically. **Scope** determines which users will trigger an automatic workflow, and **Start when** determines the events that will cause the workflow to run. Automatic workflows are important and can be confusing at first. We will spend plenty of time on them, both in this and subsequent chapters, but let's start with three of the most important points about them.

1. *Scope only matters for automatic processes, and only if one of the **Start when** checkboxes is selected is a workflow automatic.* I talk to people all the time who find it confusing that while an on-demand process is specified with a checkbox of the same name, there's no corresponding checkbox for an automatic process. That is, you implicitly designate a process as automatic by ticking off one of the Start when checkboxes. *And only if one of the Start when triggers is selected does Scope matter*.
2. A business process *can* be both automatic and available for on-demand use. Which it *should* be depends on your business requirements, but it's important to note that both can be selected.
3. Only workflows can be automatic processes. So if you compare the *workflow* designer with the *dialog* designer the most obvious difference is that the latter doesn't have an **Options for Automatic Processes** section.

With that as background, let's cover **Scope** and **Start when** options for automatic processes.

Scope

When you create an automatic workflow for a user-owned entity, there are four values available in the Scope list: User, Business Unit, Parent: Child Business Unit, and Organization. The scope value refers to the level of "availability" of the workflow; who in the organization it will run for. Scope is analogous to the Access Level concept from the security model, although it's important to note that Scope can never supersede security. Scope refers to owner of the process itself, not the target records of the process.

Scope	Who will it run for?
User	Just the user who owns the workflow
Business Unit	The user who owns the workflow plus anybody else in the same business unit
Parent: Child Business Unit	The user who owns the workflow, anybody else in the same business unit, plus anybody in a child business unit
Organization	Everybody in the organization

While scope is analogous to the access level concept within a security role, it works somewhat differently. Here's an example to illustrate the importance of the scope concept and how it behaves differently than you might expect.

Suppose you have several different business units and each requires a different sales process. You can design an automatic workflow that runs when an opportunity record is created, but if its scope is **Organization** it will be triggered when *any* user in the entire organization creates an opportunity record. If on the other hand its scope is set to **Business Unit**, it will only be triggered when an opportunity is created by a user in the same business unit as the workflow's owner. This sounds promising, and it turns out to be the correct approach when you need to target an automatic business process like this.

But there's a catch you need to be aware of: Only the owner of a business process can activate it, and when a process is assigned it is deactivated. So, suppose you, as a system administrator in the root business unit, create an automatic workflow with a scope of business unit. If you activate it, it will only run for other users in the root business unit. If you assign it to a user in a child business unit it becomes deactivated and only the new owner can activate it. You might think that you can maintain ownership, activate it, and share it to a user or team, but sharing has no impact on scope. So, there's really no way around the requirement that department-specific processes must be owned and activated by a user in the appropriate business unit.

Triggering Automatic Workflows

After setting the Scope for an automatic workflow, you need to decide which event will cause it to run – how should the workflow be triggered?

Start When	Important Points to Keep in Mind
Record is created	Workflows triggered by **Record is created** are useful for automating everything that should happen when a new record is created. Default values in the primary or related entities, notifications, task assignments, are all good candidates for automation with this trigger.
Record status changes	The "status" referred to here is the **Status**, not the **Status Reason** we discussed above. This is an important distinction, because you will often have multiple Status Reason values for the same Status value. *Only if the Status value changes will this workflow trigger fire.*
Record is assigned	The **Record is assigned** trigger fires when the value of the **Owner** field changes. A common use is to send a notification e-mail or assign a task to the new owner of a record.
Record fields change	Use this trigger to fire a workflow when specific fields change on a record. For example, a sales process workflow written for the opportunity entity could be triggered by changes to a field tracking the sales stage. Or if a case record's priority is changed to High, an automatic workflow can route the case to an appropriate queue.
Record is deleted	This allows you to trigger an action *after* a record is deleted. It's important to stress "after", since by the time a workflow on the delete trigger runs, the record it runs against is already deleted. But the workflow engine holds all of the field values of the deleted record in memory while the workflow runs, so while you cannot use a workflow triggered by the Record is deleted trigger to roll back a delete, if necessary you can write out any of a deleted record's field values to another record.

Examples of Triggering Automatic Process

Here are several examples to illustrate the most important points about automatic workflows that might not be obvious at first (at least, they were not to me!) and that can have important implications for how they run.

Record is created vs. **Record fields change**
When a record is saved for the first time, the **Record fields change** trigger does not fire. So if you need something to happen when a field changes even if the record is being saved for the first time, you should specify both **Record is created** and **Record fields change** as **Start When** options.

Record status changes vs. **Record fields change**
If you want something to happen when a record's status changes, use the **Record status changes** trigger. If you want something to happen when the value of **Status Reason** changes, use **Record fields change**. For example, an open lead can have different Status Reason values, and you might want a workflow to send a notification email when it changes from **New** to **Contacted**. For that scenario, the Record fields change trigger should be used. But if you want to be notified when a lead is qualified or disqualified, that requires an automatic workflow using the Record status changes trigger.

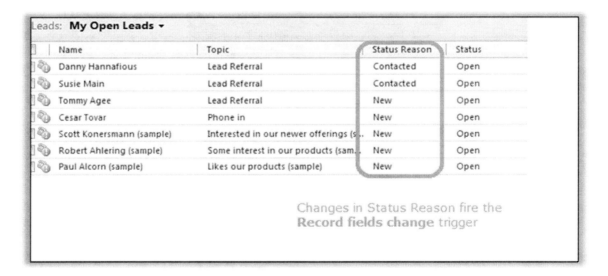

Different processes triggered by the same event
Watch out for situations when different workflow processes are triggered by the same event for the same entity. This will not necessarily cause problems, but it can. For example, an

organizational sales process workflow is often started by the **Record is created** trigger, and a different workflow started by the same trigger might perform different functions, specific to a user or a department. Workflows like that *can* co-exist peacefully, but can also conflict. For example, suppose you have two different workflow processes, each written for the case entity, each with the same scope, and each run automatically on the **Record is created** trigger.. The first one routes all cases to a specific queue, and the second one routes all cases to a different queue. That is an example of colliding workflows, and they definitely do not live in harmony!

Infinite loops

Another easily made mistake is to create an automatic workflow that triggers itself. For example, suppose you wanted to enforce your organization's naming conventions for sales opportunities. You might create an automatic workflow on the opportunity entity and have it run automatically when a record is created. You could use the **Update Record** action in the workflow designer to dynamically populate the **Topic** field with appropriate values. If a workflow like this is only triggered by the Record is created event, it will work fine. But suppose you're worried about users making *changes* to the topic field, and you decide to *also* trigger the workflow when the topic field changes. The following figure illustrates what such a workflow might look like in the designer:

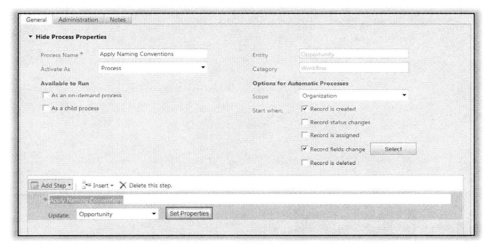

The Record fields change option is selected, and the field change that triggers it is the Topic field. But remember that the Update step *changes* the topic field, which will fire the Record fields change trigger. The following figure illustrates what this might look like from the context of an opportunity form:

Eventually the infinite loop is detected and the workflows stop firing, as you can tell by opening the very last system job (the one with the **Failed** status reason):

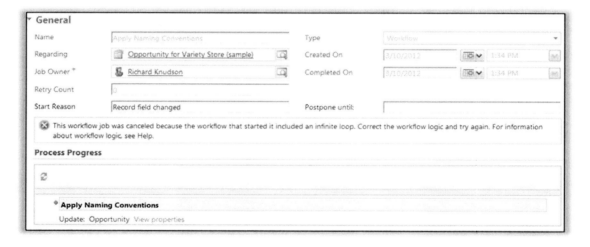

Automatic workflows are "post-event" processes

When any of these automatic workflows are triggered, the triggering event has already happened, and if any fields have been changed, the workflow engine only has access to the new values, not the old ones. It would often be convenient to have access to both the previous and the current values of changed fields, and the fact that you can't get these in a workflow does limit what you can do. For example, sales managers often want to answer questions like whether their opportunities are progressing through the stages of a sales process, or how fast they're progressing (e.g., how long on average opportunities stay in the different stages). In my experience, these are in the category of "things that business people reasonably assume Dynamics CRM can just (easily) *do*, but that it can't (easily)." In fact, this is a good example of where the workflow designer is *not* the right tool for the job, and where you'd be better off with either JavaScript (Jscript) or a Plugin. While JScript and Plugin customizations are not covered in this book, it's important for you to know what kind of problems you can solve with workflows and dialogs...as well as which ones you can't, and this is an example of the latter.

Available to Run -- On Demand

If you want a workflow to be available for a user to run manually, make sure the **As an on-demand process** checkbox is selected in the **Available to Run** section of workflow properties. If an entity has an on-demand process with a status of activated, you can run the process – whether a workflow or a dialog – by selecting it from the ribbon on the data grid or the form for the entity. The process of running an on-demand process is illustrated in the following figures.

Suppose there's an activated on-demand workflow available for the lead entity. From the leads data grid you can click the **Run Workflow** button in the **Process** section of the ribbon, highlighted here.

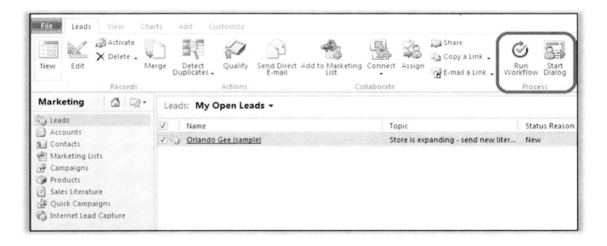

After clicking **Run Workflow** you can use the **Lookup Record** dialog to select the workflow and click **OK** to run it.

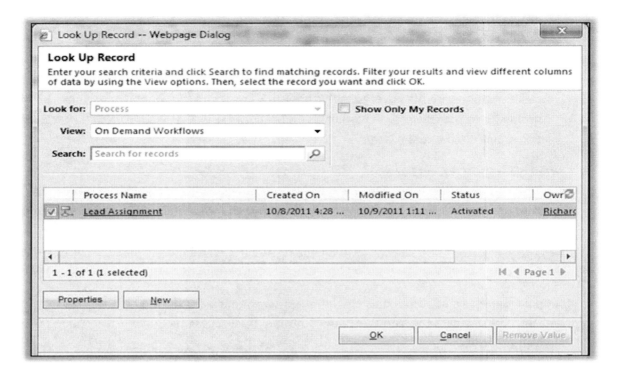

Again, the process will only appear in the list if the process is activated, and if the **As an on-demand process** option is selected, and if the current user is included in the scope of the particular workflow.

Sometimes you will have a slightly different experience, like the one illustrated in the following figure.

Notice here that the button on the ribbon is labeled **Process**, and only after clicking it do you see the **Run Workflow** and **Start Dialog** buttons. This only happens when there's not enough room to display both buttons on the ribbon; so it can be a little confusing for new users if they resize the window and see a slightly different experience.

If you want to run an on-demand process for a single record, you can also run it from the record's form.

Again, if the form is sized differently or if you're running at a lower screen resolution, those two buttons might not be on the ribbon, and only available after clicking the **Process** drop-down as shown here.

Here are some of the more common uses of on-demand processes.

Bulk Edits and Intelligent Data Updates

Sometimes you may want to update multiple records at the same time, rather than one by one. On-demand workflows can be used for this. Sometimes "bulk-editing" of records can be used instead, but not always. Here are several scenarios that would require an on-demand workflow to edit multiple records in one pass.

- Suppose you're the System Administrator and you need to make bulk changes to user records, such as changing address fields or e-mail access settings. Bulk edit is not available for the User entity (along with plenty of other entities in CRM), so your best option here would be an on demand workflow.
- Even for entities for which bulk edit is enabled, there are several scenarios where an on-demand workflow is a better approach.
    - Some fields cannot be changed with a bulk edit. For example, while you can perform bulk edit on contact records, you cannot change the Parent Customer lookup field (ever) with a bulk edit, but you can update it with an on-demand workflow.
    - A bulk edit can add or change values in a field, but it cannot *clear* values from a field. The workflow designer provides a handy Clear operator designed precisely for this purpose.
    - A bulk edit applies the same change to every record selected. An on-demand workflow can apply conditional logic to perform updates. So you might select several records, apply the same on-demand workflow to all of them, and the workflow itself can include conditional logic to assign them to different users based on the value of the Territory field.

Discretionary Business Processes

Sometimes business processes need to involve discretion or are difficult to automate entirely. Here are a few examples of this.

- A sales manager might want to "audit" opportunities, emailing reminders out to the sales team to close out past-due opportunity records. We'll see later how to implement this functionality as part of a process, with an automatic workflow. But with an on-demand workflow, a sales manager can reserve the option to only perform this audit periodically, making the decision when to do so based on factors that might change from time to time or might be hard to model in an automatic process.
- Even if a sales process can be entirely automated, you may sometimes implement a process after records have been created, and want to apply it to some or all of those existing records. For situations like this an automatic workflow might also be made available for occasional on-demand use.

Dialog Processes

Dialog processes – new in Dynamics CRM 2011 – cannot be run automatically and usually *must* be run as on-demand processes. I use the term usually because they can also be available to run as a child process, which is discussed next.

<table>
<tr>
<td></td>
<td>Automatic vs. On-Demand Workflow Processes
When I build and automatic process, I usually have the on-demand option selected as I'm testing it, since it can save some time to run it manually rather than having to perform whatever else needs to happen to trigger it automatically. While this testing technique usually works it doesn't always work. For example, complex workflows that combine stages and wait conditions cannot be tested by running them on demand, nor can ones that create records, create activities or send notifications.</td>
</tr>
</table>

Child Processes

The **Available to Run** section in process properties also has a checkbox labeled **As a child process**, as the following figure illustrates.

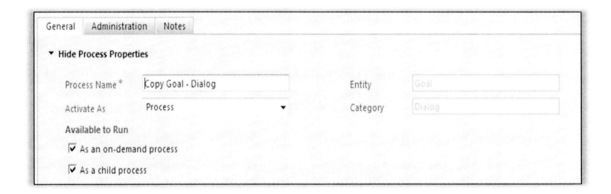

Both workflow and dialog processes can be available to run as a child process. Here are two common uses of this feature.

Re-usable Business Processes

If you find yourself recreating the same functionality in several different processes, you can break it out as a separate process and make it available to run as a child process. This technique has several benefits, generally similar to the benefits realized by breaking down large programs into smaller chunks of reusable function libraries. For example, a dialog process might prompt the user with a list of available e-mail templates, ask them to select one and then send an e-mail to a specified contact. A requirement as generic as this might come up in several different contexts. when a lead is converted to a contact, as a manual process run directly from a contact record, and so forth. Rather than create and maintain the functionality in several different processes, you can create it once and simply call it, as appropriate, from other parent processes.

Recursive Processes

Another scenario we will examine that will make use of this capability is when a workflow or dialog process needs to call itself, "recursively".

- For workflow processes, this is useful for "looping" situations, when a process needs to run continuously until some exit condition happens, and when you want some flexibility in jumping around to different stages of the process.
- A common use of this technique in dialog processes is when you want to give a user the option to repeat a process. A requirement I encounter frequently is to save users time in the creation of complex records. Not surprisingly, copying to and pasting from the Windows clipboard doesn't work well with Dynamics CRM records, but both workflows and dialogs can be used to create "copies" of existing records. And the dialog version of a record copy process might include as one of its prompts whether the user would like to create another copy after the one currently being created.

An example of a dialog process to copy a goal record (generally one of the most time-consuming of records to create, hence a good candidate for a process like this) is explained in detail later in the book. In the meantime, the following figure shows the relevant portions such a dialog process.

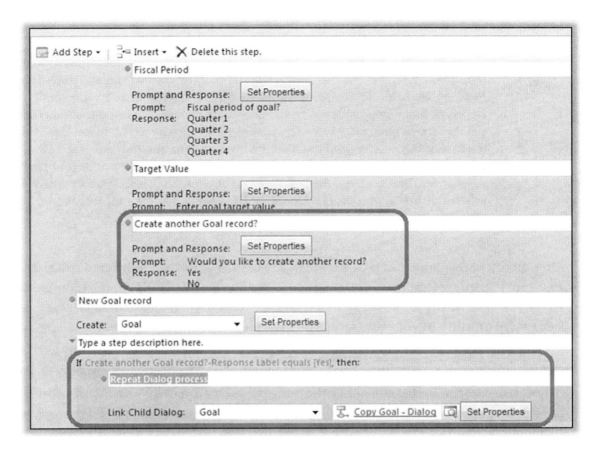

Even if you haven't seen dialog processes before, the logic is easy to follow. The first highlighted section is displayed as a prompt when the user runs the dialog on a selected goal record. If the response is "Yes", the **Link Child Dialog** action is performed against the *Copy Goal – Dialog* process. Refer back to the figure at the beginning of this section and you can see that this process is calling itself recursively. And the only reason it can is that the **As a child process** option was selected before the process was saved.

Using the Workflow Designer

 Workflows only for the rest of this chapter
I mentioned this previously but thought it was worth repeating: the topics and examples covered in the rest of this chapter and the next will be workflow-specific. Just keep in mind that dialog functionality can be thought of as a superset of workflow functionality: basically, the only thing dialogs cannot do that workflows can is run automatically. What this means is that almost all the topics discussed in the rest of this chapter and the next are important foundation skills for both workflow and dialog processes. So, even in the unlikely event that in your career as a Dynamics CRM business process designer you intend to specialize exclusively on interactive dialog processes…you still need to know all of the topics covered between here and the start of chapter 4!

After specifying the properties for a workflow, you use the Workflow Designer to add and configure the actions it will perform, and to construct the logical flow of the workflow process. To see this in action, here's a step by step example of how to create a workflow to assign new leads based on attributes of a lead record such as industry and company size.

Step by Step: Finish the Lead Assignment Workflow
Let's finish the Lead Assignment workflow with which we started the chapter. We left off after specifying its properties and minimizing the properties section, and then saving and closing it. In the following exercise we will open it up again in the workflow designer and add the logic to conditionally assign lead records to users, based on specific values of the Industry field.

This is a bit of a preview of what's to come in Chapter 3, since we have not yet covered conditional logic. But it's pretty straightforward and it will provide a good idea of what you can accomplish, so let's go ahead and go for it.

1. On the site map, click **Settings**, and then click **Processes** in the Process Center section.
2. Locate the Lead Assignment workflow in the grid, and double-click it to open the designer.
3. Click the first line in the step editor (**Select this row and click Add Step**).
4. Click the **Add Step** drop-down menu, and select **Check Condition**. At this point, the workflow designer should look like the following figure:

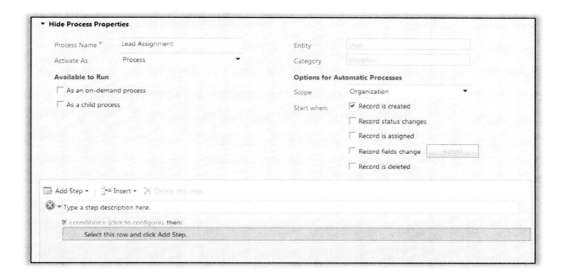

5. Now position your cursor where it says "Type a step description here", and enter descriptive text. (This is optional, but you should always do this as a best practice.)

6. Click the link labeled **<condition> (click to configure)** to access the **Specify Workflow Condition** dialog.

7. Position the cursor on the **Select** link and a drop-down menu that allows you to select from the various entities available. For now, select **Lead**, then tab to the next column.

8. A drop-down menu displays the fields for the lead entity. Select **Industry**, then tab to the next column.

9. A drop-down menu displays the *comparison operators* available for the selected field. Select **Equals**, then tab to the next column. The Specify Condition dialog should now look like this:

10. Notice that on the next column an ellipsis appears, indicating you can select from a list of values. This is because the **Industry** field is an option set, so you can specify one or more available values, any of which will satisfy the current condition. Suppose you have a vertical sales model, where certain sales reps focus on specific industries or groups of industries. Here, select multiple values such as "Accounting", "Brokers", "Business Services", and "Consulting".

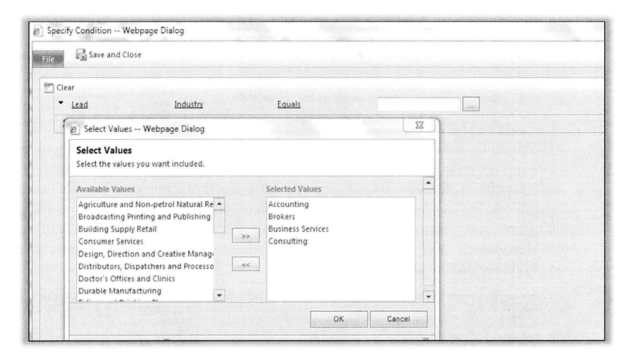

11. After selecting those values, click **OK**, and then click **Save and Close** to return to the workflow designer.

12. Now, position your cursor on the "Select this row and click Add Step" line that is indented under the condition we just specified.

13. Click **Add Step**, and from the drop-down menu select **Assign Record**.

14. Fill in the step description if you like, and then use the lookup button to select the user to which records meeting the current condition will be assigned. Again, this is not required but is a best practice.

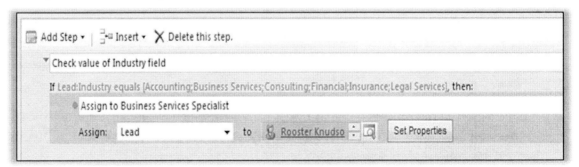

15. At this point, you should click the **Save** button. Then you can click the **Activate** button to "turn it on".

Now you can test the workflow, and verify that it works as expected. If you're wondering why the assignment logic of this workflow does not meet the requirements set forth in the Visio diagram shown earlier, it's because we aren't done yet!

In the next chapter we will review conditional logic in more detail and finish the Lead Assignment workflow, but for now, you see that without too much work we've created an automatic workflow process that will assign leads based on the value of the **Industry** field. Most Dynamics CRM record types are preconfigured with lots of fields that can be useful in workflow scenarios like this one. In fact, until you start understanding what you can do with workflow and dialog processes, you might not appreciate the value of some of the fields you have to work with. For example, the following table lists some of the other fields on the Lead entity, and how you might use them to assign records.

Fields	Use when
Annual Revenue, Number of Employees	Leads are assigned based on company size
City, State or Zip Code	Leads are assigned based on geography
Industry	Leads are assigned based on industries
Lead Source	Leads are assigned based on the channel they were created by (phone call, web, tradeshow...)

We'll see plenty of other examples like this as we move ahead.

Workflow Steps and Stages

Let's focus in just a little more on the mechanics of using the workflow designer. Just to the right of the Add Step drop-down menu, you can click **Insert**, and select one of two options: **Before Step** or **After Step**. The default value is **After Step**, and with that selected the workflow designer functions as you saw in the previous exercise, adding all new steps immediately after the currently selected step. Select **Before Step** when you want to add a step above the selected step.

One aspect of the process designer that is confusing at first is keeping track of which step you have selected, and knowing where to add new steps. Let's take a closer look at this, using the Lead Assignment workflow to illustrate.

With this selected…

…these options are available on the Add Step menu:

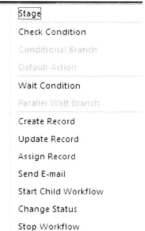

In this figure the selected line is immediately above the **If** line; think of the selection as being *outside* of the conditional block.

In this situation, the Add Step menu presents everything you can do in a workflow except for the three steps – Conditional Branch, Default Action, and Parallel Wait Branch – that only are available *inside* a conditional block.

With this selected…

…these options are available on the Add Step menu:

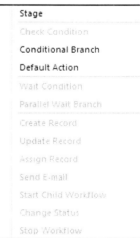

Here, the selected step is the If line. (It takes some dexterity to select this, by the way: as usual, the blue text is a link, so you have to click right on If or then in order to select the line!)

In this situation, the Add Step menu presents only the steps available in this context; since we're on the If line, it makes sense that we might add another Conditional Branch at this point.

With this selected...

...these options are available on the Add Step menu:

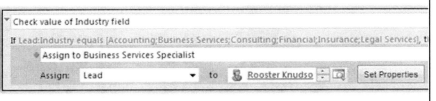

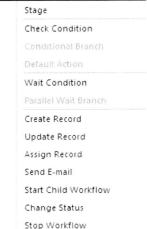

Stage

Check Condition

Conditional Branch

Default Action

Wait Condition

Parallel Wait Branch

Create Record

Update Record

Assign Record

Send E-mail

Start Child Workflow

Change Status

Stop Workflow

Here, the Assign Record step is selected, and we're inside the conditional block.

In this situation, once again all the menu options are available, except for those that are only available with the conditional block selected.

Notice that no matter what is selected, the Stages command is always available.

We mentioned before that all processes – both workflows and dialogs -- can have stages. Process *stages* are essentially containers for all of the steps in a workflow, and you can add them at any time. If you add a stage to an existing workflow, the editor will "wrap" all of the existing steps inside the new stage.

For example, in the step editor for the Lead Assignment workflow, you can select any step, and click the Add Step menu. Select Stage and you will see the following dialog:

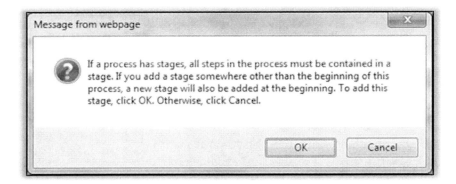

Click OK and you can see that the first stage is always added at the start of the process, with the default text, "Type a stage description here", reminding you it's a good idea to describe stages in a process.

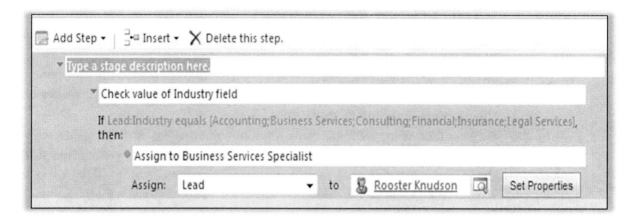

If you change your mind and decide you want to delete a stage, just select the stage, and click the Delete this step button. You will see the following descriptive dialog, telling you that deleting a stage isn't very dangerous.

 Where are Stages most useful?
Personally, I find stages much more important for dialog processes than for workflows. This is because most dialog processes have characteristic things that always happen, and always happen in the same order. Workflow processes tend to vary more from one another, and especially for small, single-purpose workflows like the Lead Assignment example, there really isn't a lot of value added by adding a single stage.

Here are a few things you should know about workflow stages in Dynamics CRM 2011.

- If you have stages in a workflow, every workflow step must be contained within a stage.
- You can add as many stages as you like, and you don't have to add steps for a stage. So, for example, you might want to start by adding all of the stages to a complex workflow before you add the steps (conditions and actions), so that you have "placeholders" for everything, and get a feel for what needs to happen where.
- You can delete a stage. If you do, all of the steps within that stage will be placed in the previous stage, rather than deleted.
- On the other hand, there are many situations where deleting *steps* will delete many other steps. For example, if you select the beginning **If** on a conditional block and delete that step, the entire conditional block – including all of the actions and any nested conditional blocks contained within it – will be deleted. This is a good way to lose a lot of hard-won work in a hurry, so be careful not to confuse deleting a step with deleting a stage!
- In Dynamics CRM 2011, stages are mainly for organizing the steps of workflows into logical groups of conditions and actions; by themselves, they don't really change the behavior of a workflow. For example, you might have a sales process workflow with multiple stages (Identify, Qualify, Propose, Negotiate, etc.). But there's nothing about stages that will make a workflow stop within a stage.

Be Aware of Process Designer Limitations
Workflow and dialog processes can achieve important results, but the design environment has certain limitations it's important to be aware of. In my view, the two most important ones to keep in mind are the following:

1. You cannot promote or demote steps. For example, if you don't quite get the logic right the first time, and want to promote a condition from a nested block to the block it's nested within...you cannot do it, so you need to delete it and add it where it belongs.
2. You cannot move steps. For example, you may have painstakingly constructed a complex Send E-mail action and decide it needs to be moved, or that it could be re-used somewhere else. Unfortunately, you will need to re-create it.

What these really mean is that you should design your business processes before diving into the Dynamics CRM process designer. Put differently, the process designer should really be thought of more as a *construction* tool than as a graphical designer. This reinforces the recommendation I made earlier about using Visio to describe your processes, but even if you don't use Visio, at least diagram processes on paper or whiteboard before diving into the Dynamics CRM process designer.

Workflow Actions

After our introduction of basic workflow properties and how to use the step editor, we can start putting workflows to work. This is where "Actions" come in. You can think of these as the "work" in workflow, the actions they can perform. (The "flow" of your workflows is controlled by "Conditions" and "Waits" – we will discuss these in the next chapter.)

A good way to see a complete list of all the actions a Dynamics CRM workflow can perform is to open up the workflow designer and click the **Add Step** menu. You will see something like the following figure, where the actions are the seven menu commands in the highlighted section.

We will discuss each of these actions in turn.

Create Record

This action allows a workflow to create a new record in Dynamics CRM. Assuming you have sufficient security privileges, you can create a new record for any custom entity, plus for most of the "core entities" of the CRM user experience.

To create a record, select **Create Record** from the **Add Step** menu, then specify which record type to create with the entity list immediately to the right of **Create**.

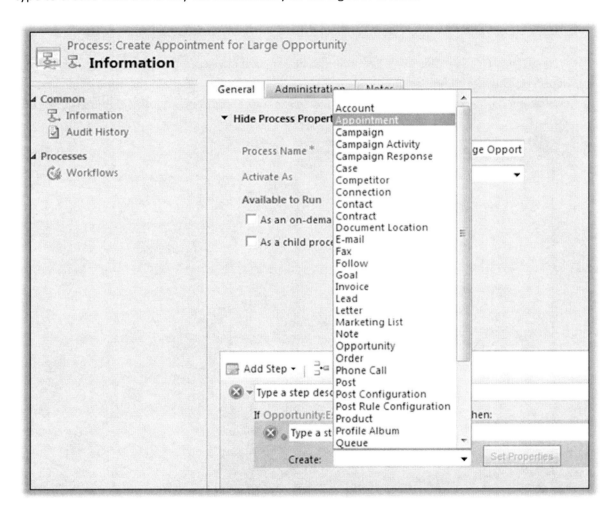

What Records can be created by Workflows and Dialogs?

All custom entities can have records created by business processes, as well as core record types such as accounts, contacts, and opportunities. Cases and all activity record types can be created, as well as many other record types.

Here is a complete list of the record types that workflows and dialogs can create.

Record Type	Record
Core	Account
	Contact
	Opportunity
	Lead
	Note
Activity	Email
	Phone Call
	Fax
	Letter
	Appointment
	Campaign Response
	Service Activity
	Task
Sales	Invoice
	Quote
	Order
	Sales Literature
	Competitor
	Product
Marketing	Marketing List
	Campaign
	Campaign Activity
Service	Case
	Contract
Miscellaneous	Territory
	Site
	Queue
New in CRM 2011, including the November 2011 Service Update	Connection
	Document Location
	Follow
	Goal
	Post
	Post Configuration
	Post Rule Configuration
	Profile Album
	Queue Item
	SharePoint Site

To give you a feel for the kinds of things you might want to use Create Record for, here are a few scenarios.

- **Create an appointment**, task or other activity when an opportunity record gets to a certain stage in a sales process.
- **Create a case record**, using some of the information contained in an incoming e-mail.
- **Create a queue item** to route an item to a queue. This is new in Dynamics CRM 2011, and reflects the enhancements to queues. This is an important topic and will be covered in detail below.
- **Create a new goal record**, based on the information contained in an existing goal. This is a common technique you can use to copy Dynamics CRM records and save yourself a lot of data entry time.
- **Create a follow or a post record.** The follow and post entities are new in the November 2011 service update, and have to do with the **Activity Feeds** feature. Because you can create these record types automatically with a workflow, you can create highly targeted activity feeds not possible with the standard configuration tools available in the UI. Be cautioned, there are a maximum number of follows of 500 records. If you are automating these, that number might creep up quickly.
- **Create a SharePoint Site or Document Location.** These are only available if you're using the SharePoint integration supported by the Dynamics CRM 2011 List Component for SharePoint 2010. At the time this was written, the list component was only supported for the on-premise version of SharePoint 2010, but Microsoft had announced that support for the online (Office 365) version of SharePoint 2010 would be added shortly.

While it's important to know which records *can* be created by workflow and dialog processes, it will probably save you more time to know which records *cannot* be created! The following table lists the most important record types you cannot create from within a Dynamics CRM 2011 business process.

Record Type	Record
System	User
	Workflow
	System Job
	Report
	Business Unit
	Security Role
	Team
Sales	Opportunity Product
	Quote Product
	Order Product
	Invoice Product
Service	Knowledge Base Article
Marketing	Marketing List Member
Miscellaneous	Goal Metric
	Rollup Query

It's important to understand the limitations of the workflow designer, if for no other reason than it will save you the time of trying to figure it out yourself! Consider the following things you might want to do...but cannot (yet) with the **Create Record** action in the workflow designer.

- I'm often asked how to schedule reports in Dynamics CRM. While the on-premise version of Dynamics CRM 2011 has a scheduling wizard you can use for this, that handy feature is not currently available in the online version. IF a workflow could create a report, that would do the trick...but as you can see in the table, that is not supported.

- If you use the product catalog and system calculated pricing, you may be familiar with line items for the four sales pipeline record types (opportunity, quote, order and invoice). There's plenty to like about using system calculated pricing and line items, but one limitation is that you cannot automate the creation of the line item records with a workflow. Effectively, you can use a workflow (or dialog) to create the "header" record, but not the line items.

- You can create a marketing list with a workflow, but you cannot use a workflow to add members to the list.

- You can use a workflow to copy a goal record and save some time in the process, but if the goal record requires a rollup query you will have to add that manually, since rollup queries cannot be created with a workflow.

Security and Business Processes

This entire discussion assumes you have security privileges to create all these records – in the real world this won't always be the case. The issue of security and business processes is important to understand both for *designing* processes and for *running* them.

For example, when you select the **Create Record** action, the workflow designer only allows you to create record types for which you have at least user-level access for the Create privilege. So, suppose you have (only) the Salesperson security role and you're using the workflow designer. Because your security role doesn't have sufficient privileges, there are plenty of record types – such as Competitor, Product, Sales Literature and Territory that you won't see after selecting Create Record. The following figure shows the relevant part of the Salesperson security role.

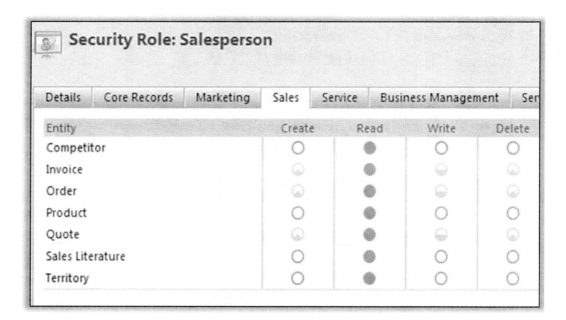

So the design experience is "trimmed" according to your security role. But that's not always the case when it comes to *running* workflows. For running workflows, the main thing to remember about security is this: *Automatic workflows run in the security context of the user who created the workflow; On Demand workflows run in the security context of the user who runs the workflow.*

This is an important topic, and we will cover it in considerably more detail below!

Working with Queue Items

Let's take a closer look at this topic, since it's both important, and significantly different in Dynamics CRM 2011 compared to earlier versions. To start, here are a few of the most important things you should know about queues and queue items in Dynamics CRM 2011:

- Queues are essentially containers for things you're working on. The "things" in this context are Dynamics CRM records, such as cases, activities, contacts, opportunities and so forth.

- Queues are similar to most records in that they can be owned by users or teams.

- Most users can only see queues they own (or that are owned by a team of which they're a member).

- In Dynamics CRM 2011, any record type can be routed to a queue. (This is different from earlier versions, when only cases and activity record types could be routed to queues.) The only records with queues enabled by default are the cases and activities, but any entity can have this enabled. Once enabled it cannot be disabled.

- When we say a record is "routed to a queue", what we really mean is that a *queue item* is created for the record. For example, if you navigate to the cases grid, select a case record and use the Add to Queue button on the ribbon to route it to a queue, a single queue item is created in that queue. This queue item is related to the underlying case record, but it's important to understand that the queue item itself is a different record: it's customizable, has its own form and views and so forth.

- A record can only have one queue item at any time, and a queue item can only exist in a single queue at a time. These two characteristics of queue items have important implications for workflows that route items such as cases to queues. Most importantly, they mean that if a workflow process routes a case to a queue, the case is *automatically removed* from any other queue it might have been in previously.

These may sound like a pretty boring recitation of "facts about queues", but they actually turn out to have important consequences for the kinds of things you can use queues for, and especially so in the context of workflow and dialog processes. Here's an example to illustrate how you can work with queues and queue items interactively. One of the example processes at the end of the chapter illustrates how to use an automatic workflow to route cases to queues.

Step by Step: Working with Queues and Queue Items

In this exercise, we'll create two queues, and then route some records to and through those queues.

1. On the site map, click **Settings**, then **Business Management**, and then click **Queues**.
2. Click **New** at the top of the grid, and type *Standard Service* in the **Name** field.
3. Click the **Save & New** button, and create one more queue, this time called *Premium Service*.
4. Click **Save & Close**.
5. Now click **Service** on the site map, and then click **Cases**.
6. Select several cases, and in the **Collaborate** section of the cases ribbon, click **Add to Queue**.
7. Use the lookup button to select the **Standard Service** queue, and click **OK** twice to add the records to the queue.
8. Now, navigate to the **Workplace** and click **Queues**. In the **Queue Items** drop-down, select All Items, and in the **Queues** drop-down, select Standard Service. You should see something like this:

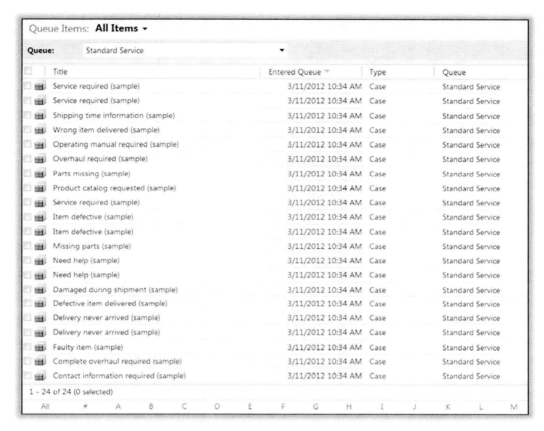

These are queue items, not cases, although it's hard to tell the difference at first! As you examine this view of queue items in the Standard Service queue, note the record count at the bottom of the data grid.

9. Now select several (but not all) of these queue items, and then click the **Routing** button on the ribbon. You should see something like this:

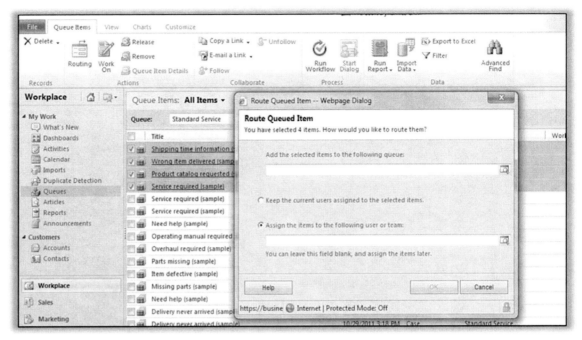

10. Use the lookup button on the **Add the selected items to the following queue** line to route these items to the Premium Service queue. After you do that, notice that the record count in the Standard Service queue drops by the number of items you routed.

11. Then select the **Premium Service** queue in the **Queue** drop-down to verify that queue items have been created in that queue.

12. Now, navigate back to the **Standard Service** queue (select it from the **Queue** drop-down), and select all the records currently in the queue.

13. Click the **Remove** button on the ribbon. Confirm by clicking OK.

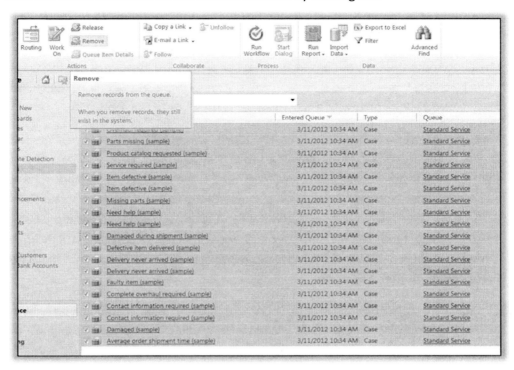

14. Now click **Advanced Find** on the ribbon, and verify that **Queue Items** is selected in the **Look for** drop-down:

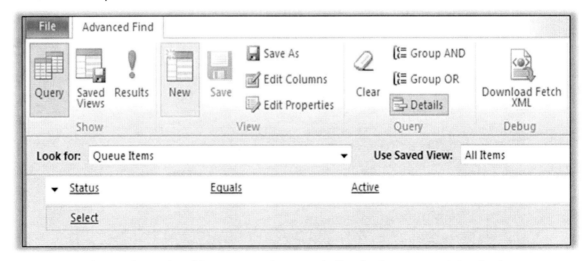

15. Click **Results**, and you should see queue items only for the items remaining in the **Premium Service** queue.

This exercise is intended to illustrate several of the "queue facts" mentioned above. Most importantly, that queue items are distinct from the underlying record they are created for, and that an underlying record can only have a single queue item, in a single queue, at any time.

When you route items to queues in workflow or dialog processes, you use the Create Record action to create a new queue item. You will see an example at the end of the chapter that uses this to route case records with a workflow.

Working with Activity Feeds

Activity Feeds are an important new feature in the November 2011 service update for Dynamics CRM 2011, and while a comprehensive treatment is out of scope for the book, I will provide a brief introduction and then focus in on a couple of topics particularly important in the context of this book: that is, how you can use workflow and dialog processes to get more value out of the baseline activity feeds feature set.   As of this writing Activity Feeds are strictly an internal facing communication tool, but Microsoft has discussed plans to include external social posts such as via Facebook, Twitter or LinkedIn.

Let's start with some basic concepts. Suppose you're all up and running with activity feeds. If you click on the **Workplace** and then click **What's New,** you might see something like the following figure.

This is what's referred to as a user's personal *page*, but I've also seen it referred to as a *wall*. Either way, it gives you a single place where you can do things like these:

- To share an insight with your colleagues, type up to 250 characters in the text box at the top, press **Enter**. Colleagues who are following you will see this on their walls.
- Edit your profile picture.
- See which records (users, contacts, cases, etc.) you're following.
- View posts on items you're following.

For our business process-centric discussion of activity feeds, the most interesting features are the following.

- **Post** is a new record type. With reference to the previous figure, each of the three posts shown are post records. The wall is only *one* of the ways post records are exposed. For example, as with other record types, you can open up Advanced Find and create a query for posts. *You can also use the **Create Record** action to create post records in a workflow or dialog process.*
- **Follow** is a new record type as well. It sounds a little odd at first, and I suppose it's because most entities in Dynamics CRM are named after nouns, and follow is a verb, but I digress. In any event, when you follow a record such as a contact or an account, a new follow record is created. The following two figures (not *that* following!) shows an Advanced Find query on the Follow entity.

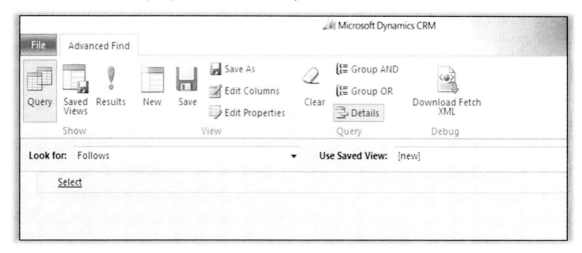

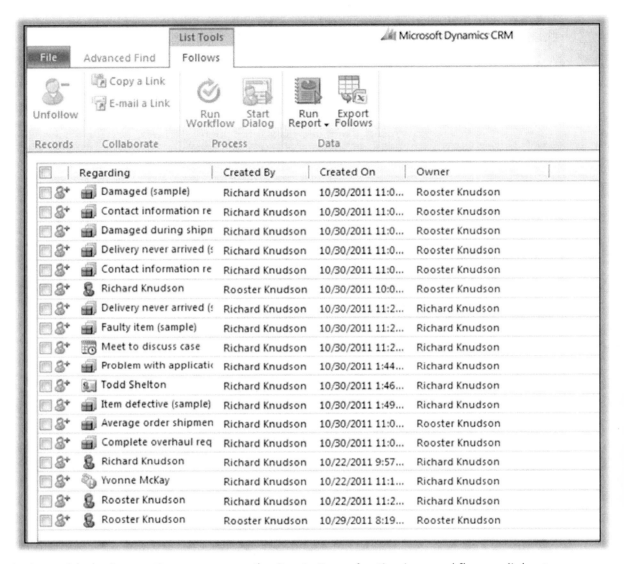

*And, as with the Post entity, you can use the **Create Record** action in a workflow or dialog to create a follows record.*

So...apart from getting really good at Dynamics CRM 2011 Business Process Jeopardy, why does it matter that you can use Create Record to create a post or follow record in a workflow? What's the use case?

Actually, it turns out to be quite useful! For example, here's a problem that can be solved with a workflow that creates these record types under certain conditions.

For certain record types (case, opportunity, and lead to name three) there are default "Activity Feeds Rules". If these are active, a post will automatically be created and pushed out to your wall when certain things happen (this is referred to as an auto post). The following figure illustrates the default rules for the case record type after they've been activated:

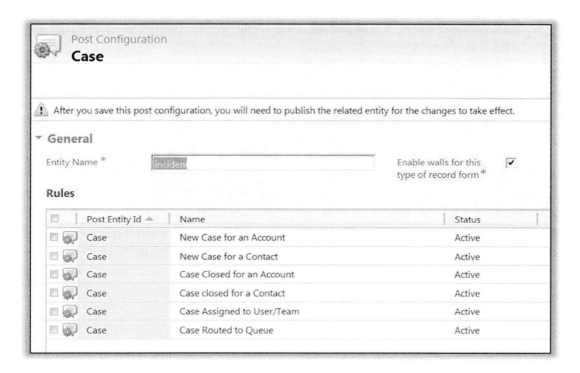

The problem with these default rules is that they have a "shotgun" quality: they post to everybody's wall. For example, the default rules for cases indicate that all users with the minimum permissions required for activity feeds will see auto posts on their walls for *every* case record created, closed, assigned or routed. In the sample workflows at the end of this chapter, you will see a workflow that solves this problem.

Update Record

Use this action when you want a workflow to change values of fields for a record. You can change the values of fields for the entity the workflow is created on, as well as for any parent entities of the record. The data context of a running workflow is an important concept to understand and we discuss it in more detail in the next chapter. For now, here's an example to illustrate the point. Suppose you've created a workflow for the opportunity entity. What fields can such a workflow update?

- It can update fields on the specific opportunity record the workflow is running against.
- It can update fields on any of the opportunity record's parent records, such as the account or contact specified in the Potential Customer lookup field, the user selected in the Owner field, or the parent record of a custom entity with a 1:N relationship to opportunity. (Only immediate parent records can be updated; so if a contact has been selected as the potential customer, a workflow cannot update the parent account record of the contact! More on this below.)
- It cannot update child records of the opportunity, such as opportunity products, or quotes that are related to it.

Here are a couple of important topics that arise in the context of updating records, which as you will see are important in many other workflow scenarios:

The "Additional Fields" tab. Much of your work in creating workflows will take place in the workflow version of the entity forms. These look superficially similar to the user experience of working with records through an entity's main form, but they are actually quite different. One of the most obvious things you notice in the workflow design environment is the **Additional Fields** tab. For example, the following figure shows this tab for the opportunity record:

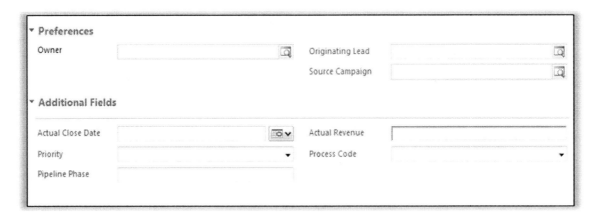

The importance of the **Additional Fields** tab is that it gives you as the workflow designer the ability to update fields that are not exposed as part of the user experience of updating a record. So you can take out of the hands of users much of the data entry associated with updating Opportunities (or any other record) that might be tedious or error prone. Here are two scenarios I frequently encounter that make me glad this feature is available.

- Notice in the previous figure the **Pipeline Phase** text field is exposed. Many people are initially confused by the system provided Sales Pipeline charts that figure prominently in the out of the box charts and dashboards for the opportunity record type. The reason it's confusing is that they are all based on this Pipeline Phase text field, which is nicely populated with values in the sample data set...but which is not available on any forms! So in order for the system sales pipeline charts to make sense, you either have to modify them to use a different field for the sales stage, or have an automatic workflow update Pipeline Phase in the background.
- Opportunity records have a text field, **Topic**, which acts as the name of a record. Cases have **Title**, leads have **Topic**, and custom entities, by default, all have a **Name** field. All of these fields serve the same purpose, providing a short name for a record. The problem is, without agreed-upon naming conventions, every user simply "types stuff in" and you end up with an ad-hoc mish-mash of personal naming conventions. Even if you have naming conventions, you still have to rely on a user typing correctly, and they waste time typing in the meantime. For case records, the Title is often meaningful – for example, if an experienced customer service rep enters the text "Customer is super upset and really needs management attention asap!!!" in a case record's Title field, it's probably higher impact than simply selecting High in the Priority option set field. But for most other situations, create a workflow to enforce naming conventions and save your users' time!

Step by Step: Create an Automatic Workflow to Name Opportunity Records

To create a workflow that automatically fills in the Topic field when a new opportunity record is created, follow these steps:

1. On the site map, click **Settings,** and then click **Processes.**
2. Click **New**. The Create Process dialog appears.
3. Select **Workflow** in the **Category** field, **Opportunity** as the Entity, and provide an appropriate value in the Name field.

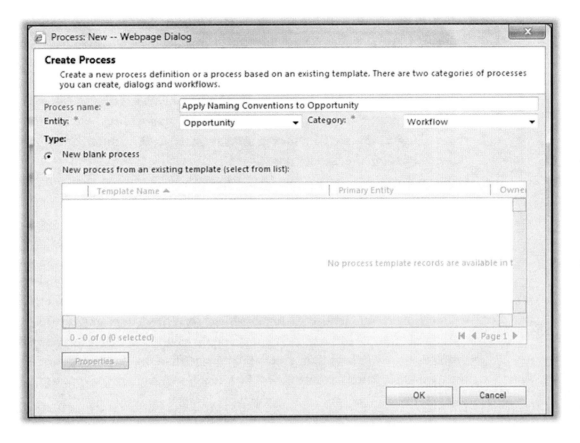

4. Click **OK** to save the new workflow and access the workflow designer.

5. Select **Organization** in the Scope field, select the **Record is created** option in **Start when**, and select **As an on-demand process** in the **Available to Run** section. (For a workflow like this one, I would generally leave the on-demand option selected even after the process is thoroughly tested and activated in a production environment. That's because all the workflow does is update the value of the topic field, a relatively innocuous thing. As mentioned previously, workflows that are more complex, create records, send notification emails and the like should not generally be available for on-demand use after they're in production.)

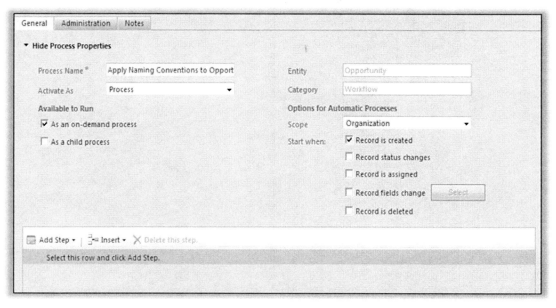

6. Next, click the **Add Step** menu and select **Update Record**.
7. The opportunity record type is the primary entity of the workflow, and will be the default selection on the Update line. Leave that as is, and click **Set Properties**.
8. In the **Topic** field, enter the text ***Opportunity for***.
9. In the **Dynamic Values** section of the Form Assistant, click the field list immediately beneath Opportunity in the Look for section.

10. From the field list, select **Potential Customer**, and then click the **Add** button. That will move the field into the selected field list.

11. Now, click back inside the **Topic** field, after the static text you entered in step 8, and make sure to leave a space after the text. Then click **OK** in the **Dynamic Values** section. The end result should be something like this:

12. Finally, click **Save and Close** twice, then activate the process.

While it's true that giving all of your opportunities Topic values such as "Opportunity for Acme" isn't the most creative naming convention, it will impart consistency to your naming conventions. We'll cover Dynamic Values in more detail below, and then you can get more creative.

When to use Update Record, Assign Record, Change Status
You might wonder why there are separate workflow actions for Update Record, Assign Record, and Change Status. After all, aren't assigning records and changing their status values really just specific kinds of updates? While that may be true, they are specific enough to have their own workflow actions, and if those are the things you want to do, you must use those actions!

As a general rule, just remember that that you need to use the Update Record action to change the value of any field on a record…EXCEPT for Status (that's what Change Status is for), and Owner (that's what Assign Record is for).

Assign Record
In Dynamics CRM 2011 most records can be assigned to either a user or a team, and in both workflow and dialog processes you can use the **Assign Record** action for that purpose. When you select Assign Record from the step menu, you will see two controls at the right of the record selector.

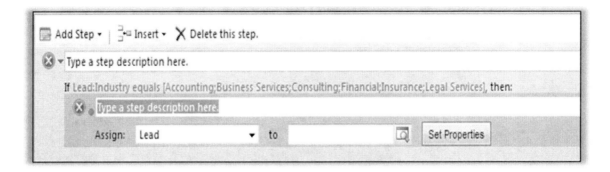

Use the **Lookup** control and select a user or a team if you always know who to select. Use **Set Properties** if you need to figure it out dynamically. For example, if a certain sales representative specializes in an industry vertical, use the lookup to select and assign a record to that user.

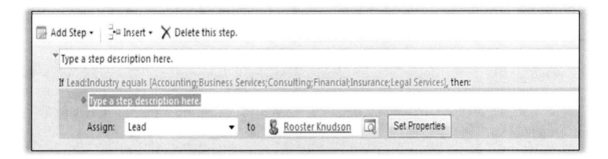

On the other hand, suppose whenever a new contact record is created, you want to assign it to the same user that owns the account record the contact is associated with. In this case, you click **Set Properties** to access dynamic values. The following figure shows an example of this, with the **Edit Assign Step Parameters** dialog open and dynamic values used to assign the contact record to the owner of its parent account.

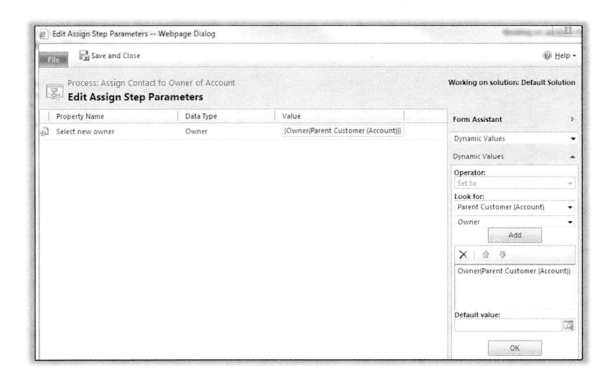

Assuming the Contact record being created by the workflow actually contains a value in the Parent Customer field, this workflow will work correctly, assigning the Contact record to the same user who is the Owner of the Parent Customer. But what if the Contact record is created as a "standalone" record; that is, without anything in the Parent Customer field? Here's an instructive exercise you should try various permutations on, to see how workflows adapt to unexpected conditions.

1. Create a workflow like the one we just showed, and run it against a contact record that has a parent customer. You will see that it works as expected.
2. Now run it for a standalone contact record – one that does not have anything in the **Parent Customer** field. From the contact record click Workflows in the Processes section and you can see the workflow is stuck with a status of **Waiting** since it doesn't know who to assign the record to. Double-click the workflow and you will see the **System Job** form, as the following figure illustrates:

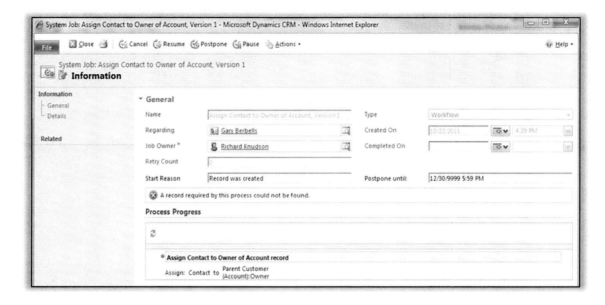

3. Switch back to the **Contact** form; assign it to a parent customer, and **save** the record.
4. Then switch back to the **System Job** form and click **Resume** on the ribbon. You'll see that after resuming, it works correctly and the contact record will be assigned to the same owner as the account record!

This is another example of how you can monitor and troubleshoot and sometimes fix (!) workflows as they run. Workflows can be monitored from a number of different places. In the current example, viewing a workflow from the contact record, you can see all instances of any workflows that have been (or are running) for the specific contact record.

As an alternative, you could navigate to **Settings** and then **System Jobs**, and then **filter** the list to see a view like the following:

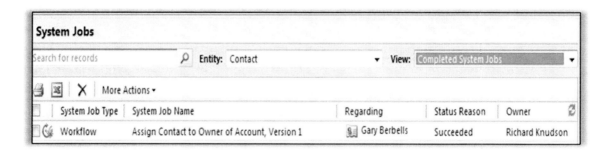

You can also use Advanced Find to create and save very specific views of workflows. In a production environment with many users and automatic workflows this is a common requirement, and system administrators often create reports to flag potential problem situations. We will give this important topic a more detailed treatment later in the book, but if you want to work ahead the following figure shows an Advanced Find view that might give you some ideas.

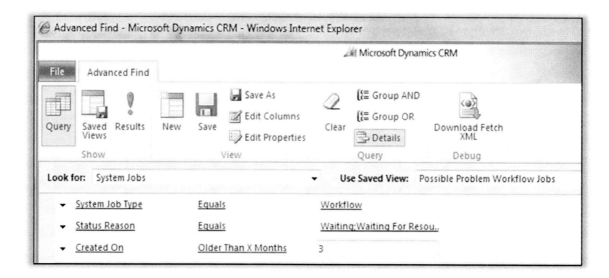

Send E-Mail
Use this action to send an email message automatically as part of a workflow. You can either create a new e-mail message, or use an existing e-mail template for the entity the workflow is created for.

Starting in the Step Editor, follow these steps to use the Send E-Mail action to create a new e-mail and send it.

1. Click **Add Step**, and select **Send E-mail**.
2. On the Send e-mail line, click the drop-down menu and select **Create New Message.**

You can configure the email – who it will go to, the subject and body of the message, and so forth, by clicking the **Set Properties** button. The next figure shows an example of the workflow design form for an e-mail being created for a custom entity.

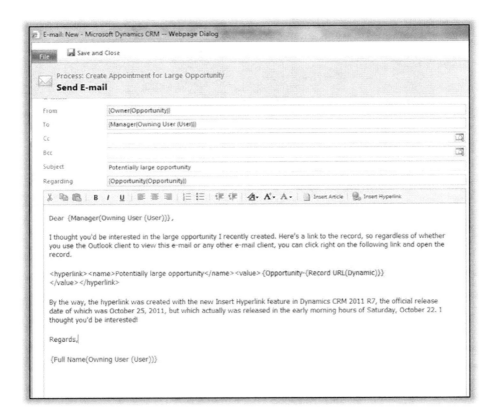

Insert Hyperlink and Dynamic Record URL

Notice the **Insert Hyperlink** command on the toolbar, and the special hyperlink text in the body of the e-mail. Here's what the **Insert Hyperlink** dialog looks like for this example:

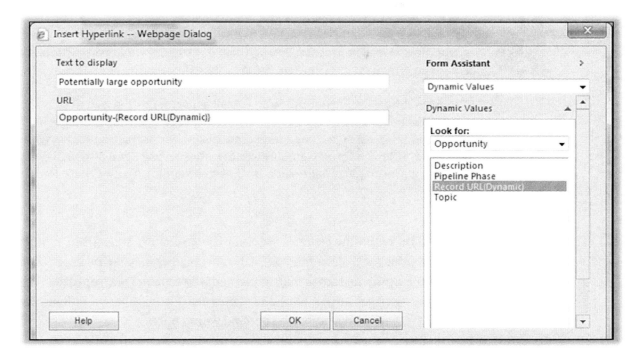

As the text in the e-mail notes, the **Insert Hyperlink** command is an important new feature included in the November 2011 Service Update. This example uses it in combination with the **Record URL (Dynamic) field** available for all records now in the Dynamic Values section. So now you can simply include a hyperlink to any Dynamics CRM record in an e-mail, and not have to rely on a user having the Outlook client for the Regarding link to work!

Some of the other advantages of using an e-mail template to send an e-mail include

- The E-Mail Template Editor lets you create formatted templates, including graphic images, layout tables and the like.
- E-mail templates also support file attachments.
- Published Knowledge Base articles can also be inserted directly into the body of an e-mail.

Later in the book, we will examine in more detail how you can send template e-mails from workflows and dialogs.

Send E-Mail, or Create Record?
You can use the **Send E-Mail** action to directly send an e-mail record from within a workflow or dialog process. You can also use the **Create Record** action to create an e-mail record. Hmmm...What's the difference?

The main difference is that the Send E-Mail action sends the e-mail directly; Create Record simply creates an e-mail activity record without sending it. For automated processes such as a lead auto-responder or a sales process where you want to send a formatted quote automatically, use **Send E-mail**. If you want to allow a user to personalize an e-mail before sending it, use **Create Record**.

Start Child Workflow

As it sounds, the **Start Child Workflow** action is used to execute one workflow from another. One situation you can use this for is a common piece of functionality that can be used by many different workflows. In this scenario, rather than implement the functionality repeated times in many different workflows, you can write it once and simply call it from other workflows. Then, if you ever need to change it, you change it in one spot and you're done.

The records you can start a child workflow for include the primary entity the workflow is written for, any parent record types, and any records created by the workflow process.

Another example is for what is generally referred to as a "recursive" workflow: a workflow that calls itself. This is often used for "escalating" scenarios. For example, if a case is created and not resolved within a certain period of time, you might need a workflow to progressively escalate the case – perhaps alerting supervisors, assigning it to different users or queues, etc. Here's an example of what the Step Editor might look like in such a scenario. Focus for now on the last step shown in the next figure, where you can see that the **Start Child Workflow** action is used to call the Escalate Case workflow from within the Escalate Case workflow – the definition of "recursion" in this context.

Note that a workflow can only be called in this way if the **As a child process** option is selected in the **Available to Run** section. We will discuss this topic more thoroughly in the next chapter, and will see lots of examples of the general technique.

Change Status

Use the **Change Status** action when you want a workflow to change either the **Status** or the **Status Reason** of a Dynamics CRM record. Although this might sound obvious, there are some subtleties around this important workflow action. Probably the easiest thing to get confused about is the distinction between the "Status" and "Status Reason" attributes. These attributes exist for every entity in Dynamics CRM, and in all cases work the same way: for each value of the Status attribute, there are one or more values of the Status Reason attribute, one of which must be selected to change the Status value. For example, an opportunity record can only have one of three potential values for the Status field: Open, Lost, or Won. *These values can never be customized*. But for each of these Status values, you can have one or many Status Reason values, and these *can* be customized.

These are especially important to understand in the workflow context, because changes in status – when an Opportunity is Won or Lost, when a Case is Resolved, or when a Lead is Qualified – are often important triggers for business processes, or important outcomes of a process.

Consider the following figure, which shows a **Change Status** step for a workflow on the Lead entity.

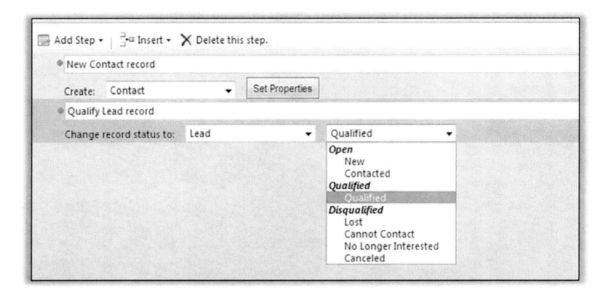

The pull down list allows you to select the value you want for the Status Reason attribute; since it *determines* the Status (Open, Qualified or Disqualified for leads), you don't select Status directly. Here are a few items to remember about the **Change Status** action

- Use **Change Status** when you need a process to update either the **Status** field or **Status Reason**.
- If you need to update the Status field, you don't select it directly: you must select one of the Status Reason values associated with the Status and the system will update it automatically.
- This is the *only* way you can change Status or Status Reason in a workflow or dialog process. You might think, for example, that you could use the Update Record action and update Status Reason. But if you try that, you might spend a lot of time looking for the Status or Status Reason fields on the workflow designer form...since they aren't exposed in the workflow designer form!

Changing Status with Dialog Processes

In several commonly encountered situations, Dynamics CRM uses a "hard-wired" process to change record status. For example, the Lead Conversion, Opportunity Close, and Case Resolution processes all use special-purpose dialog boxes to gather information required to properly move the respective record types from one status to another.

In most cases, a *workflow* process is not very good at changing the status of records like these, since important information must be supplied by the user and workflow processes do not support user interaction.

However, if the default processes do not satisfy your organization's requirements, you *can* build a custom *dialog* process. These can provide an effective way to convert leads or close opportunities or cases, and we will review some examples of this later in the book.

Stop Workflow

The **Stop Workflow** action performs as advertised, stopping the current workflow. Sometimes this is a housekeeping exercise at the end of a workflow. Sometimes it's not, however. For example, with recursive workflows, it might be important to explicitly stop a process that has "recursed" too many times. For example, the Escalate Case workflow we discussed previously could be extended to check the number of times a case has been escalated, and stop the process if it's been escalated more than some threshold value.

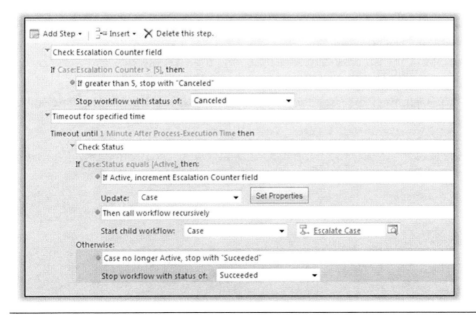

Note that when you use Stop Workflow, you also must specify whether the "status" the process is stopping with. The available options are **Succeeded** and **Canceled**. Two sentences back I put the word "status" in quotes because, as you will shortly see, those really aren't **Status** values – they're **Status Reason** values. Believe me: the related Status and Status Reason fields have a long history of being referred to somewhat inconsistently in various places throughout the Dynamics CRM UI, and this is yet another example. My advice on this topic: don't worry too much about it, you get used to it!

Monitoring Workflows

In Dynamics CRM a special application known as a service (specifically, the Microsoft CRM Asynchronous Processing Service) runs behind the scenes, evaluating and monitoring workflows along with any other CRM function that run asynchronously. This architecture makes it easy to monitor workflows from within the CRM user interface. There are three basic ways you can see the progress of workflows:

1. Navigate to the workflow record and monitor all instances of the workflow that either have run or are running.
2. Open the form for a record and monitor all workflow jobs for that record.
3. Use Advanced Find to query System Jobs and monitor the progress of all workflows.

Monitoring Workflows from the Workflow Record
To monitor workflow jobs from the workflow record, follow this step by step procedure.

Step by Step: Monitor Workflows
1. On the site map, click **Settings**.
2. Click **Processes** in the **Process Center** section, and then double-click the workflow you're interested in.
3. Click **Workflows** in the **Processes** section. The **Workflow Job Associated View** will be displayed.

The following figure shows the Workflow Job Associated View for a custom entity, Work Items, in my company's production Dynamics CRM organization.

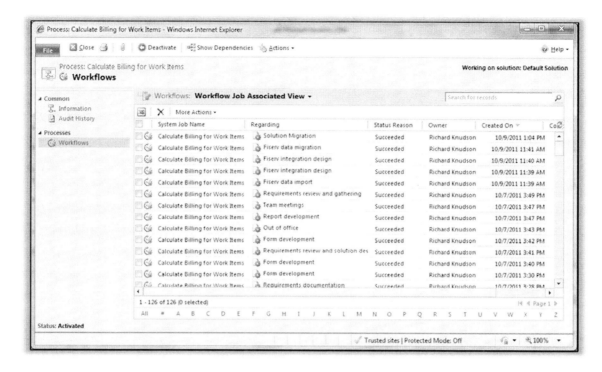

This displays a list of all running and executed instances ("jobs") of that workflow. If a workflow is still running, you can open up the record for that job and see what it's currently doing. If a workflow is completed, you can open up the record and see whether it was successful, what actions were taken and so forth.

Monitoring Workflows from a Record Form

Alternatively, you can navigate to a specific record on which a workflow has been run or is running, and click **Workflows** in the **Processes** section of left navigation to see a list of all the running or completed workflow jobs.

The following figure shows an example of this, using the Work Items custom entity mentioned above.

Using Advanced Find to Monitor System Jobs

Advanced Find queries provide an important technique to monitor workflows, especially if you've got lots of workflows running for lots of users. (I realize that's not a very precise formulation! More details later on the general topic of "how much is a lot" when it comes to workflows.)

In Chapter 7 we will examine this topic in considerably more detail; in the meantime here's a step by step example to show you how to do this:

Step by Step: Build an Advanced Find Query to Monitor Workflows

1. From anywhere in CRM, click **Advanced Find**.
2. In the **Look For** drop-down, select **System Jobs.**
3. Click the **Clear** button on the ribbon to clear any existing filters.
4. Click **Select** on the first line beneath the Look for and select **System Job Type**.
5. Press **Tab** twice and click the **Ellipsis** button
6. Scroll to the bottom of the **Available Values** list and select Workflow, then click **OK**.
7. Click the **Results** button to see all workflow system jobs.
8. After examining the results, click the **Query** button.

9. Add another filter on the second line, following steps 4-7 to add a filter for certain Status Reason values.

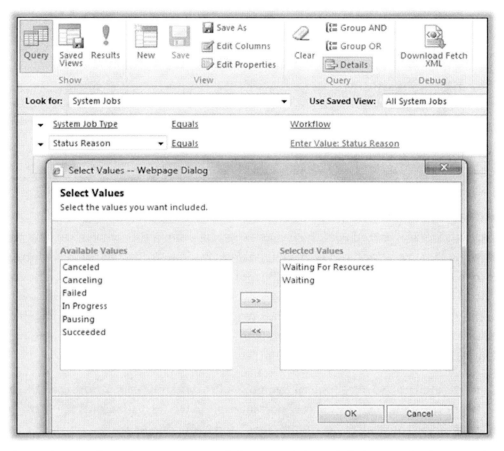

10. After selecting the values you want, click **OK**, and then click the **Results** button. This time you will see a different set of results. For example:

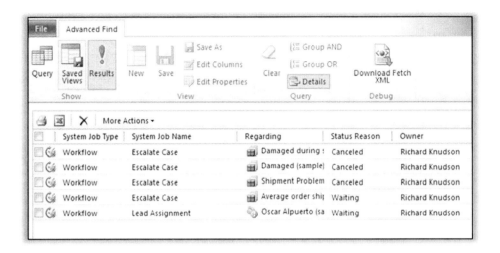

Summary

In this chapter we started with the basics – the properties a dialog can have, and some typical scenarios that can be addressed by workflows with those properties. Next we introduced the mechanics of using the "Step Editor". Most of your work as a designer of workflows will be performed in the Step Editor, so you need to be familiar with it. After that we covered in some detail the seven actions an out of the box workflow can perform; finally we ended up with a discussion of how you can monitor workflows, and some of the most important improvements of monitoring in CRM compared to the previous version.

As I mentioned, the seven actions a Dynamics CRM workflow can perform can be thought of as the "work" in workflow. The most important topic in the next chapter is the "flow" in workflow, represented by so-called "Check Conditions" and "Wait Conditions".

Before going on, make sure you review the examples for Chapter 2. A few of the examples include conditional checking and some other topics that will be covered in detail in the next Chapter. I did that on purpose, partly to make the demonstrations more interesting, and partly to pique your interest for the discussion in the next chapter. I kept them pretty basic, however, so if necessary, review them quickly for now, and come back and study them in more detail after Chapter 3.

Chapter 3 - Dynamic Values and Business Process Logic

Introduction

In the previous chapter we showed a few examples of workflow processes that relied on dynamic values. In this chapter we will cover that important foundation skill in more detail. Next we will cover the conditional logic that provides the *flow* of your workflows. There are two main types of conditional logic: **Check Conditions** can instruct a process to perform an action if a condition is met. **Wait Conditions** add a time dimension, and allow processes to wait until a condition is met, or wait for a period of time.

Dynamic Values

To review, we've seen that there are two main work areas in the workflow design environment: the **Properties** section and the **Step Editor**. Most of the work in building processes is in the step editor, and much of that work is in the workflow designer version of CRM entity forms. The entity forms in the workflow designer look somewhat similar to their corresponding user forms, but they serve a different purpose: rather than enter data as on a regular form, these forms are used to specify how a process will automatically update values as it runs. The following two figures illustrate these concepts, starting with the workflow designer:

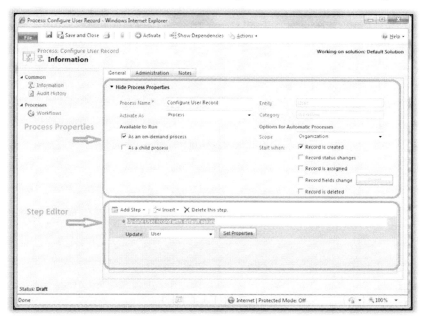

In the previous figure, if you click **Set Properties** on the Update User step the workflow designer version of the user form opens, shown here with the **Dynamic Values** section and key settings highlighted:

Referring to the figure, these dynamic values settings are explained next.

1. **Operator.** Determines which operation will be performed against the currently selected field. **Set to** is the default operator. **Increment by, Decrement by,** and **Multiply by** are all available only for numeric fields when the Update Record action has been selected. **Clear** removes any existing value from the field, and is only available for the Update Record action. **Append With** is available only for text fields, and is used to append text after, and without removing, existing text.

2. The **Look for** section has two drop-down lists. The first one allows you to select the primary entity, any related entities, or options in the Local Values section. (We'll discuss Local Values in a separate section.) For brevity going forward, let's refer to the first drop-down as the **entity drop-down**.

3. The second drop-down in the Look for section depends on what you select in the first one. If you select the primary or a related entity, you use it to select fields from the selected entity. We will refer to this one as the **field drop-down**.

4. **Dynamic Values box.** Once you've selected the Operator and Look for values, click the Add button to move them into the Dynamic Values box. Once they're in the Dynamic

Values box you can click the OK button to insert them into the selected field. This UI device seems cumbersome at first, but you get used to it the more you do it.

5. **Default value.** This is important when the dynamic value you've configured might not contain data. For example, the figure shows a common scenario: we want an email to start with "Dear", and then concatenate a contact's first name, but substitute "colleague" if there's no value in the first name field.

The most obvious differences between the run-time and the designer versions of forms are that data aren't exposed, the form toolbar isn't exposed, and the Details and other sections for related records aren't exposed on the workflow version of the form. Slightly more subtle differences are that the Notes tab isn't exposed on the workflow form, and that the workflow form has an additional tab – "Additional Fields" – that is used to expose all of the fields that are NOT exposed on the user form. We'll discuss that in detail later.

Another difference is that the **Form Assistant** is more important in the process design than in the user experience. In Dynamics CRM 2011 the form assistant has been *deprecated*, so it isn't even available on most forms in the user experience. (The case and product forms are exceptions.) But because the form assistant exposes the dynamic values feature you can't get by without it when designing workflow and dialog processes. It allows you to update field values dynamically, from other fields in the same or related records, to increment or decrement numeric fields, and to assign complex "wait" conditions to date/time fields.

Dynamic Values plays a role in workflow design similar to Advanced Find in the user experience: it's a foundation tool you will use over and over again, in many different contexts. Dynamic values can be confusing at first, partly because they are context sensitive: the field type you have selected in the workflow designer determines the dynamic values that are available for you to select.

Selected Field Data Type	Dynamic Values Available
Text	All fields (text, date/time, numeric)
Date/Time	Date/Time fields only
Numeric	Numeric fields only
Customer ("Composite Customer" record) Lookup	Customer Lookup only
User Lookup	User Lookup only
From, To, CC, etc.	Related records supporting e-mail

Dynamic values are a foundation skill for successfully using the process designer, but I find a solid understanding of how to use them especially important for sending e-mails. One reason for this is that sending e-mails is a pretty common requirement for processes; another is that the body of an e-mail message (the **Description** field) is often a complex combination of static text and dynamic values pulled from many different related entities. Let's extend the Lead Assignment workflow from the previous chapter by adding an e-mail notification for the new owner of the lead. It will include summary information about the record, and a hyperlink that can be clicked to access the lead record form, regardless of the e-mail client being used to view it.

Step by Step: Use Dynamic Values to Send E-Mails

1. Navigate to the processes grid and open the Lead Assignment workflow in the process designer.
2. If necessary, click **Deactivate** on the toolbar so you can make changes to the workflow.
3. Select the last step in the workflow and click the **Add Step** menu.
4. Select **Send E-mail**. Click the Send e-mail step and the step editor should look like this:

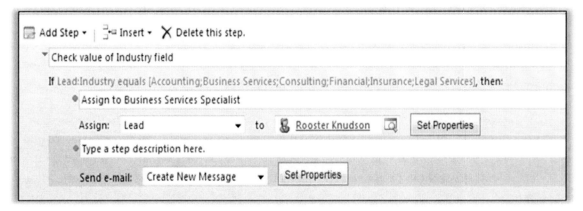

5. Click **Set Properties** to open the New E-mail dialog:

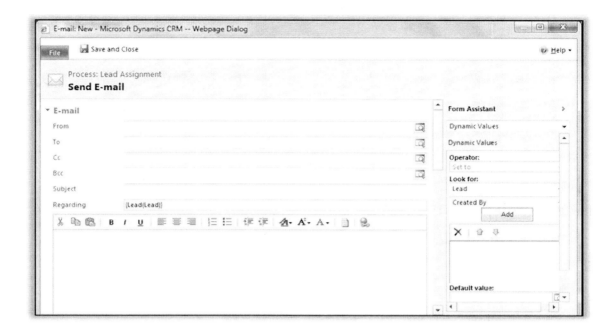

6. If you leave the **From** field empty the e-mail will be sent from the owner of the workflow, not necessarily the owner of any of the records targeted by the workflow. In this case that's fine, since the owner of the workflow is playing the role of sales manager, but this will depend on business requirements.

7. Click in the **To** field and then in the Dynamic Values section, click the second drop-down list in the **Look for** section.

8. Select **Owner**, and then click the **Add** button:

9. Click **OK** and you should see highlighted yellow text in the **To** field, like this:

10. Click inside the Subject line, and enter the text ***A new lead has been assigned to you***.
11. Position the cursor in the message body, and type the static text ***Dear*** and then press the space bar.
12. In the Dynamic Values Look for section, click the first drop-down list, and select **Owning User (User).**
13. In the next drop-down list select the **First Name** field, and then click Add.
14. Click inside the **Default Value** field and type ***colleague***. This is important for situations when there might not be a value in the selected field; then the default value will be substituted instead, then click **OK** to add.
15. Then type a comma as static text, and your form should look like this:

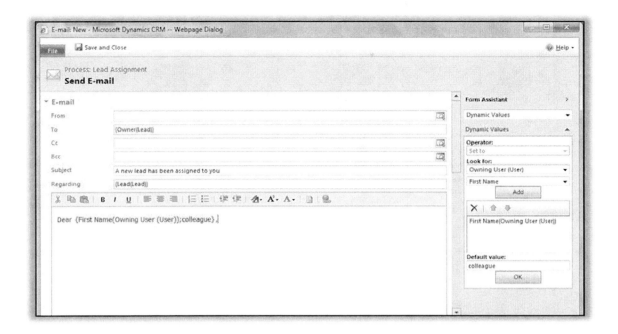

16. Skip a couple of lines and type the following text: *Lead summary information:*

17. On the next line, type *Lead Name:*

18. Click immediately to the right of that static text, and select Lead in the first list in the Look for section.

19. Then select Name in the next list in the Look for section. Click Add and then click OK, and the form should look like this:

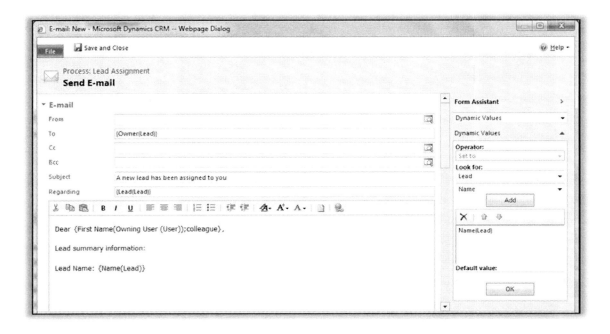

20. Repeat steps 17-19 to add as many additional fields you like in the Lead summary information section. By default, if you press the Enter key at the end of a line in the text editor, and "hard return" is used and what looks like an extra line is added. I generally press the Shift+Enter combination for things like this that I want to appear closer together. Here's what my example looks like after adding a few more fields:

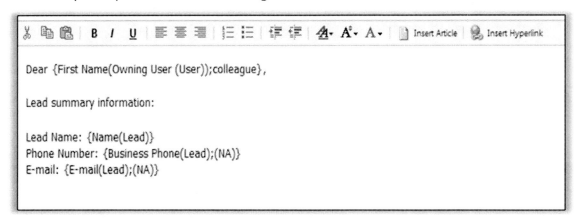

Note the liberal use of "NA" for default values. Click **Save and Close**, and then **Save and Close** again. You can activate the workflow and test it at this point, and a perfectly functional e-mail notification should be sent to the owner of the lead.

New Feature in Dynamics CRM 2011 November 2011 Service Update: Insert Hyperlink
When viewing e-mails generated by Dynamics CRM it's often convenient for users to be able to click a hyperlink and navigate directly to a record. The Regarding field provides this functionality, so if you view an e-mail generated by this workflow and happen to be using the web client for Dynamics CRM, you will see something like the following figure and be able to click the Regarding link:

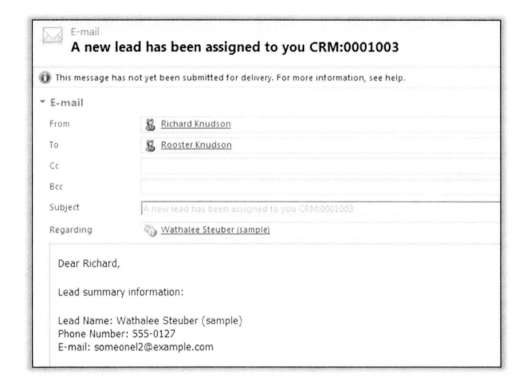

But the Regarding field only works if a user happens to be using the web client or the Outlook client for Dynamics CRM. Other e-mail clients (including, notably, Outlook Web Access) won't know how to render that as a hyperlink. There are various other ways people have added links to, such as using Jscript code to create URLs for every record, storing that information in a custom field, and the like. Fortunately, starting in November 2011 we no longer have to use those approaches because a handy, built-in field is now included for it!

Step by Step: Using Hyperlinks and Record URLs

Follow these steps to add a hyperlink to the e-mail generated in the Lead Assignment workflow:

1. Navigate to the processes grid and open the Lead Assignment workflow in the process designer.
2. If necessary, click Deactivate on the toolbar so you can make changes to the workflow.
3. Click Set Properties on the Send e-mail line to open the e-mail editor.
4. Click in the editor a couple lines below the Summary information section, and type *Click.*
5. Then press the space bar, and click **Insert Hyperlink** on the toolbar. The **Insert Hyperlink** dialog appears.
6. Type *this link* in the **Text to display** field.
7. Then tab to the **URL** field. Immediately beneath the entity list in the **Look for** section is the field list. Locate the **Record URL (Dynamic)** field and single-click it to select it:

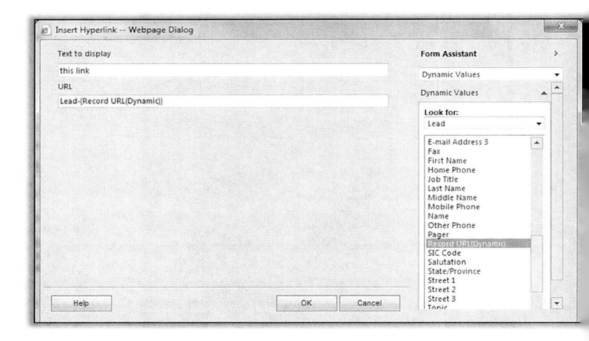

8. Then click **OK**. The hyperlink is inserted in a special markup language into the body of the e-mail.

9. Immediately after the hyperlink tag, you can finish off the sentence with static text, such as the following figure illustrates:

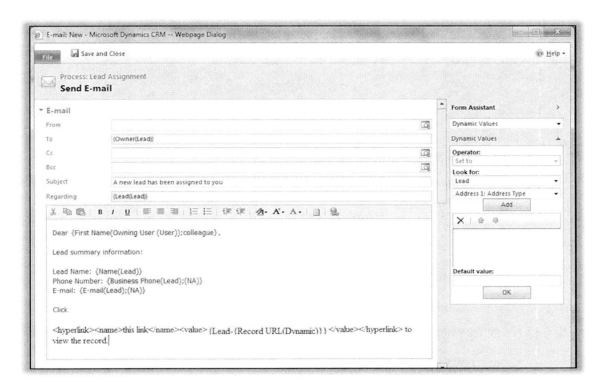

10. Notice that the inserted text isn't necessarily in the same font as the rest of the e-mail. When this happens, select all the text, and then change everything at once so it all matches. (I usually use Verdana 10-pt)

11. Finally, add a perky signature, and you're done. Click **Save and Close** twice and activate the workflow for testing.

After running this workflow on a lead record with the appropriate values for the Industry field, here's what one of the generated e-mail messages looks like now:

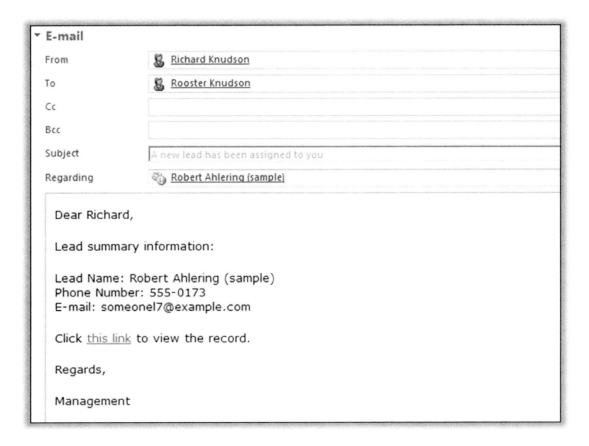

So now, even if you cannot see the Regarding field, you will always be able to click the link to view the record.

Insert Knowledge Base Articles into Process-Generated E-mails
Another useful technique is to insert a Knowledge Base (KB) article into the text of an e-mail generated by a workflow or dialog process. Let's see an example of how this works, but first, two things to keep in mind about KB articles in case you don't have much experience with them.

- This only works with published articles. In the KB world, this means that the article's status is *Published*, and it's available via KB search to anybody with Read privileges on articles.
- KB articles must be based on article *templates*. You will save yourself lots of potential e-mail formatting frustration if you make sure the template uses the same typeface and size of the font you want in your e-mails!

Now, suppose you've created an auto-responder workflow for a certain type of lead record. For example, somebody might fill out a form on your web site, requesting information on how to insert a Dynamics CRM Knowledge Base article into a workflow generated e-mail. (Don't laugh – it *could* happen!)

The following figure shows an automatic workflow on the lead entity that first performs a conditional check on the lead Topic field. If a certain value is found, an appropriate e-mail is sent:

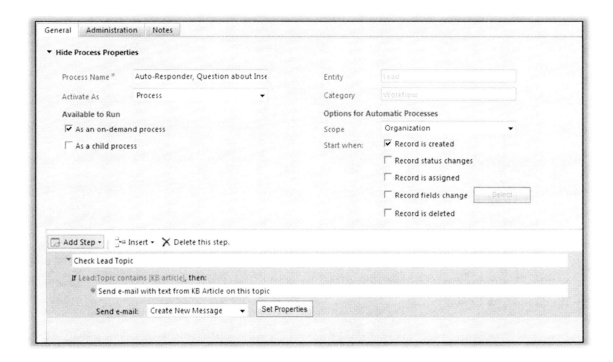

To understand how you'd configure the e-mail to leverage an existing article from the KB, consider the following figure, which is the E-mail Properties dialog you'd access by clicking **Set Properties** on the Send e-mail step in the designer:

In this illustration, dynamic values have been used to fill in the To and Regarding fields, and to create a salutation that will either include the lead's first name, or the static text "colleague" if the first name field is empty.

After the first sentence of static text, the KB article was then inserted by clicking the Insert Article button (highlighted), and using the standard KB search functions to locate the article.

Which to Use: E-Mail Templates or KB Articles?

Previously, I pointed out that with the Send E-Mail action, you can either create the message within the workflow, or use a previously existing e-mail template. We just saw an example of an alternative way of using previously created content, by using a KB article. These seem like two different ways of doing the same thing. Which one is better?

Well, it depends. Many organizations that primarily use the sales functions of

Dynamics CRM don't use the Knowledge Base. For organizations like that e-mail, templates are probably the better way to go, since they are somewhat easier to set up and a little more accessible than KB articles. On the other hand, for organizations that *do* use the Knowledge Base, it's a lot better to re-use KB article content than it is to re-create it in a different format!

Now you know both approaches are available, so you can pick the best one for your organization.

Using Increment, Decrement and Multiply Operators

So far we've examined the default **Set to** operator. When working with numeric fields, you can use the **Increment by**, **Decrement by** and **Multiply by** operators, and we will examine those in detail now.

Using Increment by to add values to numeric fields

One good example of when you might need to do this is for a "recursive" workflow – one that calls itself repeatedly. You can use recursive workflows to implement escalation business processes. For example, you might have a service level agreement that specifies a case must be resolved within a certain period of time, or it gets escalated to a senior support technician. There are many scenarios that require this kind of recursive workflow and we will look at some in detail later in the book.

Regardless of the specifics of the business process, it is often important to know how many times one of these recursive workflows has "recursed", and the **Increment by** operator gives us a way to do that.

To illustrate with an example we will finish later, let's take a sneak peak at the Escalate Case workflow. The following figure shows the process designer version of the case form open, with three items of special note.

- A custom field – Escalation Counter – highlighted on the form.
- The Dynamic Values section is also highlighted. Notice that rather than the default Set to operator, in the figure Increment by is selected.
- Also in Dynamic Values, notice that the value 1 is entered in the Default value field, and that nothing else has been added to the field list.

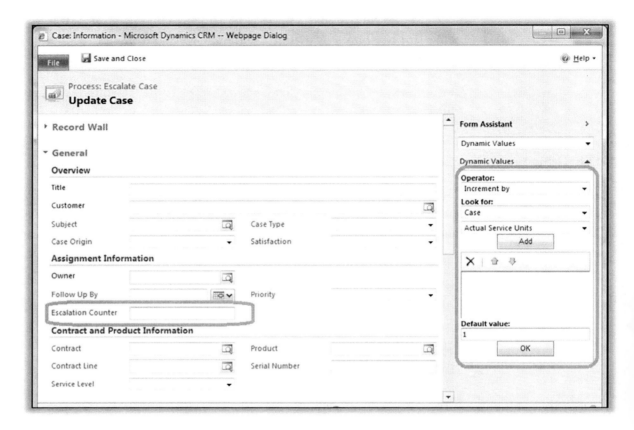

If you set things up as in the previous figure, and then click OK, the Escalation Counter field will fill in like this:

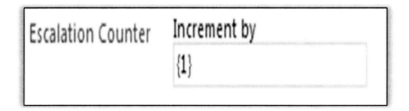

This technique gets around a problem you tend to run into in situations where one instance of a workflow needs to know something about another instance. In this example, what we want to know is "how many times has a case been escalated?" The problem is, every instance of a workflow is independent of every other one, so we need to add something like this Escalation

Counter field to keep track of it for us. More on this later, though, as we don't want to get ahead of ourselves!

Using Multiply by

Dynamics CRM does not have a built-in "calculated" field type, but you can use the **Multiply by** operator and a workflow to get something close to it. For example, the Opportunity entity has built in attributes Est. Revenue (schema name estimatedvalue) and Probability (schema name closeprobability). Suppose you wanted a "probability-weighted" revenue forecast. You can create a custom attribute, and then use a workflow to multiply the built-in fields by each other to update the custom attribute. Here are the three attributes I will use to illustrate, all on the Opportunity entity:

Attribute Display Name (Schema Name)	Data Type	Description
Est. Revenue (estimatedvalue)	Currency	Built-in
Probability (closeprobability)	Int	Built-in
Weighted Revenue (new_weightedrevenue)	Currency	Custom attribute to update in workflow. The value it contains should be Est. Revenue multiplied by Probability

After adding the custom attribute, we need to build a workflow to update its value with the product of the "Est. Revenue" and "Probability" attributes. The Multiply by operator works by multiplying the current value of a field by a *single numeric value*. What this means is that you cannot enter a formula as you might think. My inclination was to have a workflow update the weighted revenue value with something like this:

=(est. revenue)*(probability)

Unfortunately it's not quite that easy! Since the Multiply by operator only allows you to update the current value by multiplying it by something else, the workflow needs to perform three consecutive Update actions:

1. Update weighted revenue with the current value of Est. Revenue.
2. Update its new value by multiplying it by Probability.
3. Update its new value by multiplying it by .01 (since Probability is an integer value!)

The following figure shows a simple example of this, with three **Update** actions generously commented to make it somewhat self-documenting.

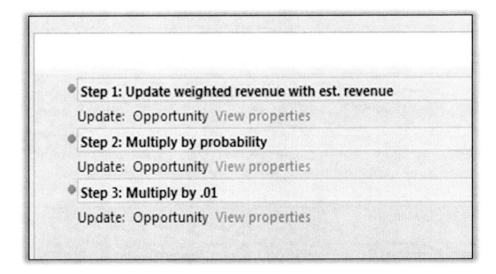

The following three figures show the successive steps in detail

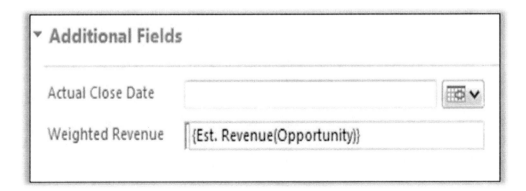

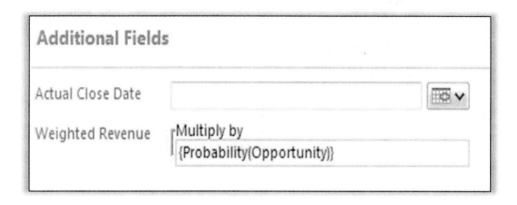

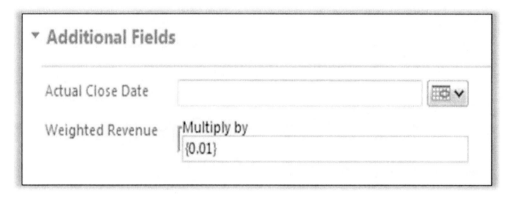

Here are a few points to consider when implementing functionality like this using workflows:

- The reason it takes three Update Record actions to perform the calculation is that you're always updating the current value of the field, and you can only perform one operation at a time. It would be better if you could use formulas, but you can't.

- You can imagine a more complicated calculation might take many more Update Record actions. This can become somewhat tedious using the workflow approach discussed here.

- Another disadvantage of the workflow approach to calculating fields is the latency problem: Dynamics CRM workflows run asynchronously, one implication of which is that calculated fields will take some time to update on the form, generally from 15 to 30 seconds. If you use the workflow approach, you will probably want to take the calculated field off the form, or maybe "hide it" on another tab.

- How should a workflow like this one be triggered? You might need to run it manually for records that were created before you implemented it. On an ongoing basis you might want to run it when a new record is created, or when the **Est. Revenue** or **Probability** attributes change. Again, the specifics will be determined by your business requirements. This figure shows what would be a reasonable configuration of an automatic workflow to do this:

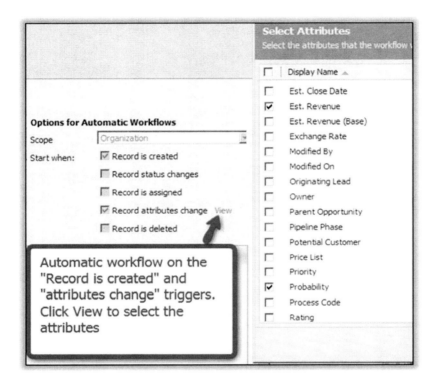

Which to Use: Workflows or Alternative Approaches

As mentioned above, using the process designer to create complex calculated fields can be tedious and some cases impractical. Then there's the latency issue with workflow-calculated values: if a user needs to see a quick refresh of a field on a form, the workflow approach is not ideal. There are alternatives:

- One is to call a JScript function from the change event of the appropriate field on a form. That's not foolproof, however, since field values can change without the form being loaded, in which case the function never gets called.

- Another is to write a Plug-in (a compiled .NET assembly). Plug-ins, unlike JScript, can be made to be foolproof: they are not run on the client and do not require the form to be loaded. However...they are also out of reach technically for many people who *can* write workflows. Sometimes, the preferred method will be dictated by the resources you have access to!

Although a detailed treatment of topics like those is not in scope for the book, I will include some more guidance on how to select the right approach, and in the Advanced Topics section below include some relatively simple JScript examples to illustrate a direct comparison of approaches.

Using Append With on text fields

While in Dynamics CRM 4.0 the **Increment by** operator could be used on both numeric and text fields, in the 2011 version it's only available for numeric fields. To append text at the end of existing text, Dynamics CRM 2011 introduced the **Append With** operator. One common example is to use Append With on a record's Description field, to create an informal audit-trail regarding status changes and so forth.

For example, the following figure shows how you might use an **Update Record** action to update the **Description** field on the Campaign entity with information from a *Campaign Activity* record.

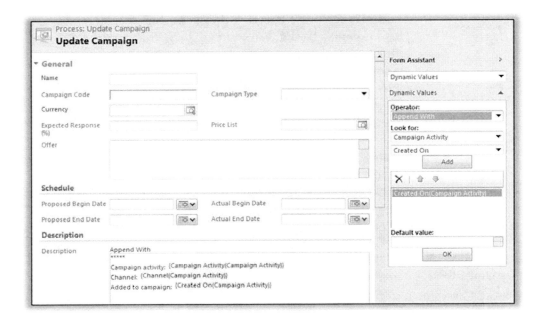

The key thing to note here is that if you use **Append With** rather than the default **Set to**, the text you increment by gets concatenated at the end of any previously existing text; if you use **Set to** it will replace it. The workflow I discuss here is created for the Campaign Activity entity. Since every Campaign Activity is associated with a Parent Campaign record, a workflow running against Campaign Activity can update the Parent Campaign.

Dynamic Values: Related Entities and Data Context

One of the most important features of Dynamics CRM is how easy it is to create relationships between entities. In an important sense, Dynamics CRM can be thought of as a development platform for custom database applications. In all relational databases, including Dynamics CRM, the most common relationship between entities is a "one-to-many", or "parent-child" relationship, such as exists out of the box in CRM between accounts and contacts, accounts and cases, and so forth. The jargon around this can be inconsistent; for example sometimes the entity on the "1" side of a "1:N" relationship will be referred to as the Primary entity, sometimes as the Parent, and so forth.

It's especially important to understand how entities are related in Dynamics CRM when you're designing workflow and dialog processes. I refer to this as the *data context* of a Dynamics CRM 2011 business process. As we saw previously, every business process is created for a "primary entity". For example, the primary entity of the Lead Assignment workflow discussed previously is the lead entity. By data context, I mean which records a running instance of a workflow knows about, relative to the record it is running on. This can be confusing at first, because the term *primary entity* in this context refers to the record the workflow is written for, rather than its relationship to any other records.

For example, a workflow written for the opportunity entity refers to opportunity as the primary entity in the workflow designer. But the opportunity entity is a child entity of many of the other entities you need to interact with in the designer!

To clarify this point, examine the stylized entity relationship diagram in the following figure:

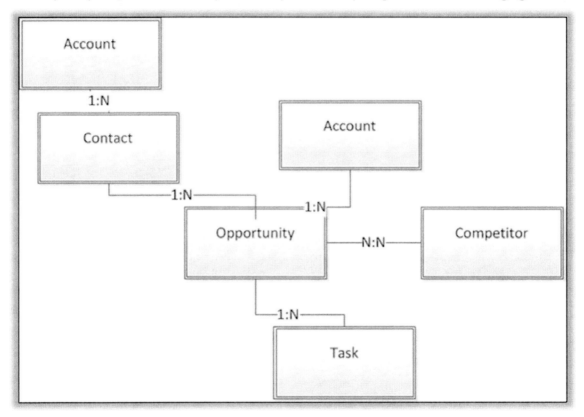

A workflow written for the opportunity entity has that record type as its "primary entity", but as you can see from the diagram, the opportunity entity's place in the overall ER scheme of things in Dynamics CRM is complex:

- Sometimes it's a parent record, as in its 1:N relationship to task.

- Sometimes it's a child record, as in its N:1 relationship to the customer records (Contact and Account).
- Sometimes it's the child record of a child record (if it's associated with a contact, which in turn is associated with an account).
- And sometimes, it's got a many-to-many (N:N, for short) relationship to another record, such as its system relationship to competitor.

Let's review a specific example so we can see what the limitations are. Suppose you have an opportunity record with a contact entered in the **Potential Customer** lookup field, like the one shown in the following figure:

In this case, the contact record is the parent of the opportunity, and if the contact is associated with an account, that makes the account record a parent record of the parent record. Here's a more specific version of the previous ER to illustrate the relationships:

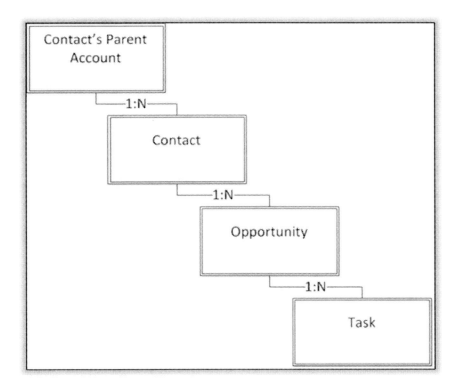

So in this example, the question of data context boils down to this: *what does a running instance of an opportunity workflow know about its immediate parent record, the parent of its parent, and any of its children?*

For these records	Which fields does the workflow have access to?	Which fields can be filtered on?
Parent records of parent records	None	None
Parent records	All	All
Record workflow running on	All	All
Child records	None, *unless child record is created by workflow*	None, *unless child record is created by workflow*

Note that Advanced Find works slightly differently. If you're using Advanced Find to build a query on the opportunity record type, you can filter on and display columns from its parent records, and you can filter on columns from parent records one or *more* levels removed from opportunity. Its' easy to get in the habit of thinking that Advanced Find and workflows essentially "work the same" when it comes to data context. But they do not, and the differences can be important. For example, the following Advanced Find query, on the Opportunity record type, effectively drills back up through two relationship levels: first through the Potential Customer (Contact), and then through the contact's parent account record:

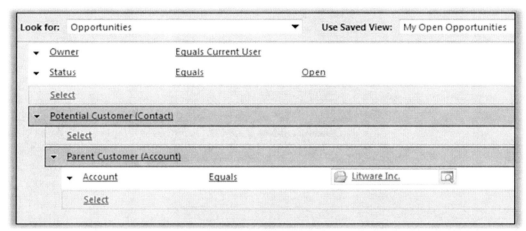

But if you create a workflow for the opportunity record type, assuming that you can conditionally check for a specific value on the parent record of a parent record, you might spend some head-scratching time when you get to a figure like the following:

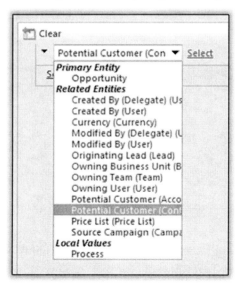

This is the **Specify Condition** dialog in the business process designer, which we will cover in detail next. For now, the key point is that it does not currently have the full flexibility of Advanced Find, and it does sometimes limit what you can accomplish within the process designer.

Dynamic Values: Local Values

In the following figure you can see that the Dynamic Values **Look for** drop-down menu has a **Local Values** section. Local Values always includes a selection for **Process**.

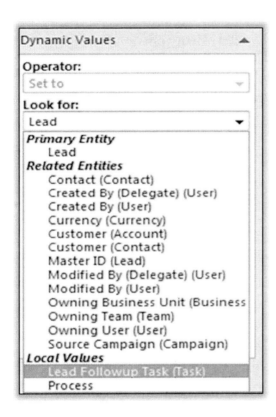

We will discuss **Process** options later in the book. Here I want to focus on the **Lead Followup Task (Task) option**. In addition to the Workflow options, the Local Values section gives you access to any records that have been created within the *running workflow*. This is important because it allows your workflows to respond to and interact with records created within the workflow, even if they don't have a relationship to the workflow's primary entity! We will see many examples of this throughout the rest of the book; for now I want to make two related points on this topic:

- **You will only see Local Values (other than the Workflow options) if you are at or after the workflow Step in which they are created.** For example, if you are working within a multiple stage workflow and have Task records created in each stage, you will only be able to select tasks that were created in previous stages.
- **The name of the Local Values you select from is the descriptive text for the** task (or any other record you create). So even though this descriptive text is "optional", you should always use a good, systematic naming convention. It's especially important in a scenario like this one where you might need to select from multiple Local Values in different contexts. In the worst case, if you left them all blank – as you can do since they are optional – you'll find yourself selecting from a list like this one:

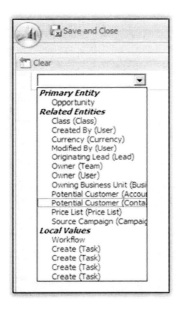

Logic – Check Condition

You can include conditional logic in your workflow and dialog processes to control the flow, specifying the conditions under which specific actions will take place. **Check Condition** provides the fundamental construct for building out the logic of your processes, and consists of three different branches.

- **Check Condition** is the first branch of a conditional block. Gets things started and performs the first *if* check.
- **Conditional Branch** provides an *else if* check. This is optional, but if included it can only be included within a check condition block.

- **Default Action** is the last branch and can specify a default action that should happen if none of the previous conditions were satisfied. This is also optional and like the conditional branch can only be included within a check condition block.

In the Step Editor, these are accessible from the Add Step menu. In the second section of that menu you'll see commands for **Check Condition**, **Conditional Branch**, and **Default Action**. Notice that unless you already have a Condition line selected in the editor, Conditional Branch and Default Action will be unavailable. Also, if you haven't selected a step at which it's possible to insert a conditional, even the Check Condition command will be unavailable.

Check Condition: Building out your Workflow Logic

Let's revisit the Case Routing workflow example discussed at the end of the previous chapter for a closer look at how conditional logic works. The following figure shows the conditional block, which first checks the value of the priority field. If the priority is high, a queue item is created in the Premium Service queue. All other cases are routed to the Standard Service queue.

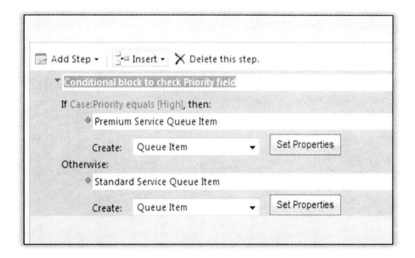

This takes a little getting used to, partly because the menu options don't use the same terminology you see in the step editor:

- Check Condition creates the **If <condition>, then:** branch.
- Conditional Branch creates the **Else <condition>, then:** branch.
- Default Action creates the **Otherwise:** branch.

Let's examine the various options we have with this basic logical construct, using the lead assignment workflow discussed previously to illustrate the various options available. The following figure shows the conditional logic for a basic lead assignment scenario, where leads are assigned to designated users, depending on the value of the industry field.

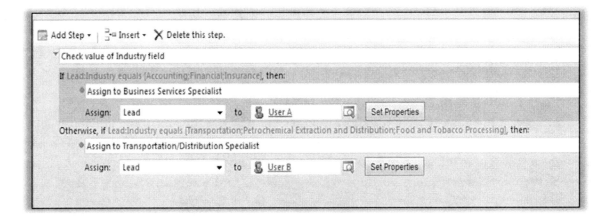

The first thing to notice is that when you specify conditions for option set (picklist) or lookup fields, the functionality is essentially an *Or* condition. In this example, clicking the link on the If branch opens the **Specify Condition** dialog you see here.

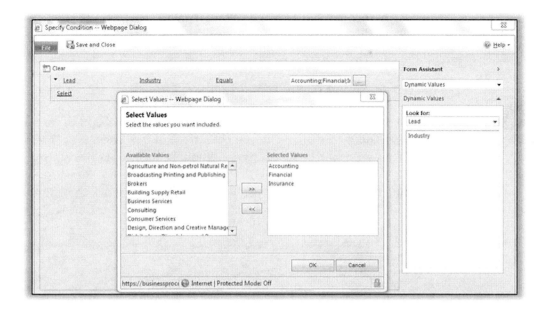

The first time you see this it might look like an *And*, but it's not. If the industry field contains any of those three values, the condition will evaluate to true and the lead will be assigned to User A.

The next thing to note is that the way this conditional block is written, if neither of the conditions are satisfied, the lead will not be assigned. So for example, suppose the workflow is run on a lead record owned by User C, and the industry field is either empty or set to a value other than the ones specified in these conditions. In this scenario the lead will remain assigned to User C.

But consider the following permutation on this conditional block.

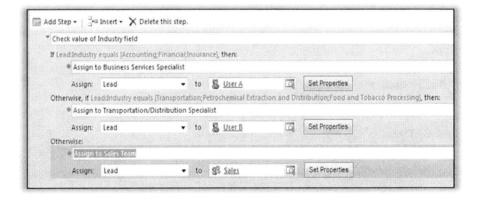

This version has an *Otherwise* branch (added with the **Default Action** step), so after the workflow runs, the lead record will **not** be assigned to User C: if neither the *If* nor the *Otherwise, if* branches are satisfied, the *Otherwise* branch will assign the lead to the (default) sales team.

For Predictable Results, Use Mutually Exclusive Conditions!

In the previous example, since the Industry field is a single-valued option set field, the conditions checked by the different branches are mutually exclusive. This is a good thing, since it means the order of the conditional checks does not matter.

But if you examine the following figure you'll see a conditional block that, although it doesn't have any problems from a technical standpoint, from a business standpoint is at best hard to understand!

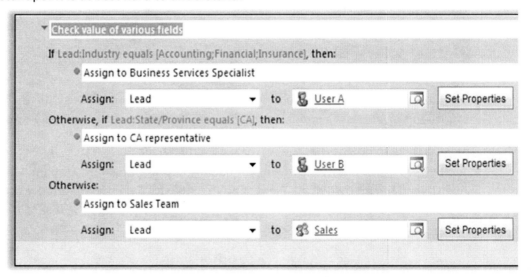

One of the problems with conditional blocks like this; that is, ones not based on a set of mutually exclusive conditions, is that the order of the conditions matters. In this case, even if the lead is from California, it will never be assigned to User B if any of the conditions in the *If* branch are satisfied. There may situations when an approach like this is the best way to go, but I'd consider those exceptions to the general rule that mutually exclusive conditions are preferred.

Nesting Conditional Branches

You can also nest conditional branches within a workflow or dialog. Nesting is useful when you need to check for conditions at different levels. For example, in the previous Case assignment workflow, suppose you want to route all high priority cases to a specific queue, but for cases that are not high priority, you want to route or assign them based on other criteria.

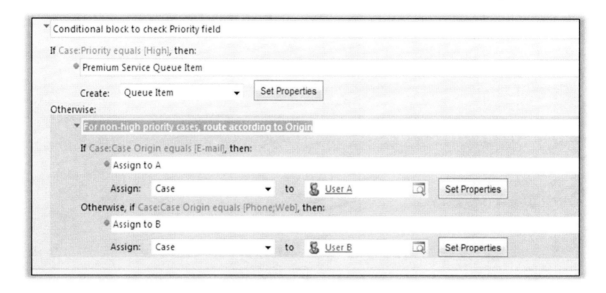

These nested conditionals can get confusing, so it's a good idea to map out your logic beforehand. And there are plenty of things you cannot do in the process design environment that you don't want to discover after it's too late! For example:

- You cannot promote or demote actions or conditions.
- You cannot move a step from one place to another.

Logic - Wait Conditions

The Check Condition logic just discussed simply checks for a condition and performs an appropriate action if the condition is true. Sometimes, however, you need to *stop* a workflow and *wait* until something happens before proceeding. This is what the Wait condition is for. To insert a wait condition into a workflow, click the **Add Step** drop-down and select **Wait Condition**.

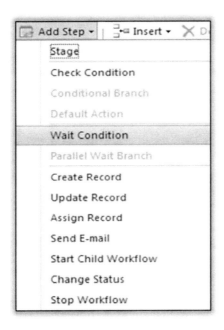

As you can see from the figure, a wait condition has a **Parallel Wait Branch**, which is analogous to the role played by Conditional Branch and Default Action for Check Condition. Personally, I've always found it harder to explain the various options available for wait conditions than for check conditions, so the following table has some examples.

Condition	Option	Use this to...	Examples
Wait Condition	Wait until	wait until a condition is true	• Wait until a task is completed before advancing to the next stage in a sales process.
	Wait timeout	wait for a specified period of time, or until the system time equals a date value in CRM	• Wait for one day after a case is created and then check whether it is resolved. If not, take appropriate corrective action. • Wait until one day before an opportunity's estimated close date and send a reminder e-mail to the owner of the record.
Parallel Wait Branch			• While waiting for a task to be completed, a parallel wait branch can specify corrective action to be taken if the task is NOT completed after a specified amount of time.

Using Wait Conditions in a Sales Process Workflow

Let's step through an example to illustrate. A commonly encountered requirement for wait conditions is encountered in sales processes. For example, suppose your business uses a simple 3-stage sales process with a workflow like the one illustrated in the following diagram.

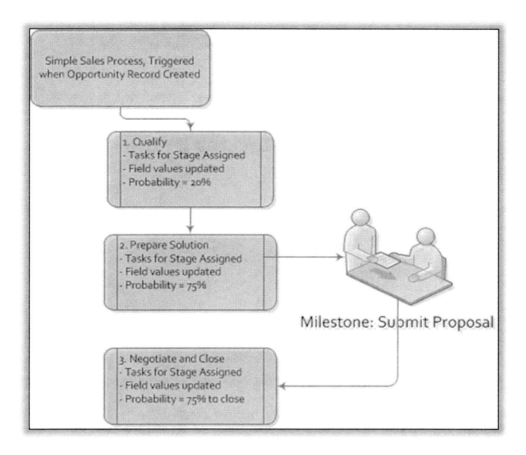

You might start out by creating a Dynamics CRM workflow.

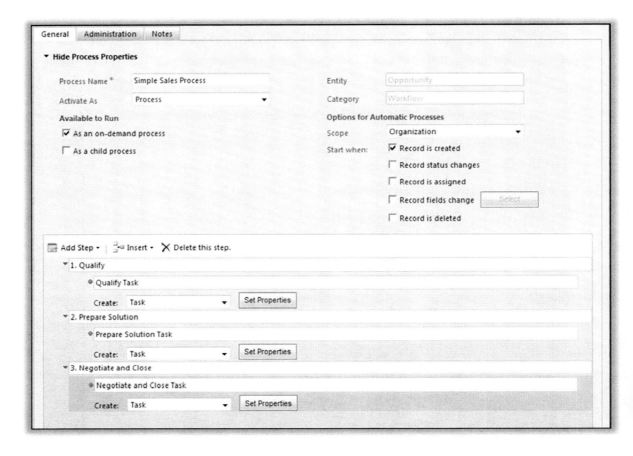

This is a simple workflow (too simple, as you will see in a minute!) with the following features:

- It runs automatically, when a new opportunity record is created.
- The scope of organization means that it will run when any user in the CRM organization creates an opportunity.
- It's also available to run as an on-demand process. Sometimes when I write a workflow like this I'll include that option at first, as I'm testing and troubleshooting. But for a workflow like this one that assigns tasks and the like, it almost never makes sense to keep on-demand turned on once it's in production.
- Being a staged sales process, the workflow can be easily divided into stages in the workflow designer as you can see in the figure.

For the current discussion, the most important point to make about this workflow is that by themselves, the stages don't have any impact on the way the workflow runs. In particular, there's nothing about a staged workflow to make it stop within a stage. So if you actually ran a workflow like the one shown above, it wouldn't stop: it would simply run, top to bottom, create three task records and then finish with a status of succeeded. Not much of a sales process!

That's where wait conditions come in. The following figure illustrates how a wait condition might look in a workflow like this.

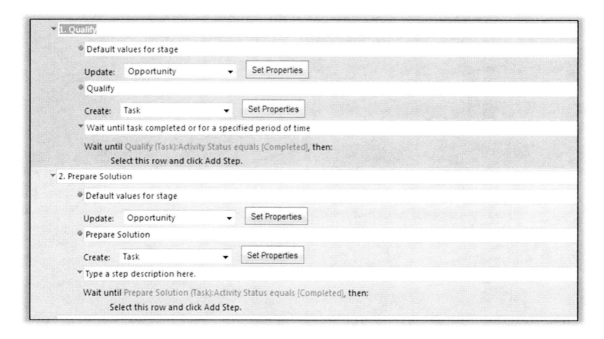

This is one of the most common uses of a wait condition: the workflow creates a task record appropriate for the stage, and immediately hits the wait condition. The wait condition will kick in before stage two is reached, so until the Qualify task is completed, none of the steps in stage two are executed. If you activate a workflow like this and then create an opportunity record, a very definite sequence of events will occur, so let's step through them in detail.

1. After creating a new record and waiting a few seconds for the workflow to fire, click Activities on the form and you should see the task record created by the workflow. Notice that so far, only the task for the first stage is created.

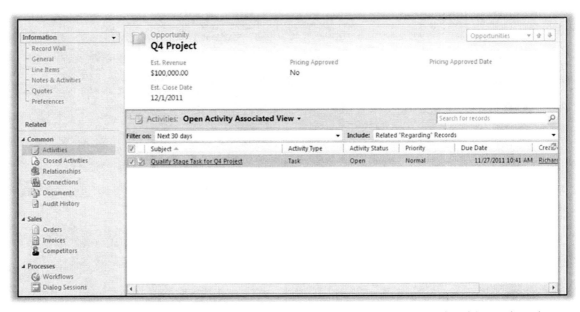

2. In the Processes section of form navigation, click **Workflows** and you should see that the workflow process is running with a Status Reason of **Waiting**.

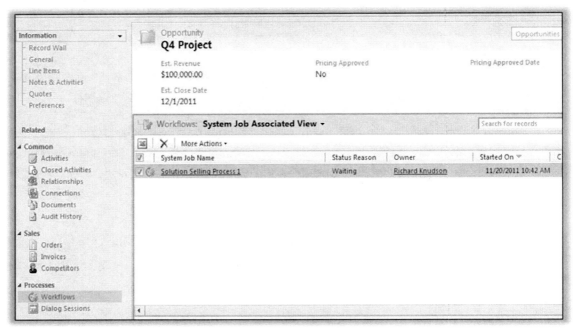

3. To better understand how a wait condition works, click the link in the **System Job Name** column and examine the visualization provided in the **Process Progress** section of the form.

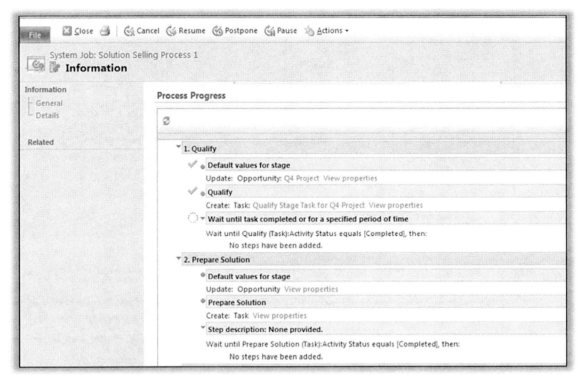

4. Close that window and then navigate to the stage one task and click the **Mark Complete** button. Click Closed Activities to see the completed task, and click Activities to note that now, the stage two task is open. Click Workflows again and then click the link in the **System Job Name** column. Once again the workflow is waiting, but now it's waiting for the stage two task to be completed.

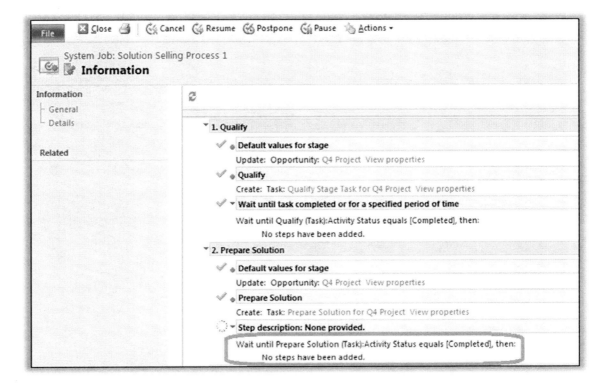

At first it might seem a little odd that the *Wait until <condition>, then:* block doesn't have any steps added for it (highlighted in the previous figure). The logic is correct, at least for this simple example. Here, the only purpose of the wait condition is to pause the sales process until the task is completed. Once the task is completed, the process simply proceeds to the next stage.

Configuring Wait Conditions

Adding a Wait Condition is the easy part. Configuring them to accommodate all the things that can happen in the complicated real world of business takes a little more work! There are two basic wait conditions: waiting for a condition to be satisfied, and waiting for a period of time to pass. Let's illustrate these next with several examples.

Waiting for Conditions

A condition like the one we just reviewed would typically be described as "wait until the task is complete before proceeding", and indeed, that's how that simple example was configured. But in most cases, a wait condition like this should be configured differently: rather than wait for the task to be *completed*, you generally want to wait until the task status is *not open*. This is to account for the possibility that the task might never be completed: that is, it might be canceled instead. If you configure the wait condition like this, then you've got the flexibility to take appropriate action whether the task is completed or canceled.

This is also a good example of how conditional blocks must often be nested to implement custom process logic, so let's implement a slightly more complex (and flexible) version of the Solution Selling Process workflow.

1. Starting with the previous version of the workflow, I'll deactivate it, open it in the designer, and select the wait condition in the first stage:

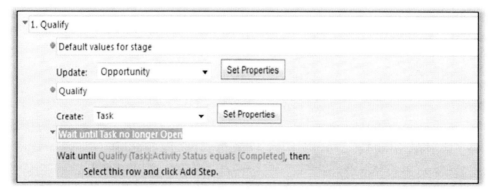

2. Next we need to change that condition, so click the link to open the **Specify Condition** dialog. Instead of waiting until the task is completed, we want to wait until it is not open, so change the operator to **Does Not Equal** and the status value to check for to **Open.**

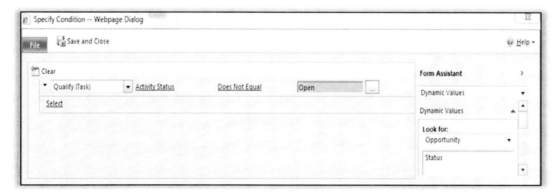

3. Click **Save and Close** to return to the step editor. Then select the line immediately beneath the condition, click the **Add Step** menu and select **Check Condition**. When you do this you will see the scary red x's as in the following figure, which indicate there's something lacking in your workflow that would prevent you from activating it.

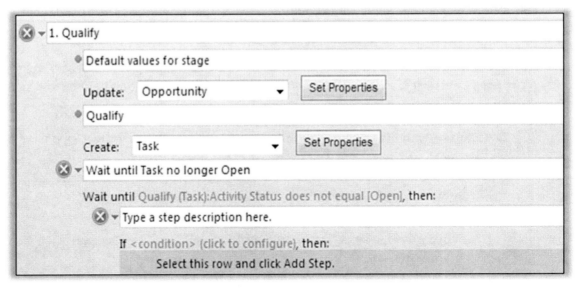

4. In this case we need to configure the nested condition we've just inserted. To do that, click the link on the *If…, then* step and use the **Specify Condition** dialog to check for the possibility the task is canceled rather than completed. After doing that and clicking **Save and Close** you should see the following.

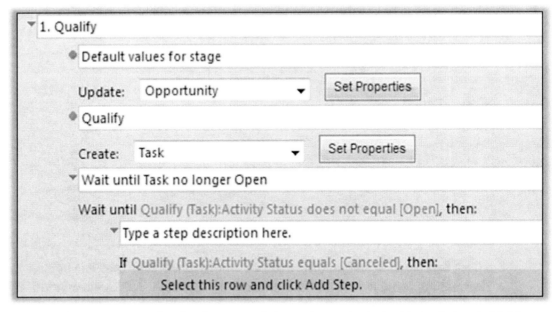

5. Now it's time to specify what happens if the task is canceled. This is obviously highly business-specific, and remember that when you're writing sales process workflows on

the opportunity entity you're exploring some of the most potentially contentious territory in the entire business world: sales representatives and their deals! With that in mind, let's venture bravely forth and put a stake in the sales process ground, in the form of some hard and fast rules on the importance of dealing properly with assigned tasks.

6. With the step selected as in the previous figure, click **Add Step and** select the **Change Status** action. Accept the default value of Opportunity in the entity column, and then in the next column select Canceled in the drop-down list. Notice that by selecting **Canceled** (the Status Reason field value); you effectively force a closing of the Opportunity record with a Status value of **Lost**.

7. Next, click **Add Step** and select **Stop Workflow**. Select **Canceled** in the Stop workflow with status of list, and you should see the following in the step editor.

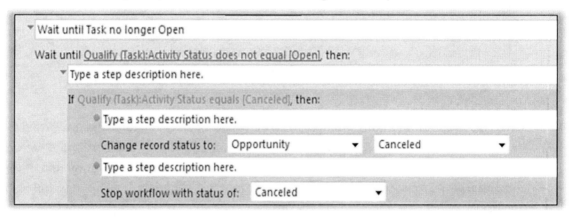

8. Now, make sure that the nested *If..., then* branch is selected and click Add Step. Select Conditional Branch and then use the Specify Condition dialog as before, to check for the possibility that the task might actually be completed.

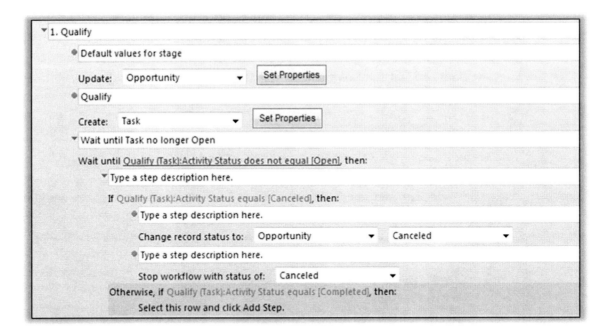

Now you're essentially done. Remember that the wait condition here serves a gating function. The process won't proceed until it gets out of the wait condition, and here there are only two ways of getting out: if the task status isn't open, it's either canceled or completed. If canceled, the opportunity's closed and the workflow's stopped. If completed, proceed to the next sales stage.

Waiting for Timeouts

Timeouts come in two basic flavors: timeout for a specified period of time, and timeout until a date milestone is reached (i.e., the system clock meets a condition relative to a date field). Since these can be confusing at first, I want to present the essentials of each with a couple of simple examples, this time using the case entity to illustrate.

Example 1: Timeout for a Specified Period of Time

Suppose you have a service process that under certain conditions requires a case to be resolved within a certain period of time. If not resolved, some kind of escalation might be performed. This is a common requirement in many service scenarios and we can use a special kind of Wait condition to implement it in a workflow process. This is illustrated in the following example.

1. Create a new workflow for the case entity that runs automatically when a record is created.
2. Select the first line in the step editor and click **Add Step**.
3. Select **Wait Condition** and you will see something like the following figure.

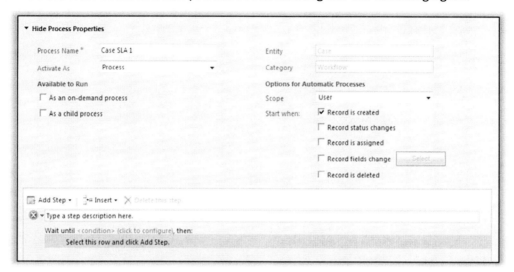

4. Click the link on the *Wait until ..., then:* step to access the **Specify Condition** dialog. In the first column click the drop-down list and select **Process**. In the second column click the drop-down and select **Timeout**:

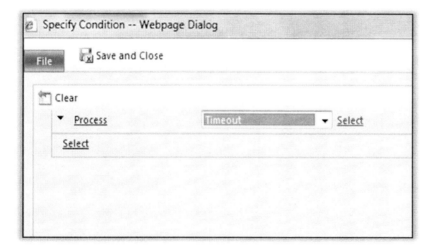

5. Tab to the next column and select **Equals** (the only option), then tab to the next column. This is a date field and is used to specify the timeout logic. In this case we want to wait for a period of time, so specify the following options in the dynamic values section,

a. Select 1 in the **Day** drop-down
b. Select **After** in the drop-down on the next line
c. Click **Created On** in the box below the entity selector

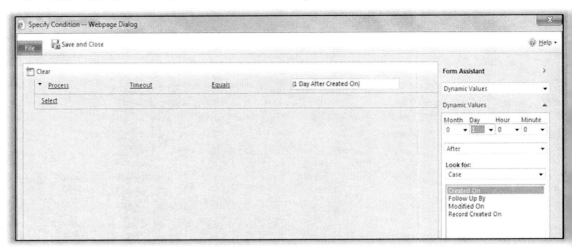

6. Click **Save and Close** to return to the step editor. From here it's easy to understand how these work.

Of course we haven't specified anything to do yet, but we will shortly!

Example 2: Timeout until a Date Milestone is Reached

Waiting for a specific period of time to pass is relatively easy to understand, but there's another kind of wait condition that is a little trickier (at least it was for me!) and at least as common. This is when you're waiting for what I refer to as a *date milestone*. Here are a few examples of what I mean.

- Wait until a case is past its due date.
- Wait until an opportunity is past its estimated close date.
- Wait until a task is overdue.
- Wait until a subscription is one month from its expiration date.

The common thread in all these examples (and the infinite number of other ones that are essentially similar) is that we need to compare the system time, that is, whatever the current time is, with a date field on a Dynamics CRM record.

The following figure shows an example of this using the case workflow just discussed.

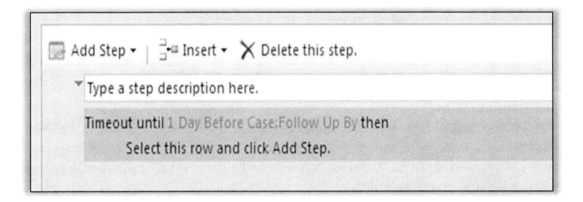

It doesn't look very different, and it's pretty much the same process to configure this (just select **Before** instead of **After** and the **Follow Up By** field instead of **Created On**), but it's different in one important way: unlike **Created On,** you don't know what the **Follow Up By** date will be. For example, Follow Up By might change as a process is running. This has important implications for how processes must be written and we'll examine some of those below.

The following table shows another example of the distinction, this time using a workflow on the opportunity entity.

What it looks like in the Step Editor	Example of how to use it

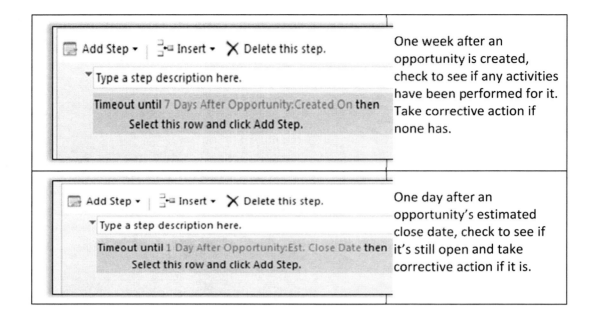

One week after an opportunity is created, check to see if any activities have been performed for it. Take corrective action if none has.

One day after an opportunity's estimated close date, check to see if it's still open and take corrective action if it is.

Parallel Wait Branch

A Parallel Wait Branch for a Wait Condition is analogous to a Conditional Branch for a Check Condition. A common requirement for a parallel wait branch is to add a time dimension when you're waiting for a condition. For example, consider the simplest version of the sales process workflow we examined previously.

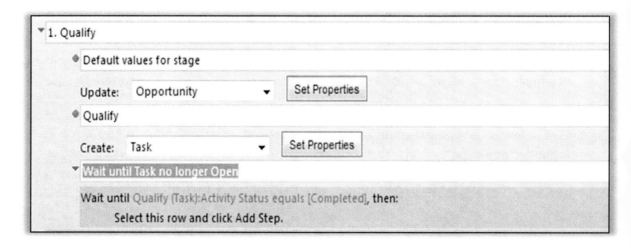

In that *Wait until…, then* branch we're waiting for a condition to be satisfied. If we want to add a time dimension to a process like this one, we can add a parallel wait branch to specify what happens if the condition isn't satisfied within a certain period of time:

> ▼ **Wait until task completed or for a specified period of time**
>
> **Wait until** Qualify (Task):Activity Status equals [Completed], **then:**
>> Select this row and click Add Step.
>
> **Timeout until** 7 Days After Qualify (Task):Created On **then**
>> Select this row and click Add Step.

When you first encounter them, the "parallel wait branch" concept sounds exotic and complex, but after you work through a few examples you'll realize how frequently you'll encounter these in the real world. Here are two examples to illustrate the point:

- A lead is assigned to a sales rep, and a "Call Lead" phone call activity is automatically created and assigned to the sales rep. When the phone call activity is completed, the lead qualification process continues to the next step…unless the phone call activity is not completed within a certain amount of time, in which case the lead is reassigned and routed to the "neglected leads" queue.
- When an email marketing blast goes out, you want sales reps to be automatically notified if an email bounces, or if a recipient opens and then clicks a link in the email. But if after a certain period of time a recipient did not open the email, you want to send a followup email at a different time of day or with a different subject line. (This is an example of what can be referred to as "nurture marketing".)

Nested Conditional Logic

We've already seen a few examples of this, and in production-caliber workflows you're probably a lot more likely to require complex nested processes than not, so let's examine nested conditional logic more closely. Let's start with a few important points to keep in mind on the topic.

- As noted previously, the process designer does not support things like promoting, demoting or moving steps, including conditional branches or the steps contained within them. In my experience, what this really means is that the complexity of the processes you are capable of creating can outstrip the editing capabilities of the designer. So while you *can* create complex, deeply nested processes… if you get to a point where it's hard to follow the logic of one, you might want to break your *uber*-process down into smaller sub-processes.

- If you delete a stage none of the steps in the stage are deleted; they just get moved to the previous stage. However, if you delete a conditional branch all of the steps in the branch are deleted. So be careful when deleting conditional branches!
- Also noted previously is the importance of having the branches within a conditional block be mutually exclusive. Again, this is not a requirement, and there are probably situations when non-exclusive conditional branching is required. But situations like that are hard to understand and troubleshoot, so at the very least I'd consider it a potential red flag.

Let's examine a more completely defined sales process, building on the example discussed previously. This time what we'll do is step through a completed version of the process (Solution Selling Process 3). In particular, I'll walk you through an exercise I find invaluable when I need to figure out how one of these things works: stepping through it branch by branch, using the ability to expand and collapse branches so we can focus just on the logic contained in each one at a time.

Step by Step: Walk through Conditional Logic in Solution Selling Process 3

1. Make sure the Solution Selling Process 3 workflow is deactivated and open it in the workflow designer.
2. In the first stage of the process, collapse the steps under the *Wait until…, then:* and *Timeout until…,then:* branches so that it looks like the following figure.

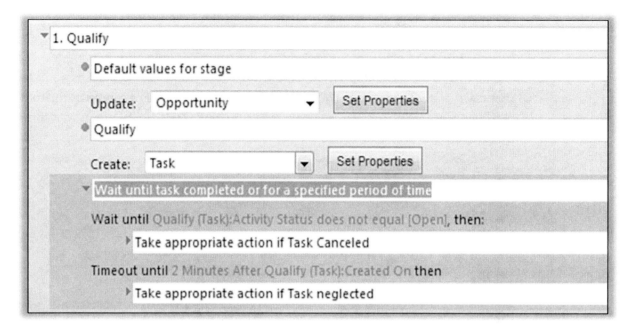

3. Click the blue arrow to expand the steps underneath the *Wait until..., then:* branch. This is the logic we discussed previously.

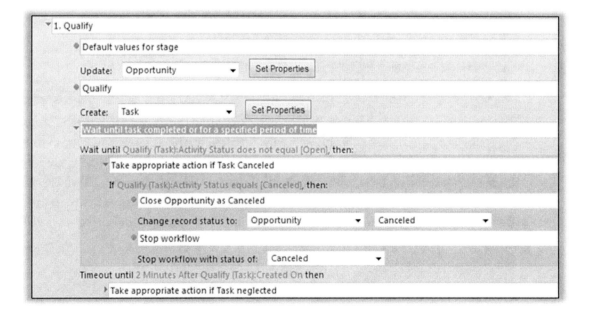

4. Collapse those steps and expand the steps under the *Timeout until…, then* branch. This is the parallel wait branch discussed in the previous section. Notice that the *If…, then:* branch checks the status of the task a specified period of time after it is created. In the example here it checks after two minutes. Most real-world sales processes don't require that rapid of a response, but if you're testing a process like this it can be useful to work with short intervals like that! The logic of this process sends a reminder e-mail if the task is still open.

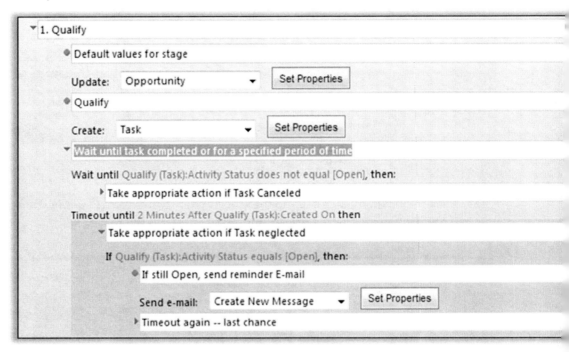

5. Then notice that there's another collapsed block *within* this *If…, then:* branch. Expand it. The following figure shows this branch only. Effectively, this repeats the logic in the previous Timeout branch, with one exception: the Timeout until condition is based on the process execution time, rather than the date the task was created. There are a number of ways to handle situations like this, but using the **Process** entity to get to the special **Execution Time** variable is one of the most frequently encountered.

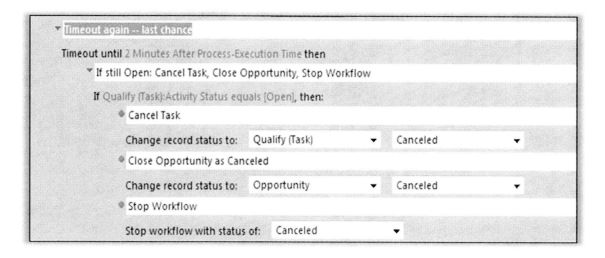

Activity Tracking and Reporting

Dynamics CRM does a great job of tracking activities. For example, you can easily see all of the appointments, phone calls and emails for any customer by opening the form and clicking **Activities** in left navigation. You can develop reports for activities, view some of the out of the box charts available for the activity pointer record type, or build your own custom charts for appointments, phone calls and so forth. Some of the default dashboards have useful visualizations of activities, or you can create your own custom dashboards.

So with all of that built in activity functionality, why do I have a topic like this one in a book about business processes? Well, as it turns out, there are plenty of common activity tracking requirements organizations have that are *not* available by default. And some of these gaps are surprising, judging by the reaction I get from customers when I explain that while these are generally not *complicated* customizations...they do require just a little bit of extra work.

The first example I describe here seems to be in the "golly, shouldn't it just do that?" category. It comes in various flavors, but generally has to do with how recently a customer or lead was contacted. Suppose you want an easy, visually obvious way of seeing which customers have been contacted recently or perhaps more importantly, which ones have *not* been contacted.

Recently I helped a customer develop a view of *neglected accounts*, defined as ones that have had no activities (e.g., appointments or phone calls) for more than nine months. Seems like it should be easy: you can quickly build an advanced find query of all account records that have had activities in the last nine months, as the following figure illustrates:

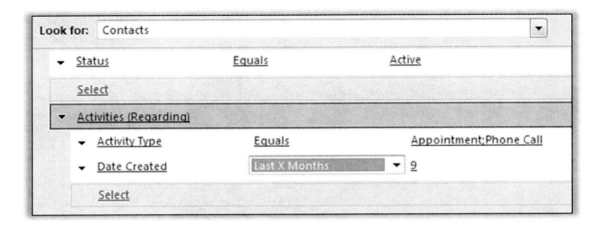

So far so good. And we can do the following easily enough as well:

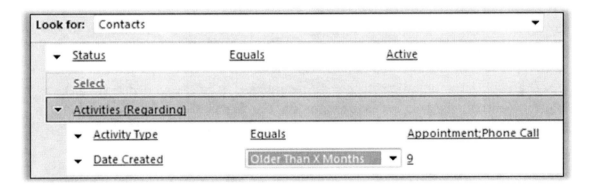

Unfortunately, the second one does not give us our neglected contacts, since all it does is return contacts with activities created more than 9 months ago: it does not exclude contacts with activities *since then*, thus while some of the contacts returned by the query may be neglected, many will not be. In fact, the problem is a limitation of the advanced find UI: you cannot perform a NOT IN query.

You can perform a workaround like the following, if you have the patience:

1. Build a marketing list based on the first of the two queries just shown. This gives you all contacts who have been contacted in the last nine months.
2. Then build a marketing list of all contacts.
3. Then remove all members from the second list that are in the first list, and you're left with... neglected contacts.

The problem with that approach is it only works with static marketing lists, so you have to repeat the process any time you want an accurate count. Not good.

Anyway, in less than the time it would take you to fiddle around with those marketing lists, you can implement the approach I describe next and generate dynamic lists of neglected accounts, contacts, leads, what have you.

Build a Workflow to Update Last Activity Date

Dynamics CRM records have a system field, **Modified On**, that contains the date and time the record was last modified. Unfortunately, it only gets updated by direct changes to fields on the record; adding an activity like a phone call or appointment does not update the Modified On field on the record the activity is regarding.

The basic tactic I describe here is simple: add a custom field, **Last Activity Date**, to any entity you want to track, and then build an automatic workflow that updates that field with the system date whenever an activity is performed. Your business rules will determine the specifics of how you do this; in this example we have the goal of tracking neglected leads, and we will update the last activity date field whenever an appointment or phone call is completed for a lead record.

The following figure illustrates a relatively simple workflow that updates the Last Activity Date field on a lead record when a phone call is closed as completed.

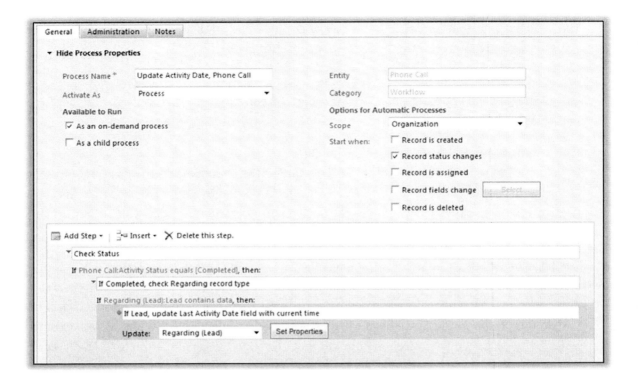

The workflow is written for the Phone Call entity, and it runs automatically on the **Record status changes** trigger. It implements the following logic:

- The first **If ... then** condition checks the value of the Activity Status field.
  - If it's completed, the nested **If...then** condition checks if the appointment is regarding a lead record.
    - If it is, a single **Update** step is used to update the **Last Activity Date** field with the process execution time.

By now the creation of the nested conditional logic should be straightforward, so I won't list the complete step by step process of creating the workflow. However, inserting the process execution time into the Last Activity Date field can be tricky the first time you do it so let's step through how you do that.

1. Click the **Set Properties** on the **Update** step.
2. Locate the Last Activity Date field and click inside it.

3. In the Dynamic Values section, select **Process** in the **Look for** drop-down, and in the next drop-down select **Execution Time**.

4. Then click the **Add** button. You should see the following:

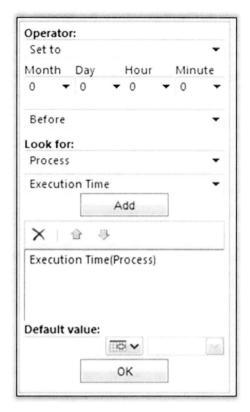

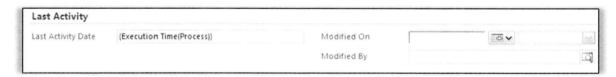

5. Then click OK, and you should see the execution time variable in the date field:

Then you can save and activate the workflow. Here are a few of the interesting points raised by this example:

- Note that in the example I showed, the workflow is both automatic and available to run on demand. I often do this when I'm testing a process like this, but I usually turn off the on demand property in production.
- The example I showed was for the phone call entity. What about the other activities you might want to track in this way? You might think you could create the workflow for the **Activity** record type (the so-called activity pointer), have it check the type of activity, and update the last activity date field for whichever activity types you want to include. Unfortunately, you cannot do this, because you cannot create a workflow for the Activity record type; you can only create processes for the specific activity types, such as appointment, phone call and so forth. What this means is that you need to create a separate workflow, with exactly the same structure, for each activity type you want to take into account when figuring out which leads have been "neglected". Some organizations might only include appointments, others might include both appointments and phone calls, and others might add emails or letters to the list. Your business rules, your call.
- If you want to implement this functionality, should you place the **Last Activity Date** field on the lead form? As we've seen, processes can update fields regardless of whether they're on the form. And certainly once a workflow like this one is in production you don't want users to be able to manually edit the last activity date field! So you have a few options:
  - You might place it on the form somewhere, but if you do you should make it read only. An issue you might encounter here is that while workflow processes can certainly update read-only fields, the designer will not let you access them! This is surprising the first time you encounter it, and in Chapter 7 I explain how to deal with that issue.
  - You might place it in the form header or footer. These form sections are always read-only, so in a sense they're designed for fields like this, that should be featured prominently but not updated interactively.

Understanding Activity Date Fields

In the workflow we just examined, you might wonder why I updated the last activity date field with the time the process executed, rather than with the date of the activity record itself. After all, what if a phone call activity took place on Monday but you didn't click the Mark Complete button until your end of the week CRM housekeeping session Friday afternoon? In that case, the last activity date field would indicate some time on Friday afternoon (the process execution time) rather than Monday, when the call actually took place. And while the commonsense interpretation of "last activity date" in this scenario would probably be when the call took place, you need to understand some details about activity date fields to account for the different requirements you will encounter...and to avoid some commonly encountered mistakes!

To understand this, consider the following two illustrations. The first one is of the default appointment form:

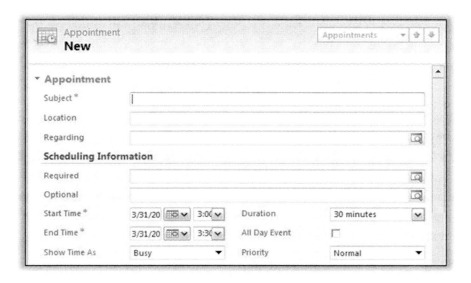

The second one is the default phone call form:

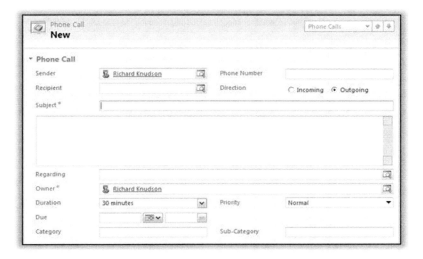

While all activity types are in many ways similar, there are important differences as well. For example, on the appointment form notice that the **Start Time** and **End Time** fields are auto-filled (with the next nearest half-hour block) and that they are both required. On the phone call form there's a single date field, **Due**, and it's *neither auto-filled nor required.* In practice, what this means is that a significant number of phone calls will be saved and eventually marked complete with nothing in the Due field.

With this in mind, you can appreciate why I used the process execution time to update the last activity date field in the previous workflow process: because even though it might not be as "correct" as the date the phone call took place, at least you know the last activity date will have a value!

The most obvious fix is to make the appropriate date fields required on the activity types you're most interested in. If you customize any of the activity entities, you'll discover that they all have the same set of date fields, even though – as we just saw -- they're handled inconsistently on the forms. For example, the schema name of the End Time field on the appointment form is **scheduledend**; the schema name of the Due field on the phone call form is also **scheduledend**. You can probably guess now that every activity type has **scheduledstart** and **scheduledend** fields, as well as **actualstart** and **actualend** fields.

If you need to track and report on when activities actually took place, the best approach is usually to make the Due field (schema name scheduledend) required on the appropriate activity forms. (The single exception will be the appointment form, where it's already required but referred to as End Time.)

If, on the other hand, you really **do** want to know when users are closing activities, you can use the **actualend** field.

Armed with this drill-down knowledge of how activity date fields work, you could build a variation of the previous workflow to update the last activity date field on a lead record. The following illustration shows an example:

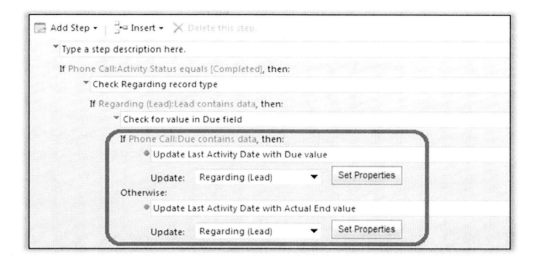

The highlighted If…then, Otherwise block first checks to see if the **Due** field contains a value; if so, the lead record is updated with the value of the field. Since we know that the **Actual End** field always contains a value when an activity is marked complete, we can use the Otherwise default action to fill it with that value, just in case there's nothing in the Due field.

Wait a Second. I thought you said the Due field was required!
Remember, I said I was going to try to help you avoid some commonly encountered mistakes. (OK, maybe they're just commonly encountered by *me*, but let's not go there!)

Suppose you've modified the Requirement Level setting on the Due field and set it to Business Required. It's tempting to think this means you'll always have a value in that field, in which case you wouldn't need the conditional logic in the version of the workflow we just examined. That's not true though, so if you really, *really* need a value in the last activity date field, you should include that logic.

The key thing to remember is that *Requirement Level settings configured through the standard customization UI are enforced at the form level*. So if a record is created other than interactively with a form, these settings are not enforced. Here are two examples:

- If you create records by importing them, requirement level settings for a field such as Due in this example will not be enforced.
- If records are created by a workflow process, forms never open and

requirement settings are not enforced. Suppose for example you want a workflow process to automatically create a scheduled phone call when an account is assigned to a new user. If the Due field is required when you create the workflow, the workflow designer will force you to supply a value for the Due field. But that is really enforcement at the form level. You can see this if you create the workflow first and activate it, and *then* change the requirement setting of the Due field. If you do that, the workflow will continue to work, and it will create phone call records with nothing in the Due field, even though it's required.

Sales Processes

Most organizations with anything more than a moderately complex selling cycle use some variant of a sales process. Benefits of a well-defined sales process can include the following:

- By appropriately qualifying a potential deal, salespeople can allocate more time to promising opportunities and spend less on time on deals unlikely to close.
- Having a consistent and shared sales process can make it easier to train new salespeople, and potentially reduce an organization's reliance on a small number of "superstar" sales reps.
- Clearly defined tasks for each stage of a sales process can increase efficiency and reduce sales cycle time.
- Templates ("job aids") can be created for customer documents to be delivered in various stages of the cycle.
- Clearly defined sales stages can provide improved management reporting.

Many organizations develop their own sales processes, but several off the shelf sales processes are available from companies in the "sales performance improvement" business. For example, one of the most popular is the solution selling process, developed and popularized by Mike Bosworth[9] and later sold to Sales Performance International[10].

---

[9] http://mikebosworth.com
[10] http://www.spisales.com/

Questions to Ask when Designing your Sales Process

In this section I will present a Dynamics CRM workflow implementation of a simplified solution selling process, but before diving in let's take a step back and ask a few basic questions you should be able to answer before building your sales process in CRM.

Does your organization _have_ a sales process? (Be honest – it's okay; I won't make fun!) In my experience, most organizations really don't have a well-defined sales process, in the sense that, for example, everybody in the company can sit down independently and write out the same thirteen stages of the process. Dynamics CRM has tools you can use to create an automated version of an existing sales process, but it won't help you define your sales process! If you don't have a well-defined sales process, trying to create one on the fly in Dynamics CRM (or any other CRM) will be an exercise in frustration.

What is the purpose of your sales process? One way to think about this is with reference to the potential benefits I outline above. For example, some organizations implement a multiple-stage sales process primarily for management reporting or pipeline management purposes. If you simply want to see potential revenue or the number of deals distributed across the stages of your process, this can be quite easily accomplished. Some of the other potential benefits, such as requiring certain tasks to be completed before advancing from one stage to the next, require a little more planning and work.

Do you have different sales processes within your organization? The larger and more departmentalized your organization, the more likely this is the case. But even a small organization might need different sales processes for different kinds of deals. Here are a couple examples to illustrate the point.

- I once managed a training business, and we made a big distinction between one-off registrations for an open enrollment class and private training classes. Open enrollment registrations were our transactional business. They often closed on the first phone call and didn't really need a sales process. Private training classes were different: they were custom, expensive, had a longer sales cycle and needed a well-defined sales process.
- More recently I've been working with several banks on their CRM deployments. One particular client has several different departments: Business Banking, Commercial Real Estate, Mortgage Lending, Non-Profits. Each focuses on different products, and each has different sales processes. One basic way these different processes are manifested is in different stages of the sales process for each department: each has its own stages, and needs to see how its pipeline is distributed across them.

Do your sales processes depend on other processes? Suppose we defined a *self-contained* sales process as one that has no dependencies on people outside the sales department. For example, a sales manager has responsibility for several salespeople, and as they're working their deals through the pipeline they may require approval from the sales manager at various points, but not from anybody external to the sales team. Self-contained processes like this are relatively simple, but in the real world it can get more complex. Here are two scenarios I've encountered where a sales process has an explicit dependency on a process external to the sales department:

- A transportation logistics firm has the salesperson manage an opportunity up to the proposal stage in the process, but then it gets handed off to the engineering team which is responsible for detailed configuration and pricing. After engineering completes its configuration and pricing processes, the deal gets handed back to sales.
- A mortgage banker gets a request from a client for a loan modification. After initial information (some of it required by regulations) is gathered by the banker, an outside appraisal is required. The mortgage banker is prohibited from having direct contact with the appraisal company, so at that point the appraisal request gets routed to the operations department at the bank. Operations then selects the appraisal company and orders the appraisal. After the appraisal comes back, operations will then attach it to the deal form and hands it back to the banker.

How does a deal advance from one stage to the next? Here are two of the ways organizations might answer this question and the implications for how they'd model their sales processes:

- **Manual sales processes.** Suppose you have a picklist field on the opportunity form representing the stages of your sales process, and the owner of the record simply selects a value to indicate the current stage of the opportunity. Let's refer to this as a *manual process*. What it lacks in rigor, a manual process makes up for in simplicity. This might be appropriate for organizations whose only (or initial) goal is pipeline reporting. Suppose the sales stage picklist is a required field, either for all opportunities or for certain types of opportunities: at the very least you'll know that 100% of your opportunities will fall into one of the stages! Again, this is a little simplistic, but for many organizations it might be an improvement compared to their current state.
- **Gated sales processes.** Many organizations require the completion of certain tasks, or the collection of certain kinds of information, before an opportunity advances from one stage of the sales process to the next. Processes like this are often referred to as *gated processes*. If defined properly a gated process can mitigate a seller's risk and improve sales efficiency, by winnowing down the number of deals at successive stages

and controlling resource expenditure on non-performing deals. The concept of stage-gating is really fundamental to the most commonly used sales process models, and underlies much of the metrics and terminology we typically apply to sales processes. For example, the commonsense notion that percentage likelihood to close *increases* at successive stages of a sales process is implied by a gating process: if a deal at the *Closing* stage is less likely to close than one at *Qualifying*, it probably shouldn't have made it through those gates! Even the out of the box pipeline chart familiar to most users of Dynamics CRM 2011 implies that successive stages are somehow smaller as deals advance through the pipeline.

For example, compare the following two images. Both are the standard sales pipeline chart, which uses a default text field (**pipeline phase**) on the opportunity entity to represent stages of the sales pipeline. This funnel chart is hardwired to represent each successive stage as a narrower wedge than the previous one, and although these two pipelines are dramatically different, unless you're used to it the visualization obscures how different they are!

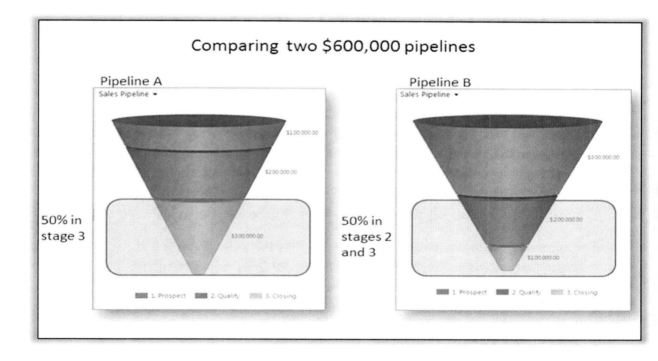

The standard funnel chart uses the *width* of the wedge to represent where opportunities are in the pipeline: early stage wedges are always wider than later stage wedges. The *height* of the wedge represents the percentage of the overall pipeline the opportunities in that stage account for, in terms of the sum of the estimated revenue values for all opportunities in the stage. In this example, $300,000 represents half the total pipeline, so $300,000 will always be represented as 50% of the height of the total pipeline chart. In pipeline A, stage 3 opportunities make up half the total. In pipeline B stage 3 opportunities only account for 1/6th of the pipeline; stage 3 plus stage 2 deals make up 50%.

What should your pipeline look like? As I mentioned, the two pipelines we just examined are dramatically different. An organization's *ideal* pipeline will depend on many factors. An excellent discussion of how to quantify the ideal pipeline for an organization was provided by C.J. Warstler, a Director at Sales Performance International[11].

That article is well worth reading, and discusses several important factors in determining what your ideal pipeline might look like:

- The complexity of your sales process
- The percentage of deals you win, and your overall sales goal
- How long, on average, does it take to close an opportunity?
- How long, on average, does a deal stay in each stage of the process?

One problem with the calculations presented in the article is that many organizations don't have these numbers. For example, I work with organizations every day that are migrating their CRM efforts to Dynamics CRM with the goal of tracking metrics like these. This obviously implies they don't already know them, and in my experience, sales managers consistently underestimate the level of discipline and commitment required to provide useful and **True** (with a capital T!) metrics for concepts like the ideal pipeline shape, pipeline velocity and so forth.

As to what the ideal pipeline should look like, one thing we can say is that if you have a gated sales process and enforce some discipline in opportunity management, the ideal pipeline will look a lot more like pipeline B than pipeline A. One of the most important reasons to put a gate between stages is to choke off the bad deals earlier rather than later, so your salespeople don't

---

[11] http://www.solutionsellingblog.com/home/tag/sales-funnel

waste time on them. Here are a few of the quantitative claims we can make about what a reasonably well-managed pipeline should look like for an organization with a gated sales process:

- Certainly you'd hope that the *number* of early stage deals is greater late stage deals.
- You would also probably expect the sum of estimated revenue to be greater in early stages than late.
- As close probability increases in successive stages, what happens to a probability-weighted revenue estimate? Well, probability is increasing; the number of deals is decreasing, so it depends.

A Few Caveats

Many an attempt at creating a solid sales process in Dynamics CRM has foundered on the rocks of poor execution, unrealistic expectations, and a lack of understanding of what's built in and what's not. Here we'll move away from the conceptual discussion of the previous section and I'll tick off a few of the more common (and important) CRM-specific things to keep in mind when designing a sales process.

- **If you can't flowchart it, don't do it**. I can't stress this one enough. Dynamics CRM is a blank slate when it comes to sales processes: unlike Salesforce.com, for example, it doesn't give you pre-defined stages or make any other assumptions about your sales process. In general, this is a good thing, and it's in keeping with Dynamics CRM's role as an application *platform*. It provides tools you can use to implement your sales process, but you need to have a sales process to implement! In particular, the workflow designer is NOT a good prototyping tool. (In my view, it's a rather bad one, but I'm hopeful that will change in future releases!) Use Visio or some other flowcharting tool to describe the business logic of your sales process before you start doing anything in Dynamics CRM.
- **Dynamics CRM does not track days in stage out of the box**. This comes up a lot: I often have conversations with sales managers who assume that something like this is "built in". It is not, and while it can be added as a customization, it's best to explain this before-hand rather than after the fact.
- **Generally speaking, the *Status Reason* field is not good to use for sales stages**. The question of what field to use to represent your sales stages is an important one, and the answer can depend on several factors. The Status Reason field is a customizable picklist ("option set" is the term we use for picklists now, and I'll switch over to the option set terminology going forward) and *could* be used to represent stages for a sales process,

but it's not usually a good idea. One problem with the status reason field is there's only one. If you start using it for a sales process, and then decide you need a second sales process with different stages, you'll need to use a different field for the second process. Now you'll have one system field used for sales process A, a custom field for sales process B, and you'll find yourself wondering if you should add a second custom field to replace status reason for process A. You probably should in that case, but it's messy to cut over…you get the point. Another reason not to use status reason is that to change it in a workflow process you need to perform a Change Status action, rather than the Update Record action used to change most fields.

- **If you want good pipeline data, make sure you have some required fields on the opportunity form**! The opportunity record type is what most organizations use to drive their sales pipeline, but by default it only has two required fields: **Topic** and **Potential Customer**.   The advantage of this is that it makes opportunity records easy to enter. The disadvantage is that most of the information needed to manage and report on a sales process will be incomplete at best. At a minimum, I advise my clients to make the estimated revenue, estimated close date and sales stage (whichever sales stage field you use!) fields required, as the following slightly customized opportunity form illustrates.

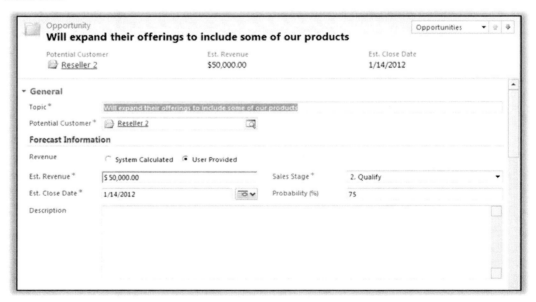

An often-encountered objection to this is that when the record is created some of those values aren't known. While that may be true, I usually counter that that's what the term *estimated* means: these are *estimates*, and in some cases may be a best guess that can be updated as more information becomes available. And if you really have *no* idea how big a potential deal is or when it's likely to close, it probably isn't a real opportunity. I don't always win that argument, but at least when the sales manager asks, months later, why her sales pipeline looks like the following figure, I'll be ready with the answer!

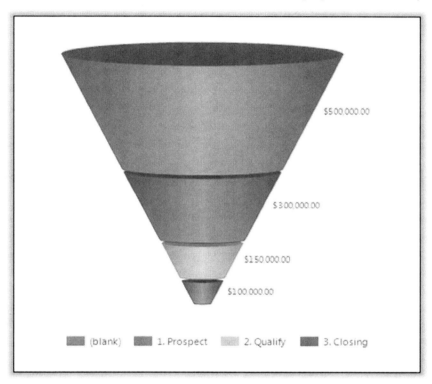

Designing a Sales Process

What stages should you have in your sales process? What tasks are required at each stage? Are close probabilities calculated automatically at each stage, and if so, what are they? These are the kinds of questions you need to answer as you design your process, and in this section we'll walk through a "typical" sales process design discussion. If you need some food for thought on topics like this, there are many good resources available. Here are a couple of my favorites:

- *Sales Process*, from Wikipedia[12]

---

[12] http://en.wikipedia.org/wiki/Sales_process

- *The Stages of Solution Selling and Supporting Job Aids*, from AgKnowlogy[13]

As you'd expect, the Wikipedia article is definitional, and include lots of links you can explore on your own. For our current purposes, the most interesting thing about this article is the various 8-9 stage sales processes it describes as being relatively typical. I think that's a bit of a stretch, since there really isn't a *typical* sales process, but still it's worth taking a look at them. For example, here's a section of the article describing two of them:

> *Specific steps or stages in a sales process vary from company to company but generally include the following elements:*
>
> 1. *Initial contact*
> 2. *Application of Initial Fit Criteria*
> 3. *Sales lead*
> 4. *Need identification*
> 5. *Qualified prospect*
> 6. *Proposal*
> 7. *Negotiation*
> 8. *Closing*
> 9. *Deal Transaction*
>
> *An alternate but similar series of steps is as follows:*
>
> 1. *Prospecting/Initial contact*
> 2. *Preapproach- planning the sale*
> 3. *Approach*
> 4. *Need assessment*
> 5. *Presentation*
> 6. *Meeting objections*
> 7. *Gaining commitment*
> 8. *Follow-up*

And the following figure shows a slightly different 9-stage process also characterized as typical:

---

[13] http://www.agknowlogy.com/ProductsServices/SolutionSelling/TheStagesofSolutionSelling/tabid/80/Default.aspx

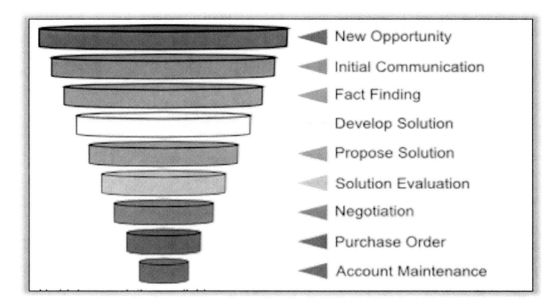

New Opportunity

Initial Communication

Fact Finding

Develop Solution

Propose Solution

Solution Evaluation

Negotiation

Purchase Order

Account Maintenance

Next let's turn to the AgKnowlogy article, which is interesting in that it's much less generic, and much more derived from a specific sales process (solution selling, in this case). It also does a good job of summarizing, by stage; many of the tasks typically required throughout the solution selling process, as well as the "Job Aids" that would be useful for salespeople to efficiently push a deal through the pipeline. The following table presents a selectively summarized version of these concepts.

Stage	Tasks	Job Aids	Summary Stage
1. Analyze	• Market share analysis • Identify specific deals	SWOT	1. Qualify
2. Plan	• Diagnose pain • Develop action plan		
3. Create	• Stimulate interest • Identify sponsor • Get client to admit pain • Agree on next steps	• Value proposition • Reference story • Opportunity assessment	
4. Develop	• Diagnose		2. Develop

				Solution
	<ul><li>admitted pain</li><li>Identify benefits to other business areas</li><li>Create shared vision of solution</li><li>Develop power sponsor</li></ul>			
5. **Prove**	<ul><li>Develop "proof of capabilities" plan</li><li>Ask for business</li></ul>	<ul><li>Evaluation plan</li><li>Proposal template</li><li>Agreed-upon success criteria</li></ul>		
6. **Close**	<ul><li>Resolve outstanding issues</li><li>Reach final agreement</li></ul>	<ul><li>Negotiating worksheet</li><li>Give-get list</li></ul>	3. Negotiate and Close	
7. **Implement**	<ul><li>Implement solution</li><li>Establish report card review schedule</li></ul>	<ul><li>Account plan</li><li>Call schedule</li></ul>		

This information is more specific, and in terms of how we might design a workflow process in Dynamics CRM, more useful. For example, the tasks could be created by a workflow process. A gated process could create and assign the tasks automatically as each stage is reached, and wait until the tasks are completed before proceeding to the next stage. The job aids – in the form of template Word documents, PowerPoint slide decks and so forth – could be automatically attached to an opportunity record, so the salesperson doesn't have to perform inefficient searches on shared drives or SharePoint sites. In my experience, having an automated process that can automatically attach the appropriate job aids at various stages of a complex sales process is one of the biggest potential payoffs of the entire effort. Below, we'll examine some approaches you can use to do that.

While most full-blown implementations of solution selling style processes are similar to the seven-stage process in the first column, I've added a simpler three-stage process in the last column, and that's the one I'll use for the examples we walk through next. Here's why I like the simpler process for our present purposes:

- First, the workflows we will review are complex enough with only three stages. Presenting a seven-stage process doesn't provide any pedagogical benefits but it does have costs, in the form of unnecessary complexity.
- Second, in my view most organizations overcomplicate their sales processes with too many stages. If you're designing your sales process, my advice is to err on the side of too simple rather than too complex. You can always add more stages later if you really need them. But if you add them in the beginning they take on a life of their own and pretty soon they're there … because they've always been there, not because they need to be.

In the examples for this chapter we will walk through in detail both a manual sales process and an automatic gated sales process.

Summary

In this chapter, we covered two of the most important foundation skills for building Dynamics CRM business processes: how to use dynamic values, and how to use conditional logic.

Dynamic values are used in many contexts when designing processes, such as creating or updating records or activities, sending emails and the like. Dynamic values can gather information from parent records of the record the process is running against, or from records created by a process. Depending on the type of field you're updating, you can use different operators with dynamic values. For example, **Set to** is the default operator and will replace the value of a field, but in a text field you can use the **Append With** operator to append text rather than replace it. In addition to Set to and Clear, numeric fields have the additional operators **Increment by**, **Decrement by** and **Multiply by**. You can also use local values to access special process variables, such as the process execution time.

Conditional logic is an important aspect of business process design, and the two main constructs available in the Dynamics CRM process designer are **Check Condition** and **Wait Condition**. Conditional blocks constructed with Check Condition are essentially *If, then, else* blocks. Use these to perform different actions depending on the value of a field. For example, you might assign a lead record to a different user or team, depending on the value of the industry or the city fields. Use Wait Condition when you need to add a time dimension to a workflow process. For example, after sending an email blast, you might have a workflow wait for two days and then send a second email if the first one wasn't opened. Parallel wait branches can be added to perform an action if some condition is met before the wait condition is met. In the email blast example, a parallel wait branch could be used to perform appropriate action if an email bounces, or if a recipient opens an email and clicks one of its links.

After covering these foundation skills, we examined how to apply them in two frequently encountered business process scenarios: activity tracking, and sales processes.

Chapter 4 – Introducing Dialog Processes

Comparing Workflow and Dialog Processes

In Microsoft Dynamics CRM 2011, *Workflows* are quite similar to their slightly less evolved CRM 4.0 ancestors. But the tools you have to automate business processes are significantly improved compared to the previous version, thanks to the introduction of the new D*ialog* process. Semantically, workflows and dialogs are each considered a type of *Business Process*. While both dialogs and workflows allow you to automate business processes, in many ways they function quite differently. The following table summarizes the differences between workflow and dialog processes.

Dialogs	Workflows
Present a wizard-like UI to the end-user, and always require user input to start and run to completion	Always run in the background, and do not support user input
Always run synchronously	Always run asynchronously
Cannot be triggered automatically; must be started by a user	Can be started by a user, or triggered automatically
Can query CRM data	Cannot query CRM data
Can call child dialogs and pass information to them	Can call child workflows but cannot pass information
Can be run only on one record at a time	Can be run on multiple records , or just a single one
Only available in language they are targeting	Language un-aware

Basically dialogs provide the ability to create wizard-style processes within Dynamics CRM. Think of dialogs as adding an information-gathering UI on top of the traditional workflow foundation. Now, in addition to automating processes in the background, you can create processes that collect information from users. Here are a few examples of what you can do with dialog processes.

- Create guided selling or service processes, with a series of questions guiding representatives through otherwise complex sales/service processes.
- Create wizard-style substitutes for traditional forms-based record creation.
- Create your own customized replacements for lead conversion, case resolution, or any other process where information on one record functions as input for the creation of another.

Dialog processes require a user to start them and to respond to the prompts they present. However, once a dialog gathers information from a user, it can do almost everything a workflow can: create, update and assign records, send e-mails, include conditional logic and so forth. Almost all of the topics covered so far in the book apply equally well to dialog processes. Before drilling down into the specifics of building dialog processes, here are a few more ways in which you can contrast workflow and dialog processes, each of which you will see illustrated shortly.

- Unlike workflows, *dialog processes cannot have wait conditions*.
- A dialog process can call a child dialog process or a workflow process. As you have seen, a workflow process can call a child workflow process but *a workflow cannot call a child dialog process*. An example of this is presented in the next chapter.
- *Dialogs can look up Dynamics CRM data* and present them to a user in a prompt. This is one of the most important capabilities supported by dialog processes and we will cover it in detail.

Properties

Primarily because they cannot be triggered automatically, dialogs do not have much in the way of properties. Here is the Process Properties section of the designer for a dialog called "Dynamics CRM Upgrade Conversation".

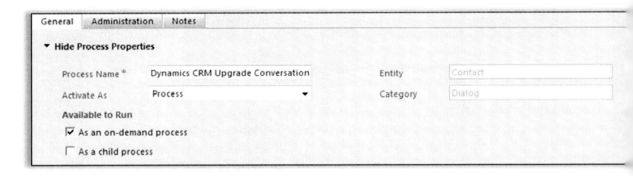

Activate As

Select **Process** if you want to activate the dialog for users to use; select **Process Template** if it is to be used as a template to create other dialogs.

Available to Run

Normally you will select **As an on-demand process**. This simply means that the dialog will be available to run when a record of the type the dialog is written for (*Contact* in the previous figure) is either selected on a data grid, or when a form is opened.

Dialogs can call child dialogs, and that's what the **As a child process** option is for. The two options in this case are:

- If only **As a child process** is selected, then the dialog will not display on the ribbon for a user to run it; in this case it can only be called by a parent dialog.
- If both **As an on-demand process** and **As a child process** are selected, the dialog will be able to call itself recursively. A common use of this technique is to create a "looping" process. For example, a dialog might walk you through the process of creating a case record for an account, and after gathering information and creating the case, ask you if you'd like to create another record. If you respond yes, the dialog calls itself as a child process and walks through another case create dialog.

Basic Constructs: Pages, Prompts and Responses

Dynamics CRM 2011 dialog processes contain one or more *pages*, which provide the visual experience for the user. Each page can contain multiple sets of *prompts* and *responses*. Prompts and responses always go together, so I often refer to them as prompt/response pairs. Pages, and prompt/response pairs, are the most fundamental difference between workflow and dialog processes. They present the user interface and gather the information that the rest of the dialog process can use to do whatever it needs to do.

One way to appreciate the fundamental rules presented in table above is to consider the following rule:

*Dialogs must contain at least one page, **and** at least one prompt/response pair.*

For example, you can create a new dialog without any pages or prompt/response pairs, and you can save it. But if you try to activate a dialog like that, you will see the following scary dialog with a very clear message:

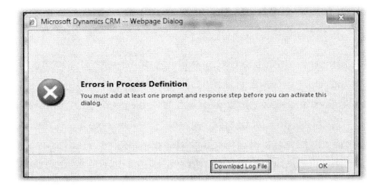

Let's walk through an example to illustrate these basic dialog constructs. The following figure shows the experience of the user running a dialog. Dialog pages are displayed one at a time, just like steps in a wizard. The page shown here has two prompt/response pairs, with the second one selected. Notice the Tip on the right side of the form.

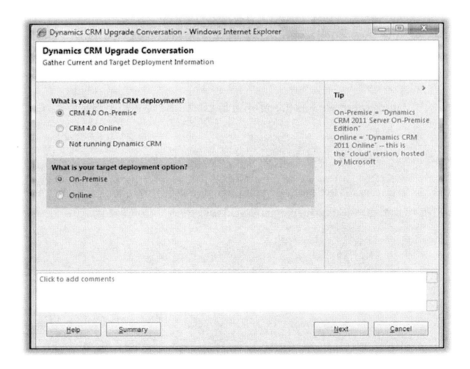

The following figure shows the same dialog, but this time in the design environment:

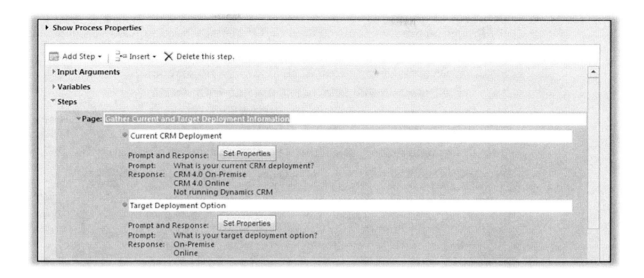

Here you see the design environment, with the Process Properties section collapsed immediately above the Step Editor. This will be familiar to anybody with CRM 4.0 workflow experience – about the only obvious difference is that wherever in CRM 4.0 the word *workflow* would have appeared you now see *process*.

But as you will see, when you start designing your first dialog process and click the Add Step drop-down list, there are lots of new actions you will not recognize from your workflow experience! Let's go through the process now of creating a simple dialog to start learning how they work.

Creating a New Dialog Process

In this exercise you will create a simple dialog to create a case record. The dialog process will be written for the Account entity, with the goal of simplifying the process of creating a new case record for an account that already exists in your Dynamics CRM. This kind of dialog process is in the category described above as "wizard-style substitutes for traditional forms-based record creation".

Note: unless otherwise noted, all of the step by step procedures in this chapter assume you are using the Dynamics CRM 2011 web client and have the System Administrator security role.

Step by Step: Create a New Dialog

1. Click **Settings** on the site map, and then click **Processes** in the **Process Center** section.
2. Immediately above the Processes grid, click New.
3. In the Create Process dialog, provide the following information:
    a. In the **Process Name** field, type *Create Case for Account*.
    b. In the **Entity** drop-down, select **Account**.
    c. In the **Category** drop-down, select **Dialog**.
    d. In the **Type** section, select the **New blank process** option.

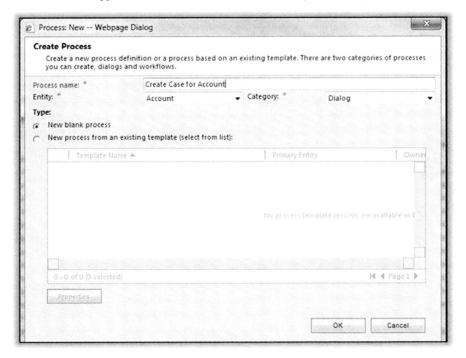

4. Click **OK**. The Process Design form opens.

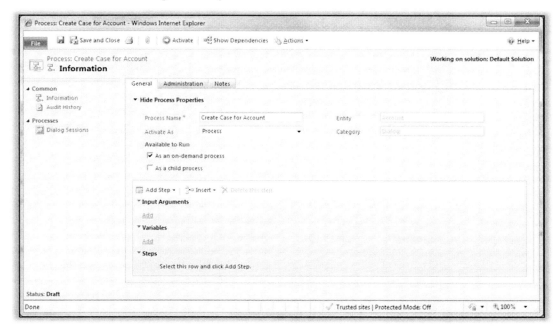

Your new dialog has been created, although of course it will not do anything yet. Again, a comparison with workflow processes will help to sharpen your understanding:

- For example, notice that unlike the workflow process designer, there is no **Options for Automatic Workflows** section. As mentioned previously, this is because dialogs must be started by a user.

- Also, notice that the **As an on-demand process** option is selected by default. If you de-select that option, and save and close the dialog, you will notice when you open it again that it's been selected again. This is because if you haven't selected the **As a child process** option, a dialog must be available as an on-demand process. We will come back to this point a little bit later.

Now let's make the dialog do something. The next exercise picks up where the previous one left off, and illustrates how to add the basic Page and Prompt/Response components.

Step by Step: Adding Pages, Prompts and Responses

1. In the Step Editor, click the line that says "**Select this row and click Add Step**".
2. Click the **Add Step** drop-down, and select **Page**. A Page component will be added.

3. With the cursor on the highlighted "Select this row and click Add Step" line, click the **Add Step** drop-down, and this time select **Prompt and Response**.

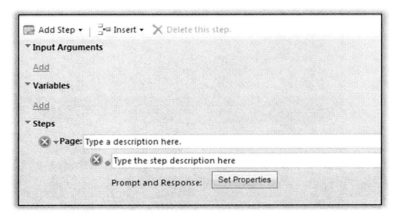

4. Click **Set Properties**. The Define Prompt and Response dialog appears. Provide the following information:
    a. In the **Statement Label** field, type *Case Title*.
    b. In the **Prompt Text** field, type *Enter a title for the case*.
    c. In the **Response Type** drop-down, select **Single Line**.

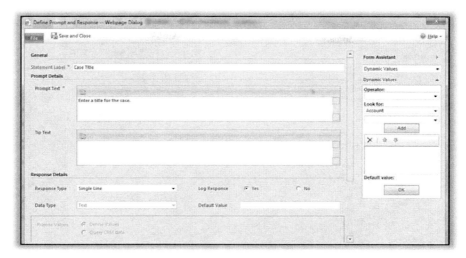

5. After entering the information, click **Save and Close**. The dialog closes and you return to the Step Editor. Notice that the text you entered in the **Prompt Text** field is automatically added in the **Description** field for the step. You can change it in either the Define Prompt and Response dialog or the Step Editor.

6. Click **Add Step**, and select **Prompt and Response** again. This time, provide the following information in the Define Prompt and Response dialog:

    a.   In the **Statement Label** field, type *Case Description*.

    b.   In the **Prompt Text** field, type *Enter a description for the case*.

    c.   In the **Response Type** drop-down, select **Multiple Lines (Text Only).**

7. Click **Save and Close**. You will return to the Step Editor, which should look like this:

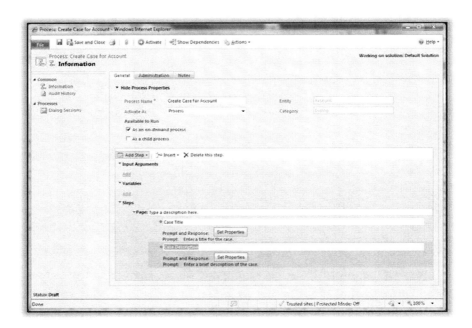

At this point, you could save the dialog, activate it, and run it. It would run, and you could see how the **Page** and **Prompt and Response** components combine to provide the user interface for the dialog. But it still wouldn't create a case record, so let's do one more exercise, picking up where we left off, to finish off and add that functionality.

Step by Step: Creating a Record with Information Gathered in a Dialog Process

1. Click on the **Page** step, and click inside the text box, where it says "Type a description here".
2. Type *Gather basic information*.
3. Make sure the Page step is still selected (the entire Page block should be highlighted in blue), then click **Add Step** and select **Create Record**.
4. Click the drop-down to the right of **Create** and select **Case**.

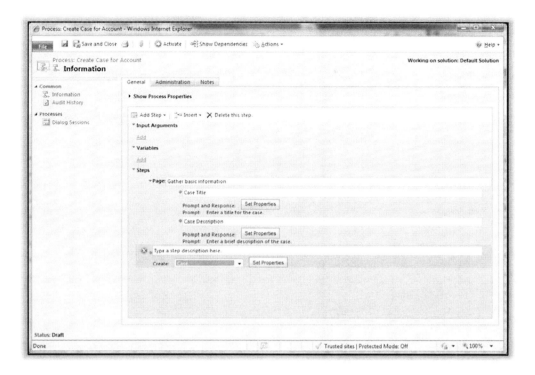

5. Click **Set Properties**. The Process form editor opens.
6. With the cursor in the **Title** field, click the **Look for** drop-down in the Dynamic Values section of the Form Assistant, and select **Case Title** in the Local Values section of the list.
7. Click the **Add** button in the Dynamic Values section.

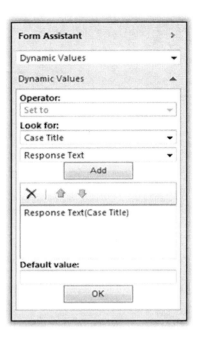

8. Click **OK**. The **Title** field is populated with **Response Text(Case Title),** which when the dialog runs will contain the text the user entered when prompted for Case Title.

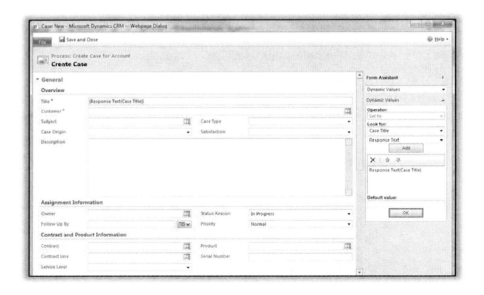

9. Click inside the Customer field. In the **Look for** drop-down, select **Account**, which is the primary entity for the dialog process. Notice that Account is automatically populated to the second drop-down list. Remember we are selecting a value for the Customer lookup field on the Case form, and the only values that can be entered are account or contact lookups.

10. Click the **Add** button.

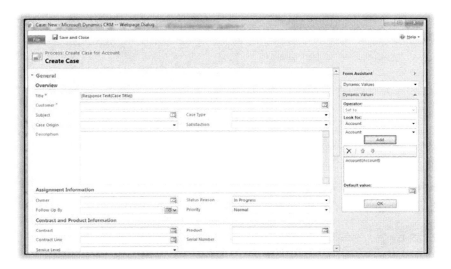

11. Click **OK**. The **Customer** field is populated with **Account(Account).** This is process design notation for "the account field (from the account entity)".

12. Click inside the Description field. In the Look for drop-down, select **Case Description** in the Local Values section, and then click **Add**.

13. Click **OK**. The Description field is populated with Response Text(Case Description), and the Process form editor should look like this:

14. Click **Save and Close** to return to the Step Editor.
15. Click inside the Create action's Description field, and type **_New Case_**.

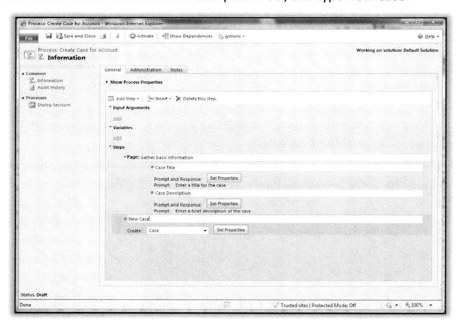

16. Click **Save and Close**, to return to the Processes grid. With the **Create Case for Account** dialog selected, click **Activate**.

17. In the Process Activate Confirmation dialog, click **OK**, and your new dialog is ready to run.

Step by Step: Running a Dialog Process

Once you've created and activated a dialog process, you can run it by following these steps, using the Create Case for Account process as an example:

1. Start the dialog using one of two methods:

    a. Navigate to the Accounts grid, select a single record, and click **Start Dialog** on the Accounts ribbon.

    b. Or, open an account form, and click **Start Dialog** on the Account ribbon:

2. Select the dialog process in the **Look Up Record** dialog, and click **OK** to run it:

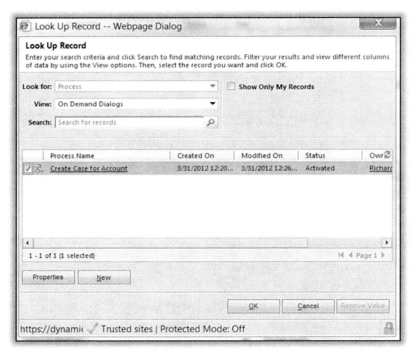

3. The first page of the dialog appears. Enter the requested information, and optionally use the text box at the bottom to enter additional information.

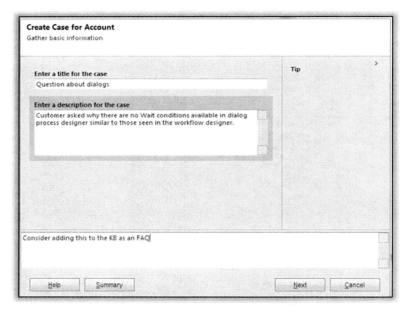

4. Click **Next**. This dialog only has one page so at this point you can click **Finish**.

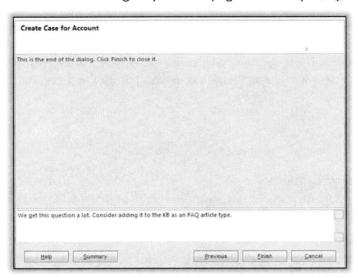

5. At this point the case record is immediately created, and associated with the account record selected when the dialog was started:

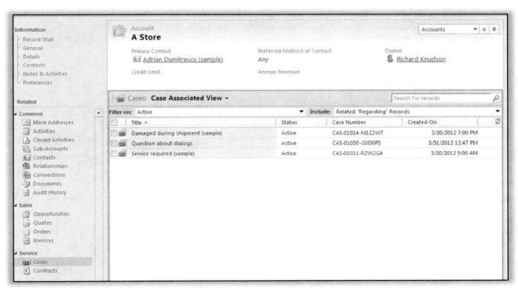

Dynamic Values: Look Familiar?
In the previous step-by-step exercise, you probably noticed how similar the dialog design experience is to the workflow design experience. That's because they are essentially the same. Even though the user experience at run time is different, the design experience is the same. In particular, the way you work with dynamic values in the process designer is exactly the same whether you're designing a workflow or dialog process.

Understanding Prompts and Responses

Pages are really just containers for the Prompt/Response pairs of a dialog process; these are where the real work takes place, so in this section we will review them more thoroughly. When you are designing a dialog process and click **Set Properties** for a Prompt and Response action, you see the Define Prompt and Response dialog. Here is the first of the two Prompt/Response pairs from the previous example:

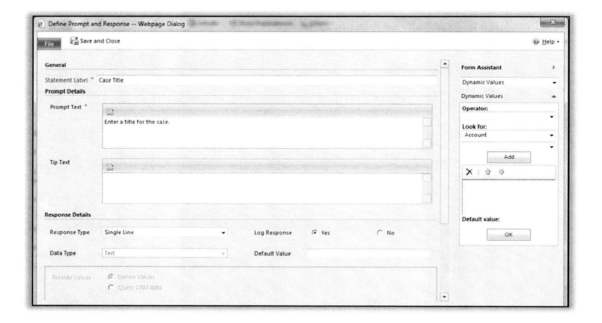

Statement Label is a required field, and as you saw previously, the value you enter in the Define Prompt and Response dialog is what appears in the Step Editor on the Description line for the Prompt and Response.

Prompt Text is also required. This is the text that instructs the user what to do. Depending on the business functionality, you may want to structure this as a question to be posed to a customer, or it may simply provide instructions for the user.

Tip Text is optional. Use it to provide additional instructions for your users. For example, in a "guided conversation" dialog, the prompt text might present the question a sales representative is instructed to ask the customer. The tip text in this case could provide internal guidance to the sales representative, such as what the goal of the question is, or some of your products/services that might be relevant to the question, or tips on how to engage the customer in conversation on the topic.

Response Details are important, and although they are not required, it's hard to imagine a scenario that would not require them. These are what allow the dialog process to *do something* with the information gathered from the user. The following table includes the possible response types.

Response Type	Data Type(s)	Provide Values	Description
None	NA	NA	
Single Line	• Text • Integer • Float	NA	Allows user to enter information in a single line text field. *Data Types described in detail below.*
Option Set (radio buttons)	• Text • Integer • Float	• Define Values • Query CRM Data	Allows user to select one of two options. Can define available values within dialog, or can query from CRM data. *Described in detail below.*
Option Set (picklist)	• Text • Integer • Float	• Define Values • Query	Allows user to select one value from a multi-valued picklist (option set)

		CRM Data	Can define available values within dialog, or can query from CRM data.
Multiple Lines (Text Only)	Text only	NA	Allows user to enter information in a multi-line text field.
Date and Time	Date and Time	NA	Provides a standard Date and Time control, stores response as Date and Time field.
Date Only	Date	NA	Provides standard Date control, stores response as Date field.
Lookup	Existing Record	NA	Provides ability to lookup records, store selected record.

The **Data Type** and **Provide Values** settings are important enough to warrant special treatment in the following two sections.

Response Details: Data Type

As indicated in the table, there are several possible values for Data Type property, depending on which Response Type value has been selected. This is important because you can only use a response to update fields of the same data type.

Let's extend the Create Case for Account dialog to understand the importance of the Data Type property. Suppose in addition to filling in the Title and Customer fields on the new case, you also wanted to fill in the Case Origin field. This is a system-defined option set field available for the case entity, and by default has values of Phone, E-Mail and Web.

Suppose you add a new prompt/response pair to the dialog, click **Set Properties**, and configure them as shown in the next figure:

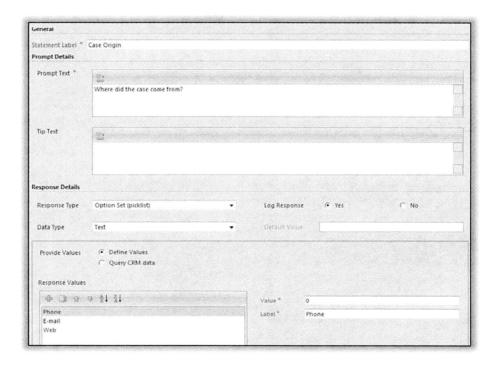

The selected Data Type here is **Text**, which is the default value. (This is one of those places in Dynamics CRM where once you save a value, it cannot be changed.) After saving and closing the Define Prompt and Response dialog, the Step Editor will look like this:

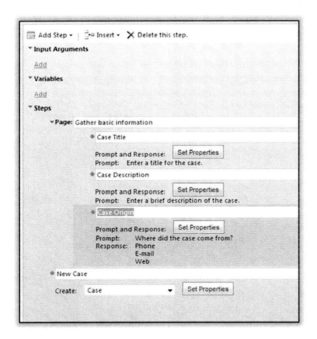

You might then click Set Properties, thinking you can use Dynamic Values to update the Case Origin field with the value selected by the user in the process. The problem is that the Case Origin field on the case entity is an option set field, which although it has a label (Phone, E-mail, Web), is actually defined as an integer field. In the dialog, this means that you cannot update the field value with the process value, since it's the wrong data type. You can see this in the following figure, where the selected field is Case Origin, and in the Dynamic Values section, the Case Origin variable has been selected in the Local Values section of the Look for drop-down.

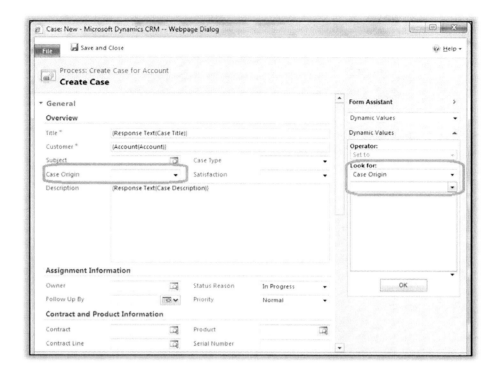

If you try this, you will notice that you cannot select anything to populate to the Case Origin field on the case form. This is the standard behavior for when data types don't match.

Now what you might try at this point is to build conditional logic into your dialog to work around this, testing for the value the user selected for the Case Origin in the dialog, and hard-wiring the entry of the corresponding option set value for Case Origin on the form. Yuck.

We will cover this in more detail below, but for now, let's look at the right way to get this done!

The key is the Response Data Type, which in this example needs to be an Integer in order to directly update the Case Origin field. You will need to delete the Prompt and Response line (since you cannot change the Data Type once it's saved), and re-do it like this.

The two most important things to notice are:

1. The selected Data Type is **Integer**. This will allow you to update the Case Origin field on the case form with the value selected by the user as the dialog runs.
2. Notice the Value of the Phone **Response Value** is 1. This must match up to the value stored by Dynamics CRM for that option set on the form.

Finally, after doing this, you can click Set Properties on the Create Case step of the dialog. The following figure illustrates that – once the correct data type is defined for the Case Origin dialog field – you can in fact directly update the Case Origin field on the case form. That's what the "Response Option Set Value" field is for.

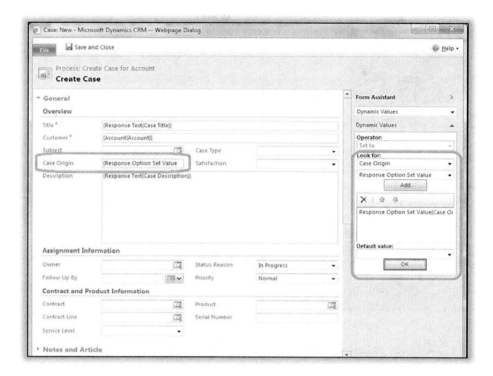

Tip: Commonly Used Option Set Values

The Dynamics CRM 2011 SDK contains a complete list of option set values for all system option set fields in the product. But that's just about as helpful as saying the dictionary contains a complete list of all the words in the English language! Like so many things, this issue – matching prompt/response values in a dialog to option set values for a Dynamics CRM field – has an 80/20 rule: most of your needs will be satisfied by a small number of the available options. In that spirit, this section includes the most frequently encountered option set fields from the *big five* customizable entities in Dynamics CRM 2011. Since we've been discussing the Case entity, we start with that one, and then proceed alphabetically with Account, Contact, Lead and Opportunity.

Commonly Used Option Set Fields for the Case Entity

Option Set Field Label (Schema Name)	Default Label	Corresponding Value
Case Origin (caseorigincode)	Phone	1
	E-mail	2
	Web	3

Case Type (casetypecode)	Question	1
	Problem	2
	Request	3
Satisfaction (customersatisfactioncode)	Very Satisfied	5
	Satisfied	4
	Neutral	3
	Dissatisfied	2
	Very Dissatisfied	1
Priority (prioritycode)	High	1
	Medium	2
	Low	3
Service Level (contractservicelevelcode)	Gold	1
	Silver	2
	Bronze	3

Commonly Used Option Set Fields for Account

Option Set Field Label (Schema Name)	Default Label	Corresponding Value
Address Type (address1_addresstypecode)	Bill To	1
	Ship To	2
	Primary	3
	Other	4
Shipping Method (address1_shippingmethodcode)	Airborne	1
	DHL	2
	FedEx	3
	UPS	4
	Postal Mail	5
	Full Load	6
	Will Call	7
Freight Terms (address1_freighttermscode)	FOB	1
	No Charge	2
Industry (industrycode)	Accounting	1
	...	...

	Wholesale	33
Ownership (ownershipcode)	Public	1
	Private	2
	Subsidiary	3
	Other	4
Relationship Type (customertypecode)	Competitor	1
	Consultant	2
	Customer	3
	Investor	4
	Partner	5
	Influencer	6
	Press	7
	Prospect	8
	Reseller	9
	Supplier	10
	Vendor	11
	Other	12
Category (accountcategorycode)	Preferred Customer	1
	Standard	2

Commonly Used Option Set Fields for Contact

Option Set Field Label (Schema Name)	Default Label	Corresponding Value
Address Type	Same as Account	
Shipping Method	Same as Account	
Freight Terms	Same as Account	
Role (accountrolecode)	Decision Maker	1
	Employee	2
	Influencer	3
Gender (gendercode)	Male	1
	Female	2
Marital Status (familystatuscode)	Single	1

	Married	2
	Divorced	3
	Widowed	4
Category (accountcategorycode)	Preferred Customer	1
	Standard	2
Contact Method (preferredcontactmethodcode)	Same as Account	

Commonly Used Option Set Fields for Lead

Option Set Field Label (Schema Name)	Default Label	Corresponding Value
Lead Source (leadsourcecode)	Advertisement	1
	Employee Referral	2
	External Referral	3
	Partner	4
	Public Relations	5
	Seminar	6
	Trade Show	7
	Web	8
	Word of Mouth	9
	Other	10
Rating (leadratingcode)	Hot	1
	Warm	2
	Cold	3
Industry (industryscode)	Same as Account	
Contact Method (preferredcontactmethodcode)	Same as Account	

Commonly Used Option Set Fields for Opportunity

Option Set Field Label (Schema Name)	Default Label	Corresponding Value
Revenue	System Calculated	1

(isrevenuesystemcalculated)	User Provided	0
Rating (opportunityratingcode)	Hot	1
	Warm	2
	Cold	3

Response Details: Provide Values

The other important option to understand when collecting response from users is whether to enter values manually as you design the process, or to get them from a CRM query. This is an important and potentially complex topic, and we will cover it in detail later in the book. For now, consider the following figure.

In the previous examples, the **Define Values** option was selected, which means you simply enter the values yourself. Here, the **Query CRM data** option is selected. This is a super-important capability of dialog processes in Dynamics CRM 2011, as it lets you build prompts based on CRM data, so as the underlying data change, your dialog processes dynamically reflect the changing information.

In the previous figure, the **Query Variable** "Practices Query" has already been defined. Query variables must always be defined before they can be used (makes sense when you think about it, right?), and in the Step Editor it might look like this.

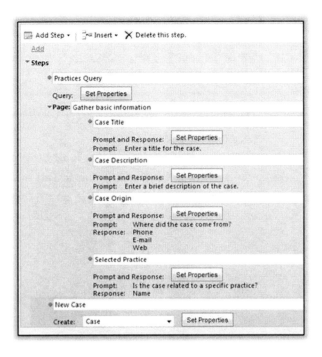

In this example, "Practices" is a custom entity my organization uses to track our different professional practice areas (e.g., CRM, Messaging…). If we want to associate a case record with a specific practice, the ability to build a query and populate a Prompt option set with all of our practices provides that ability.

Again, more details on this later, but it's important to know at this point that you won't always have to enter all of the possible option set values manually as you design the dialog process!

Response Type: Option Set (picklist) or Option Set (radio buttons)?
The only difference between the **Option Set (picklist)** and **Option Set (radio buttons)** versions are whether the prompt is presented in a drop-down list, or a set of option buttons. Suppose you use the Define Values for an **Option Set (picklist)** Response Type. As you design the dialog, the Response Details section of the Prompt and Response dialog looks like the following.

And when a user runs the dialog it looks like this:

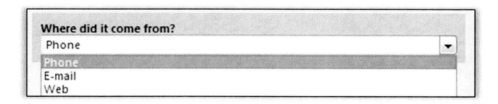

On the other hand, suppose you selected Option Set (radio buttons) in the design environment, like this.

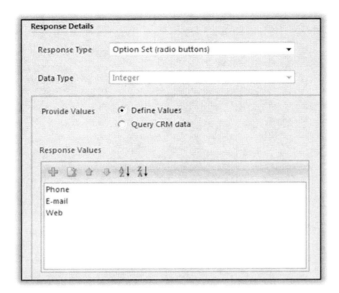

The only difference is that when the user runs the dialog, it looks like this:

Either way, you can only select a single value, and many users might not even notice the difference, although it's probably more conventional to use the radio button version when there are only two options. As a general rule, the more options you get, the more appropriate will be the use of the picklist option. For example, the here's an example that would definitely *not* be a good use of the **Option Set (radio buttons)** approach.

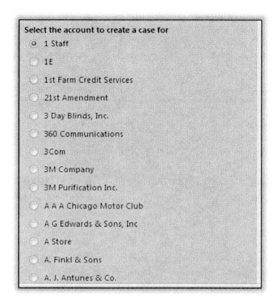

Special Topic: *Use of Hyperlinks in Prompt Text and Tip Text*

Now that we've been through the basics of creating and working with dialogs, let's examine how you can include hyperlinks to improve the user experience. In the following figure, notice that both the **Prompt Text** and the **Tip Text** fields in the dialog designer have a button you can use to enter a hyperlink.

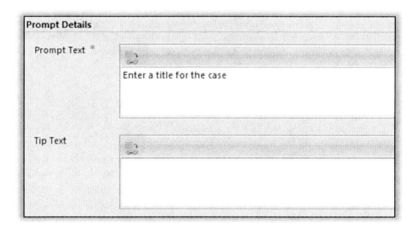

This gives you a way to use external web content to support your dialog processes, and the general rule is: as long as a user can get to the content, you can use it. For example, suppose you modify the Create Case for Account dialog by adding the following text to the Tip Text field:

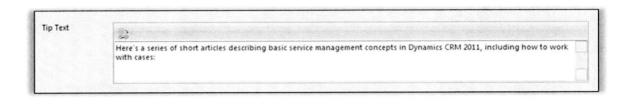

You can then position the cursor just after the "cases:" text, and click the **Insert Hyperlink** button to get the Insert Hyperlink dialog.

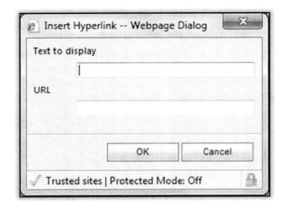

The Text to display field is the link text the user will be able to click, and the URL is where they will navigate to. For example, you might enter the following values.

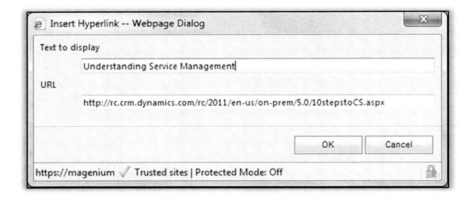

After clicking OK and returning to the Define Prompt and Response dialog, you will see the following in the Tip Text:

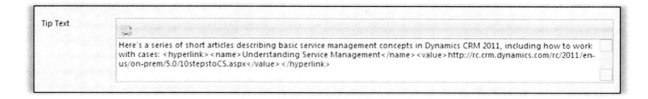

And after saving and activating the dialog, the user experience would appear like the following figure.

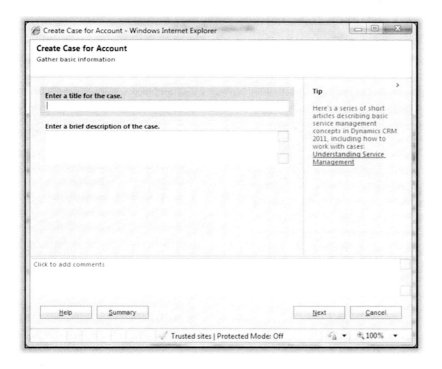

When a user clicks the link, the referenced URL will open in a new window. This gives you the ability to extend dialog processes in lots of interesting ways, including:

- Linking to special offer pages on a web site for a campaign follow-up dialog.
- Linking to Dynamics CRM forms using the "URL-addressable" forms technique that allows any record for any entity to be navigated to with its unique URL. For example, if

you use the product catalog, a specific product form could be opened with a URL like this one:

```
https://<yourorganizationhere>/main.aspx?etc=1024&extraqs=%3f_grid
Type%3d1024%26etc%3d1024%26id%3d%257bCBAC3403-1C74-E011-8947-
1CC1DEE8DAD5%257d%26rskey%3d37636470&pagetype=entityrecord
```

- Linking to a Microsoft or other Internet page for documentation, supplemental training materials and so forth. This is essentially the example shown above.
- Linking to a Web Resource HTML page contained in a Dynamics CRM 2011 solution.

Use your imagination and creativity, but remember that users must have permissions to view the hyperlink, and since the hyperlink is external to Dynamics CRM, it would be easy to include a link some users could access and others could not. For example, permissions in SharePoint and Dynamics CRM are managed separately, so you cannot assume that any user with permissions in CRM to run a dialog process will have access to a SharePoint URL you provide as a hyperlink.

The ability to create dynamic URLs, added in the November 2011 service update, gives us even more flexibility in the kinds of processes we can support with dialogs. For example, the following figure shows the dialog designer, in the process of configuring a process to gather updated information from a contact.

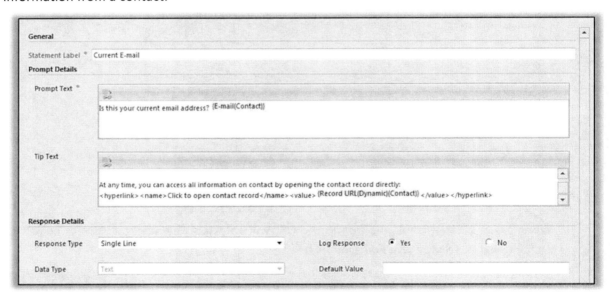

Here's what the corresponding prompt and response looks like when run by a user for a specific contact record.

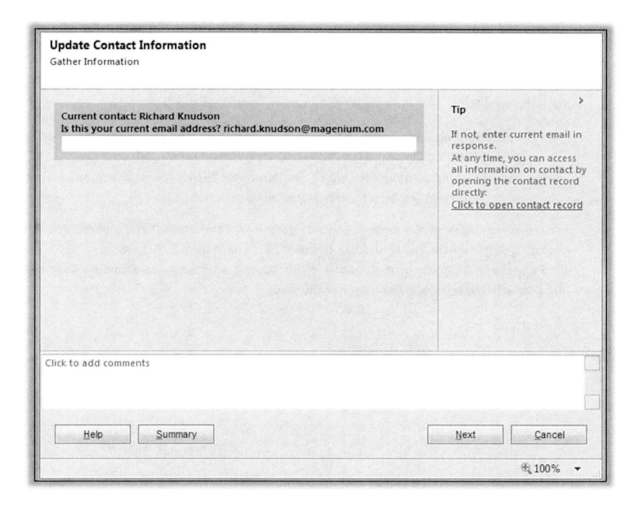

This simple example combines several of the previously discussed techniques:

- Information about the current contact is displayed dynamically in the prompt to aid the user in gathering information from the contact.
- The tip text is also constructed dynamically. In particular, the **Record URL (Dynamic)** variable is used to insert a link to the contact form. It's used in combination with the

Insert Hyperlink command discussed above to give the user a clickable link from within the dialog process.

Working with the Lookup Response Type

The **Lookup** response type, another of the important new features included in the November 2011 service update; allows a dialog process to present a user with a standard lookup view for a record type, and use the selected record later in the process.

To configure a Lookup response type, you must specify two options, the **Reference Entity** and the **Reference Field**.

- The **Reference Entity** needs to be a child record type of the record type you want to perform the lookup on.
- After selecting the reference entity, the **Reference Field** is the field from the parent record type that will be returned by the user's selection.

Let's review a couple of examples to clarify this important technique. First, suppose you want to provide a simple lookup to allow a user to select an account record. The following figure shows the Prompt and Response properties dialog with **Lookup** selected in the **Response Type** field, and **Contact** selected in the **Reference Entity** field:

Notice that the **Reference Field** drop-down allows the selection of lookup fields from record types that are parents of the contact record type. Selecting **Parent Customer** will provide a lookup to all customer records that can be parents of contact records – for most organizations, this will provide an acceptable lookup to active accounts.

Note also that once you make this selection it cannot be changed, as you can see from the following figure.

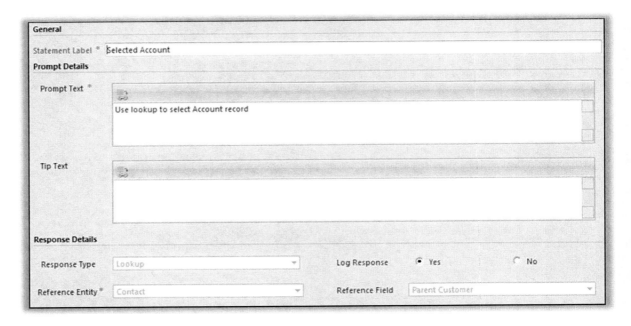

The following figure illustrates the user experience when the dialog runs; as expected, it appears to be a simple lookup to accounts.

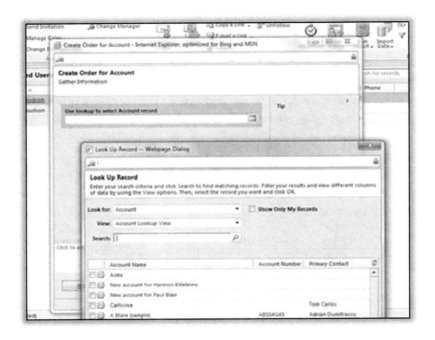

Now, suppose in addition to the lookup for account, you also want to allow the selection of a product from the product catalog. In the dialog designer, you need to select a child record of Product as the **Reference Entity. Opportunity Product** is probably the most natural choice for this, and as you can see from the following figure, selecting it then allows the selection of the **Existing Product** field in the **Reference Field** drop-down.

When this is now saved and activated, the user experience looks like this, after the user has selected from the account lookup and clicked the lookup button on the product prompt.

This approach does take some getting used to. It's the first use in Dynamics CRM (at least that I'm aware of!) of the Reference Entity and Reference Field concepts, and you may need to go through a few examples to get some intuition for it. Just remember the following:

- The first thing you select – the **Reference Entity** – must be a child record of the record you want to look up.
- The second thing – the **Reference Field** – must be a lookup field from the child record to the parent; and it's the parent record you're providing a lookup to.

Which Reference Entity to Use?

If you work through the example above you might notice that the account lookup dialog actually provides a lookup to account *or* contact.

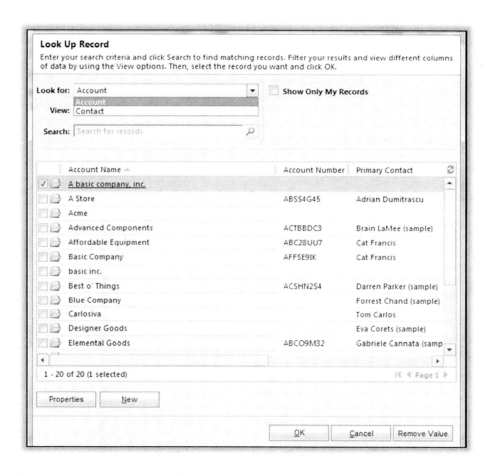

This is because the approach we took – using contact as the reference entity and parent customer as the reference field – doesn't *quite* provide a lookup to the account record type. Actually, it provides a lookup to the customer record type, also referred to as the "composite customer" record type. This is the same behavior you will see on any of the default forms with a lookup including the word "customer": **Potential Customer** on the opportunity form, **Customer** on the case form, and so on. That's why I was careful to say *for most organizations, this will provide an acceptable lookup to active accounts*. If you really want to provide a lookup only to accounts – that is, one that does not allow a user to accidentally select from a list of contacts – you can take a different approach. Suppose instead of the previous approach you selected **Account** as the **Reference Entity** and **Parent Account** as the **Reference Field**.

If you take this approach, the user can only select from active accounts, as you can see in the following figure.

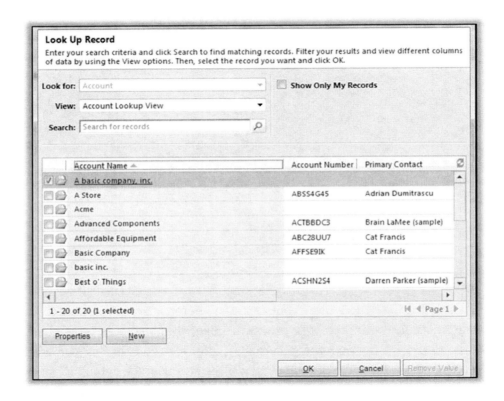

This raises an interesting question: since you have to select a child record type of the record type you want to look up…how do you know which one to select? You have to know the CRM entity relationships fairly well to know these things off the top of your head, or spend a fair amount of time experimenting! To save you some time, the following table presents, for some commonly encountered requirements, the combinations of Reference Entity and Reference Field you can use when you want to provide a lookup in a dialog process.

To provide a lookup to this entity	Use this Reference Entity	Use this Reference Field
Account	Account	Parent Account
Contact	Account	Primary Contact
Opportunity	Opportunity Relationship	Opportunity
Product	Opportunity Product	Opportunity
Lead	Opportunity	Originating Lead
Quote	Order	Quote
Order	Invoice	Order
Custom Entity A	Any custom entity with a N:1 relationship to Custom Entity A	Custom Entity A

This approach does allow you to create lookups to most record types, but evidently not to all record types. For example, the case entity does not have any out of the box child record types that uniquely identify case as the parent record. If you need to provide a lookup to cases in a dialog process, we present an approach of how to do this in the example processes at the end of the next chapter.

The accompanying solution includes a dialog process, Commonly Used Lookups, that illustrates how to configure examples such as the ones in the previous table. It's for learning purposes only, since it doesn't really do anything. But when you're learning how to create dialog processes, exercises like this can be helpful. The following figure shows what it looks like when you run it.

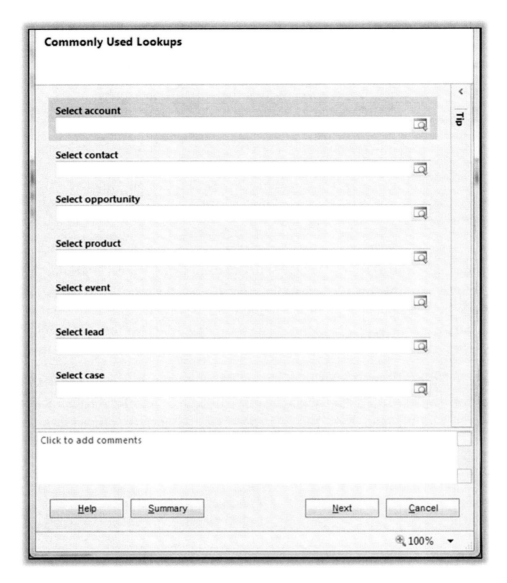

More Intuition on Dialog Lookups and CRM Data Relationships

As you may have noticed by now, I'm big on developing some intuition for how things work, and in that spirit, here's another way of understanding how lookups have been implemented in dialog processes. Remember that the reference entity must be a child entity of the entity you want to look up, and the reference field is the lookup field. I find it helpful to think of this from the context of the child form.

For example, if you review the information in the above table, you will see that the reference fields are all lookup fields. Providing as lookup fields do a reflection of the 1:N relationship from the parent to the child. So you can think of this approach as piggybacking off of existing 1:N relationships. If you want to provide a lookup in a dialog, first think of all the child entities of the record type you want to look up.

Along these same lines, you will notice that the actual look up records dialog box that users interact with is actually the system **Lookup View** for the record you're looking up. So not only does this approach re-use existing *relationships* between record types, it also leverages existing *views* to provide the look up experience. And as you will see in a subsequent exercise, if you want to provide a dialog lookup to a record type that does not have any readily available child record types, you can go ahead and create your own by creating a custom relationship!

Later in this chapter we will cover an alternative approach, **Query CRM Data,** for looking up information from CRM records within a dialog process. And after that discussion, you will be in a position to decide which of these two approaches is the most appropriate for your specific requirements.

Actions and Conditions in Dialogs

Dialogs have most of the same actions and conditions as workflows, and a few more. Here's a side-by-side comparison of what they can do, courtesy of the **Add Step** drop-down in the process Step Editor. The highlighted options are the ones each can do that the other cannot.

Add Step for Dialogs

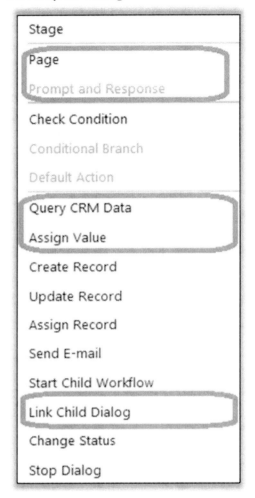

Add Step for Workflows

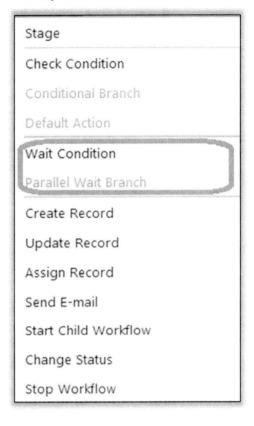

As you can see, dialogs do not have wait conditions and workflows do. This is because dialogs require user input from start to finish, so wait conditions of the type workflows have (wait until one month before a subscription expires and send a reminder e-mail, etc.) would not work very well for dialogs.

But remember that dialog processes can call child workflow processes. So you can imagine a dialog process that gathers information from a customer regarding a new subscription, and uses the information to create a new subscription record, implemented with a custom "subscription" entity. After creating the subscription record, the dialog process could then call a workflow process written for the subscription entity, which in turn implements custom wait logic regarding subscription renewal reminders and the like. This means that a dialog's inability to implement wait logic directly is not really a constraint: if you need that functionality, simply call a child workflow to implement it.

So, besides not being able to start automatically and not having wait conditions, we can say that dialogs can do everything that workflows can do, plus the following:

- As we've seen, the **Page** and **Prompt and Response** constructs present the user experience. **Prompt and Response** will be grayed out on the menu if the cursor is not inside a page.
- Dialogs can **Query CRM Data**. As was mentioned briefly above, this is an important capability and lets you present users with queries of CRM data as drop-downs from which they can select a value. This will be covered in detail in the next section.
- Dialogs also have an **Assign Value** action. This is used to update values in variables as a dialog runs. The **Variable** construct is also unique to dialogs, and will be discussed in detail later in the book.
- The **Link Child Dialog** action is similar to a workflow's ability to start a child workflow, except that a parent dialog can pass values (**Input Value**, in the Step Editor) to a child dialog. This also will be discussed in detail later in the book.

Working with Conditions in Dialogs

Conditional logic works the same in dialogs as it does in workflow processes. Since that topic has been covered previously in Chapter 3 we will start our discussion of conditional logic in dialogs by considering a conditional branching scenario unique to dialog processes: conditionally branching to pages within a process.

Conditionally Branching to Pages

One of the scenarios you will often encounter is the requirement to conditionally branch to a page based on a user's response. Suppose, in the Create Case for Account dialog discussed previously, you wanted to prompt the user for the customer's satisfaction level, and for dissatisfied customers, prompt the user for some *extra* information. Here's the logic we want to capture in the dialog process.

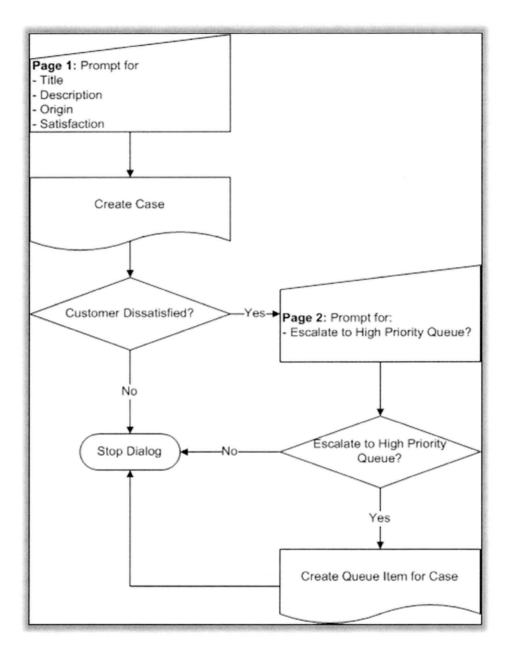

The following two figures show how to build a dialog like this one. The first one shows the first page, which has several Prompt and Response pairs, including the last one, which instructs the service representative to gauge the customer's satisfaction level.

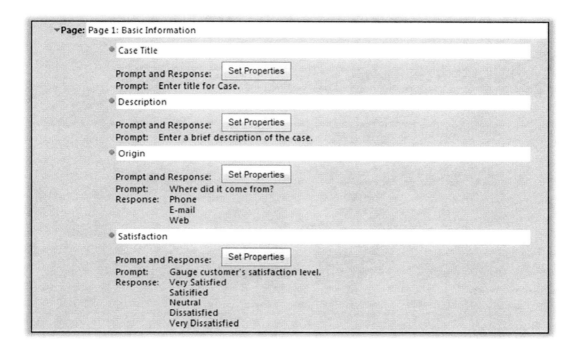

The rest of the dialog comes in three main parts. The first one creates the case record based on the gathered information. The second part (highlighted) starts with a Check Condition: if the customer is dissatisfied, we branch to the dialog's second page, which prompts for whether to escalate the case by routing it to a special queue.

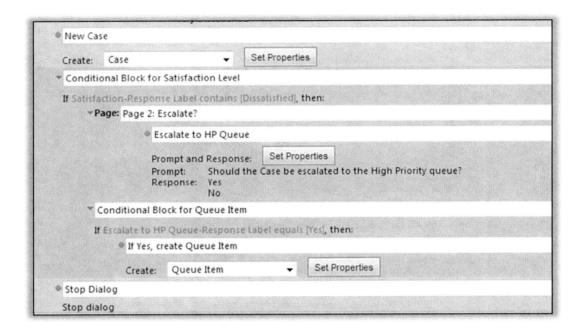

Specifying Conditions for Dialog Processes

In the Step Editor, conditional logic always has a structure similar to this:

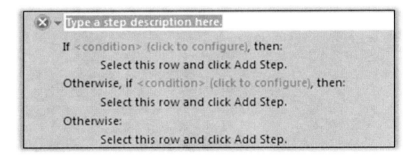

If you follow the instructions and click the <condition> (click to configure) link, the **Specify Condition** dialog appears. In general, the way you specify conditions is similar for dialogs and workflows, but there are some important new options specially designed for use in dialogs. Let's have a brief review of how to use the Specify Conditions dialog, with an emphasis on what's new for Dynamics CRM 2011 dialogs.

Continuing with our scenario of designing a dialog process to create a case record for the account entity, if you open the Specify Condition dialog and click the drop-down in the editor, you will see something like the following.

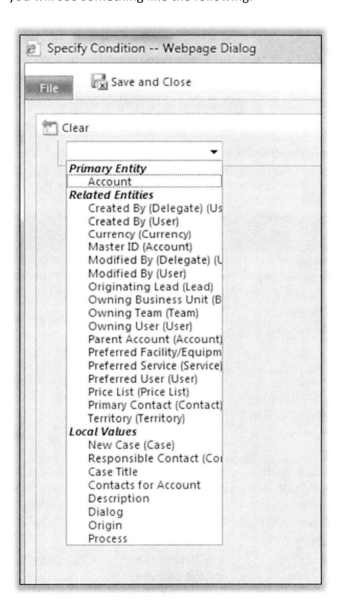

As you can see, the drop-down list has three sections. The first two – **Primary Entity** and **Related Entities** – work exactly the same for workflows and dialogs; the new stuff is in **Local Values**.

Primary Entity refers to the entity the process is written for, in this case Account. If you select it, the next column lights up and allows you to select any of the fields from the account entity, which you can then perform conditional tests on.

Related Entities refers to the entities that have a parental relationship to the primary entity of the process. So in this example, every record type that has a 1:N relationship to account is available; if you select one of these you can then perform conditional tests on any of the selected entity's fields.

Local Values presents several categories of items that can be used for conditional testing. These are listed briefly here and described in detail in the following table:

- Records created by the current process.
- **Process**. Exposes the **Execution Time**, **Activity Count**, and **Activity Count Including Process** variables.

- **Dialog**. Exposes variables defined for the dialog.
- **Responses**. Exposes the response values provided by the user.
- **Queries**. Exposes a special Records operator you can use to test how many records were returned by a **Query CRM Data** action.

As I mentioned, the most important new concepts for dialog processes are in the Local Values section, and they are important enough to deserve their very own table. In this table, I only include the items that are specially designed for use in dialog processes, and only appear when you specify conditions for dialog processes.

Local Values Item	How it's Used	Examples
Dialog	Variables are a new concept, available for storage of local values within a dialog process. If you've defined one and select **Dialog**, you can select it in the second column and test its value.	Define a variable Rating to rate a lead record. Increment its value depending on a user's responses in a dialog, using the Assign Value action. Perform conditional testing to qualify/disqualify the lead.
Responses	These are the values provided by a user to a dialog prompt. If you select a response value, the fields available in the second column depend on the type of response selected.	• Branch to specific pages based on a user's response • Prompt user to "Create additional record?" and run dialog recursively if Yes
Queries	Dialog processes have a Query CRM Data action you can use to build queries; lists of data returned by a query can be presented to a user in a prompt. If you select a query in the Local Values section, the second column exposes a special field, **Records** that you can use to test how many records the query returned.	Define a query "Contacts for Account" to display all contacts for account, prompt user to select one as "Responsible Contact" for created case record. Use Records field to verify contacts exist for the account. • If exist, prompt user with query results, update case record with selected contact. • If not, skip prompt and update.

I know these concepts might not be crystal-clear at this point, but don't worry. We will work through plenty of examples of how you can put them to work; starting in the next section, on the important topic of querying CRM data.

Querying CRM Data

Dynamics CRM 2011 dialogs can query data from your CRM organization, and the data returned in a query can be used in prompts and responses. This important feature was briefly mentioned above but deserves a more detailed treatment. Now that we've discussed prompts and responses in more detail, consider again the following figure.

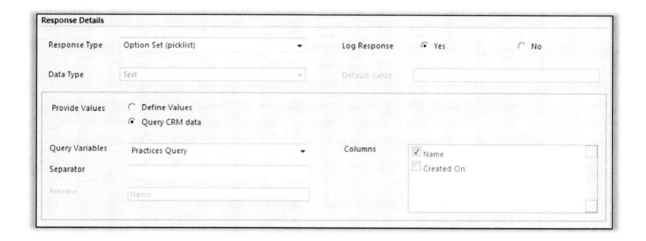

Remember from above, this is the **Response Details** section from the Prompt and Response dialog. In the figure, the **Query CRM data** option is selected for the **Provide Values** setting, instead of the alternative **Define Values** option. These options are only available for the **Option Set (picklist)** and **Option Set (radio buttons)** response types.

With the **Define Values** option, you enter the options manually; use this option for situations when the values are *not* stored as records in a Dynamics CRM entity.

Use **Query CRM data** when the values are stored as CRM records. There are several advantages to using Query CRM data, including a couple of obvious ones:

- You won't have to type as much.

- Your dialogs will always reflect up to date data, without you having to manually update the values.
- Your data will have more integrity and be less error-prone.

Others are less obvious but perhaps more important. For example, you can create dynamic, or linked queries. These are where a user's selection in query one is passed as input to query two, making the second one dynamically dependent on the first.

Here are a few examples of how you might take advantage of the ability to query CRM data in a dialog process:

- Suppose a process needs to prompt a user to select a contact associated with an account. A query can select the contacts associated with the account a dialog is running against, and present them to the user in a prompt. The user selects one, and a case record is associated with the selected contact.
- A process might allow a manager to assign cases based on criteria such as time availability. A query might select users with no scheduled activities and present the list of users in a dialog prompt; the dialog could then assign a case to the selected user.
- A process might allow a user to select from a list of e-mail templates, and use the selected template to send an appropriate follow-up e-mail to a contact. The list of e-mail templates could be created with a query in a dialog, with different criteria used to present templates appropriate for the business issue requiring follow up.

Designing CRM Queries for Use in Dialog Processes

The key to successfully using **Query CRM data** is to design your queries appropriately. Remember that the response types that can take advantage of this feature are the picklist and radio buttons options. These are not suitable for queries that return too much data, as you will see in the following simple example.

Suppose you have a dialog process a user can run from a Dynamics CRM Phone Call form. A scenario might be a receptionist receives a call, records the details with a phone call activity, and runs a dialog from the form to assist in creating a case, an opportunity, or some other record type. Let's assume that you want to present the receptionist with a list of active accounts, and allow the selection of one, for which the record will be created.

We will present a more detailed step-by-step exercise shortly, but for now let's take a high-level walk-through of how you'd build this and what it would look like.

1. Create a new dialog process, name it "Phone Intake, Create Opportunity", and base it on the Phone Call entity, and you will give you a process design form that looks like the following.

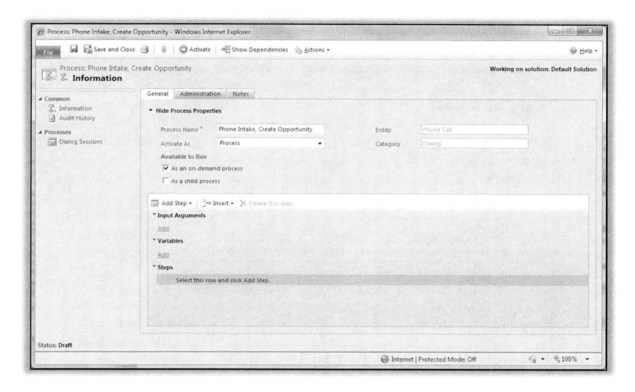

2. Now, click **Add Step** and select **Query CRM data**.

3. Click **Set Properties**, and the Define Query dialog will appear. This is the specialized version of Advanced Find you use to define the query that will provide the values to prompts presented later in the dialog. For this example, we will type "Active Accounts" in the Statement Label field, and select "Status Equals Active" in the query design section of the dialog:

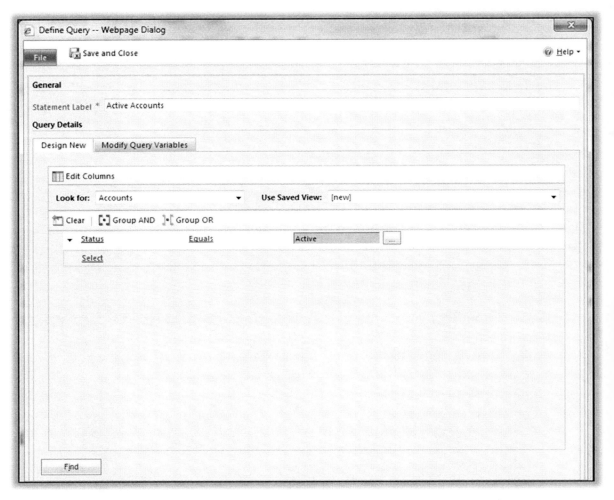

4. You can click **Find** to preview the query results, and then, as necessary, **Back to Query** to refine the query criteria.
5. Click **Save and Close**, and the Step Editor will look like this.

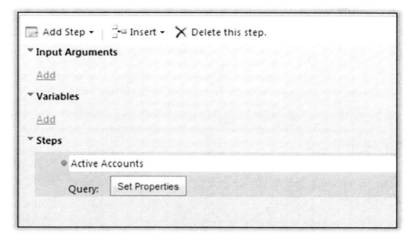

6. For this example, all we will do is add a page with a single prompt and response pair. Click the **Add Step** drop-down and select **Page.** Then, click the indented line within the Page section, click the **Add Step** drop-down again, and this time select **Prompt and Response**.

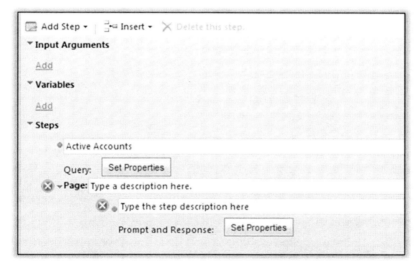

7. Click the **Set Properties** button to the right of Prompt and Response, and specify the following in the Define Prompt and Response dialog:

   a. Type *Selected Account* in the **Statement Label** field.

   b. Type appropriate text in the **Prompt Text** field.

   c. In the **Response Type** drop-down, select **Option Set (picklist)**.

   d. In the **Provide Values** option, select **Query CRM data.**

e. The **Query Variables** drop-down will then become active, and you can select the previously defined query, Active Accounts.

f. In the Columns section, select the **Account Name** column.

After doing all this, you should see something along these lines:

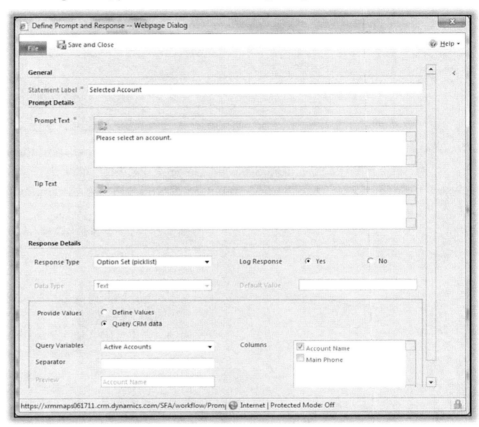

8. Finally, click **Save and Close**, then **Save and Close** again. Activate the dialog process, and from a phone call form (make sure you save it first) you should be able to click Start Dialog in the Process section of the ribbon, and select the dialog process just created.

Results will vary depending on how many accounts you have in your CRM, but you can tell from looking at the following figure that picklist or radio button controls will not be a very good way to present this list to your users!

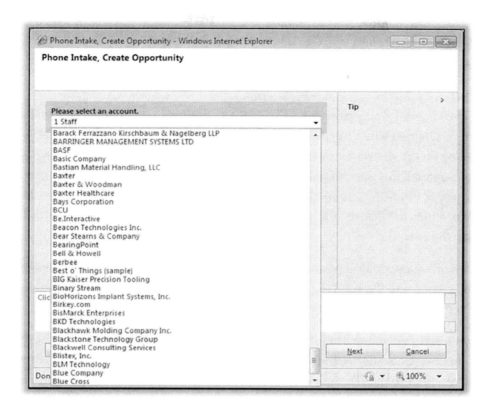

The controls we have to work with in dialog processes are drop-down lists and radio buttons, not lookups, so you will need to design queries that don't return hundreds of records. I'll spare you the radio buttons version of this, but believe me, it's even worse!

So...how many records are too many?

Well, you cannot display more than a single page of records in a dialog prompt, and since you cannot have more than two-hundred fifty records on a single page, a dialog prompt that breaks the 250 records barrier will not allow a user to select from all the available records. The *minimum* setting for **Records Per Page** is twenty-five, so if you go higher than that, there may be a few of your users who will need instructions on how to increase. On the other hand, the default setting is fifty, and a picklist with more than 25 options isn't all that unmanageable, so I'd propose fifty or so as an upper bound for the number of records to return in a query designed for this purpose.

Fortunately, there are plenty of approaches you can use to optimize queries for use in Dynamics CRM 2011 dialog processes. I'll review a couple of my favorite here, and then throughout the rest of the book we'll examine others in context.

Example: Filter a Query by the Current Record
Every dialog runs against a single record. At the risk of emphasizing the obvious, this is the record you have selected when the dialog is started. You can select a record on a data grid and click **Start Dialog** on the ribbon, or open a form and do it from there. In the workflows section of the book, we discussed in some detail how dynamic values can be used when designing a business process. For example, as an instance of a workflow runs against a record, it can access any of the field values for that record, plus any of the field values for any records with a 1:N relationship to the record.

Although there are many differences between workflow and dialog processes, there are plenty of similarities as well, and this is an important one: the business process run-time engine works the same with respect to CRM data for dialogs as it does for workflows.

So how can you exploit dynamic values and data relationships as you construct dialog queries? Let's revisit the Create Case for Account dialog we discussed previously for a good example of this. Suppose we want to modify the dialog so that in addition to prompting a user for basic information to be used to create a case for an account, it also presents a list of contacts associated with the account, and associates the selected contact as the "responsible contact" for the case record. Here are some of the important issues this new requirement raises:

- Since the dialog is written with Account as its primary entity, we can use the current account as a filter for a query of contact records. For many organizations, the number of contacts per account is small enough that it won't violate the "fifty or so" record count limit proposed earlier.
- The mechanics of constructing a query like this one take a little getting used to.
- We need a way of checking the number of contacts associated with the current account record; and in particular, if there *are* some, we need to prompt the user to select one and then update the case record. If there *no* associated contacts, we don't want to do those things. Sounds like some conditional logic in the dialog, right?

The following figure shows what a dialog like this might look like in the Step Editor. Although it's not required, this one is presented in stages to make it easier to understand.

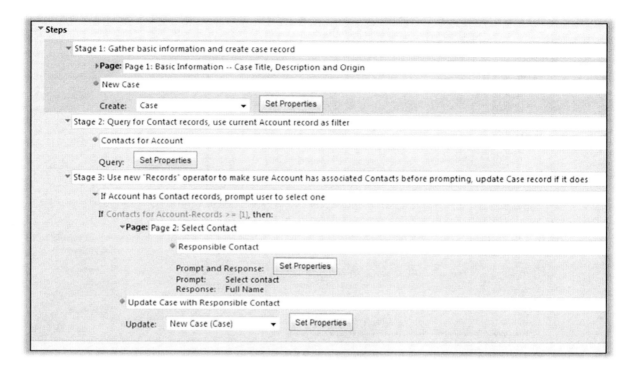

Here's an overview of each stage:

- **Stage 1** is essentially the same as the previous example. The Page is collapsed to save space, but it does the same thing as before: Prompt/Response pairs for the basic information needed to create a case record.

- **Stage 2** is where the query is constructed by passing the value of the current account record in as a filter to a query for contacts. This is new territory and is presented in detail next.

- **Stage 3** performs a conditional check to see if the account has any associated contacts. Only if there are some will the dialog prompt the user to select one of them; and only in that case will the dialog update the previously created case record with the responsible contact.

The following figure shows what a query looks like when values are substituted into it at run time. This is the finished product of stage two above; notice the Statement Label field is **Contacts for Account**, which you can also see as the label for the **Query** step in the previous figure.

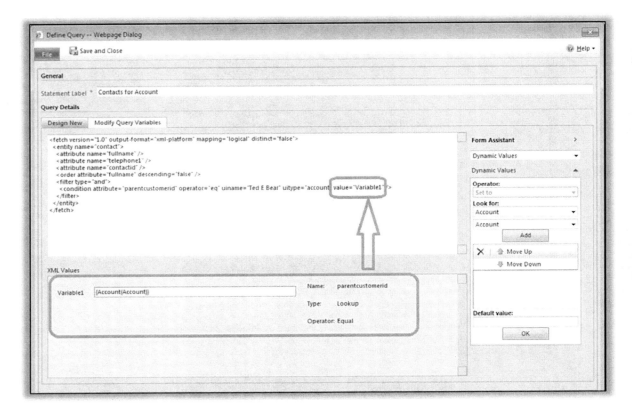

If you haven't done this before, you might not even realize there's a **Modify Query Variables** tab you can use to substitute dynamic values into a query, but here it is. Notice the highlighted areas: the Account lookup field (schema name **parentcustomerid**) is passed, via the **Variable1** variable, into the FetchXML statement. The tricky part is getting that yellow-highlighted Account(Account) dynamic value into Variable1, so here's a step-by-step exercise to walk you through it.

Step by Step: Build a Dynamic Query

Assume for the moment that you've created the previous dialog up through Stage 1: that is, you've gathered the basic/required information in a series of prompts and responses in a single page, and have created the case record. Now it's time to create the query for contacts at the current account, so position the cursor just outside of the Page block, and follow these steps:

1. Click **Add Step**, and select **Query CRM Data**.
2. Type Contacts for Account in the Statement Label field, and select Contacts in the Look for drop-down.

3. On the query designer, click **Select**, then scroll down to the **Parent Customer** field and select it.
4. Press the tab key, accept the default operator of **Equals**, and tab again into the lookup field.
5. Click the lookup button, and *select any value you like*. I know this seems odd at first, but you need to provide a placeholder here, otherwise you won't be able to perform the all-important next steps.

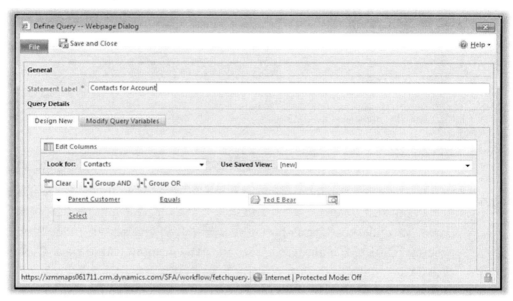

6. Now, click the **Modify Query Variables** tab and you will see this.

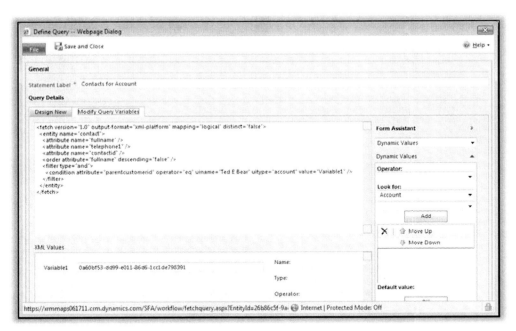

7. Here's where the dynamic values part comes in: position the cursor in the **Variable1** field in the XML Values section, and then make sure **Account** is selected in both drop-down lists underneath **Look for** in the **Dynamic Values** section. It looks odd, but the first Account refers to the entity, the second to the Account lookup field. Click **Add**, and then click **OK**.

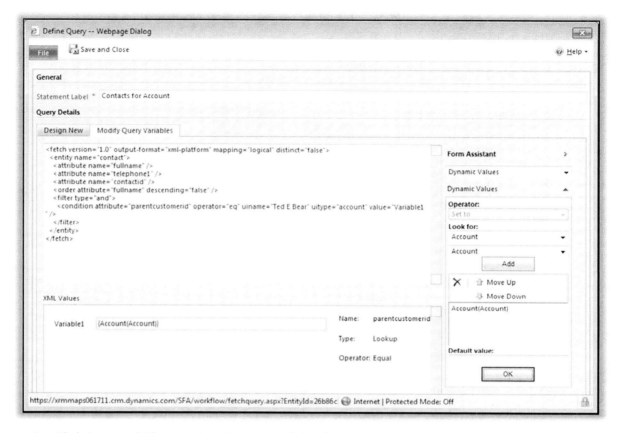

8.   Click **Save and Close** and you've created the dynamic query.

Another thing about that takes some getting used to: once you've used this **Modify Query Variables** tab to substitute a variable into the FetchXML, you cannot go back to the Design New tab. (If you click it, you'll get a warning that your work will be lost. Which it will, so don't do it unless you need more practice.)

That gets you through Stage 2 of this dialog; on to Stage 3. Refer back to the dialog overview figure above and focus on the most important thing in Stage 3, the **If** condition. This is an example of a topic I covered previously, in the section *Specifying Conditions in Dialogs*. And while the example is specific, the concept is a general one: when you construct a dynamic query, how do you know how many records will be returned? If too many are returned, you run the risk of violating the "fifty or so records max" rule of thumb discussed earlier. If too few records are returned, it gets worse, especially if there are no records returned.

The Create Case for Account example shown above already has logic built into it to manage this problem, but suppose it did not. For example, suppose you were just learning how to build Dynamics CRM 2011 dialog processes and didn't know about these things yet. You might build a dialog like the following one.

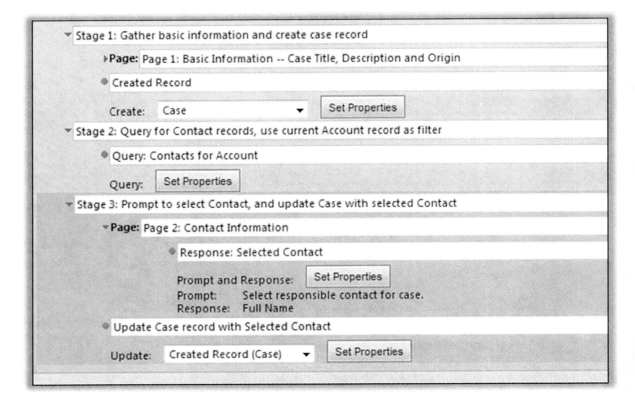

If you compare the two versions of the dialog, you'll notice that this one does not include any conditional logic in Stage 3. You might be able to guess what happens if you save and close it, activate it, and run it. If the account it runs against has associated contacts, it works fine, but if not, you see the following.

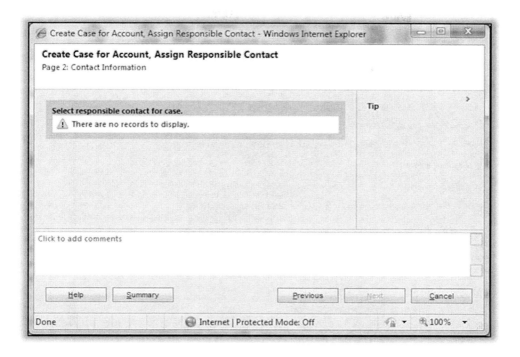

Notice that the Next button is grayed out, so you can't even complete it! In this example, the problem is that a dialog prompt cannot be displayed without any options, and since the options here are provided by a query that returns no data, the dialog cannot proceed. And that's why the special Records variable was created: so we can test how many records exist, and take appropriate action.

So how do you go about fixing a problem like this? Let's continue our example by fixing the current broken version of the Create Case for Account dialog, starting here, in the Step Editor, with the cursor positioned on the single Page in Stage 3:

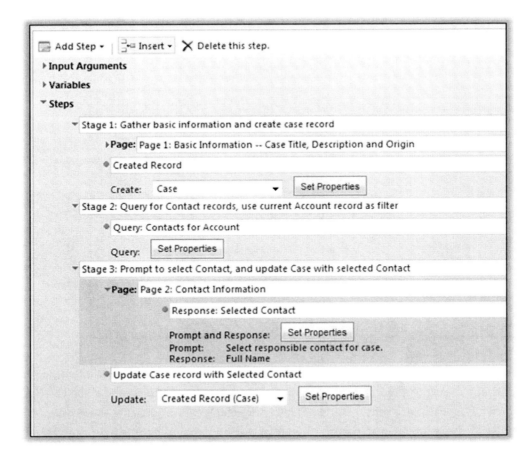

This is a real-world example, where you're fixing something that's broke, so to speak, so while you might not always take an approach like the one I do here...it's worth seeing it, just in case.

Step by Step: Build a Condition to Check Record Count

1. Click the **Insert** drop-down, and select **Before Step**.
2. Click **Add Step**, and select **Check Condition**.

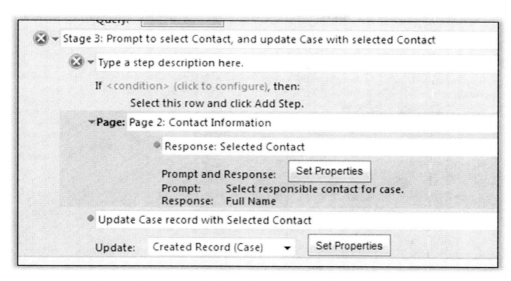

Notice that the If condition went before the Page, which in this case is what we want.

3. Click <condition> (click to configure), and the **Specify Condition** dialog will open.

4. Click Select to access the drop-down list in the first column, and select the query, which will be in the Local Values section.

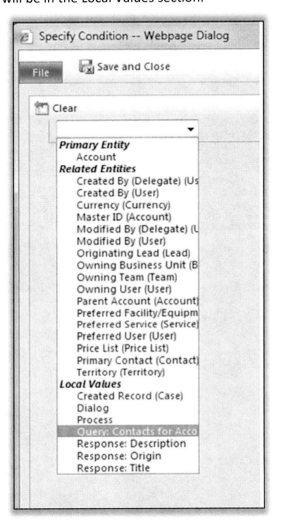

Notice that in this version of the dialog, I've prefaced the query with the text "Query: ", to make it easier to find. This is part of a naming convention I will propose a little later in the book.

5. After selecting the query, tab to the second column in the dialog, and select the only available option, **Records**.

6. Then tab to the third column and notice the available operators are the standard ones you see in Advanced Find when filtering on integer fields. This makes sense, because that's the data type of the special Records field you just selected. Select **Equals** and tab

to the value field in the next column.

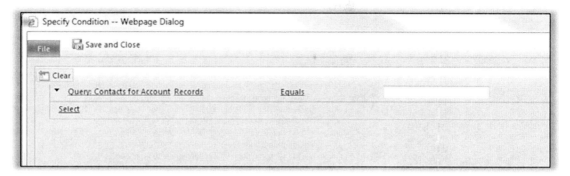

7. Enter 0 in the value field, and click **Save and Close** to return to the Step Editor.

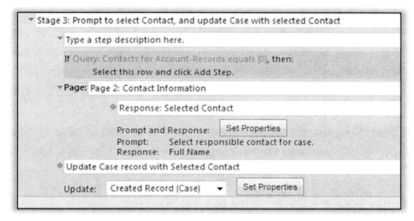

8. Click the **Select this row and click Add Step** line and click Add Step. Select the **Stop Dialog** action. That's all you really need to do, but consider adding some descriptive text, after which your Stage 3 might look like this.

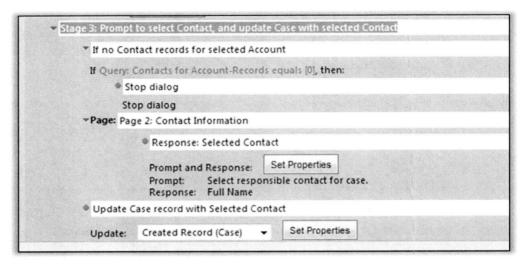

If you save and close, activate, and then run this dialog process, it will work fine regardless of whether the selected account has associated contacts or not:

- If there are no contact records, the condition evaluates to true, and the Stop dialog action is executed.
- If there are contact records, the condition evaluates to false, the Stop dialog action is skipped, and the dialog continues to the Page step, which displays the prompt and then updates the Case record with the selected contact.

Again: while this works, it's not necessarily the best way to write a process like this! It depends on what else you need to do, but in general I'd say that the approach presented at the beginning of this section (with the If condition flipped (record count >= 1), and the Page and Update Case actions *inside* the If clause) is a little easier to read, and sometimes has other advantages as well.

Tip: Understand the Difference between Filtering on Lookup and Text Fields

One of the trickiest things about building dynamic queries is in building the filter, which as we saw previously consists of two parts:

1. Adding a placeholder filter on the **Design New** tab.
2. Then using the **Modify Query Variables** tab to substitute a value at run-time into the FetchXML.

For me, one of the most confusing aspects of this at first was the difference between filtering on a lookup field – in which case you are effectively substituting in the GUID of the record to filter on – and filtering on a text field – in which case you usually want to filter on the Response Text.

The following two figures illustrate building a dynamic query where you're filtering on a lookup field. The example we discussed above – where a dialog process is written for the account entity and therefore can use the currently selected account to filter a query – is an example of using a lookup.

The first figure shows the Design New tab with Contacts selected in the Look for drop-down, and the filter being constructed on the Parent Customer lookup field. Remember that you must put something into the lookup field; otherwise you cannot access the Modify Query Variables tab. That's why I think of it as a placeholder: we aren't really going to search for contacts associated with A Store every time!

After supplying something in the lookup field, you can then click the Modify Query Variables tab. When you first open that tab you will actually see the GUID of the placeholder account in the Variable1 field. Then you should use dynamic values to substitute Account (Account) into Variable1 – you can tell if you do this right because you will see "parentcustomerid" in all the right places (that is, both on the condition line in the FetchXML and in the Name field at the right of the tab).

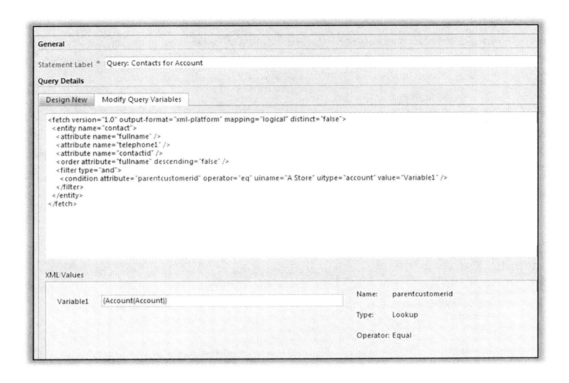

Let's contrast this with a situation where we need to filter on a text field rather than a lookup (which is really the GUID!) For example, the following figure illustrates what this might look like if a dialog process has asked the user to manually enter an account name. In this case, the dialog process is not written for the account entity, so the user types an account name. (Imagine a CSR asking a caller what company he's with, for example). Later in the process we want to query for all of the contacts associated with the account, so one might be selected as the Responsible Contact for a case record. But first we need to locate the account based on a manually entered text value, so we start the query like this.

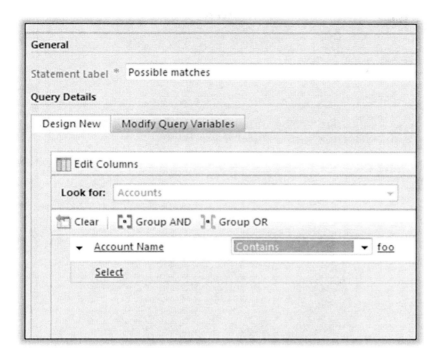

First, notice that the operator in this case is **Contains**. This is not a requirement, but it illustrates an important point, which is that when you're searching for text you don't need to be quite as precise. Second, in this situation it's more obvious that you're entering a placeholder. Now "foo" might not be your preferred placeholder naming convention, but it serves to emphasize that that text isn't really what we're going to be searching for!

As before, you must enter something in there before you can access the Modify Query Variables tab.

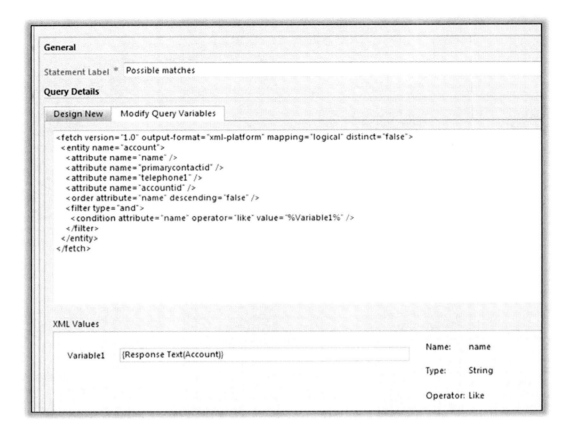

In this situation, it's probably more obvious that you want to filter on a string. Notice that the **Contains** operator gets translated to a **Like** operator in the FetchXML. Not surprisingly, close matches will be found in addition to exact ones, so if the user types "A Store" in the response text, the same query results will be returned as if they'd typed "a store".

Looking up Records: Query CRM Data, or Lookup?

We've discussed two approaches to looking up records as part of a dialog process. In the Understanding Prompts and Responses section we covered how to do this using the Lookup response type, introduced in the November 2011 service update. Then, in the Querying CRM Data section we showed how to do this with queries, using the Query CRM Data action.

Which approach is better? Well, as always with a question like that, the correct answer is "it depends."

To review, the **Lookup response type** uses the system **Look Up** view defined for the entity you want to look up. In some situations this might be what you want: users can work with it interactively, search on any columns included as view columns in the **Quick Find** view, and so forth. On the other hand, this approach can only use the Look Up view defined for the entity; an important limitation of this approach is that you cannot provide a filtered list to perform the look up against.

In contrast, the **Query CRM Data** approach presents the user with an option set populated with data returned from a query. The option set is less flexible in some ways: you cannot search or sort, and only have access to the records returned by the query. Also, as we've seen, an option set is not a very good way to navigate hundreds, let alone thousands, of records! On the other hand, in contrast to using the Lookup response type, this approach does support filtered lookups. This is probably the biggest advantage of using queries, and leads to at least a couple of definitive guidelines.

- If you want users to be able to search and select from a look up of all active records, you must use the Lookup response type approach.
- If you want to provide more structure to a look up and present users with pre-filtered or dynamically filtered lists to select from, you must use the Query CRM Data approach.

Querying CRM Data and CRM Data Relationships
In the previous discussion of the Lookup response type, I described that approach as piggybacking off of existing entity relationships. It's worth contrasting that dependence on *existing* data relationships with what you've just seen can be accomplished by querying data. With the **Query CRM Data** approach, you are not limited to existing relationships, and can in fact build a query for any record type you can get to through Advanced Find. You can see this in the Define Query dialog.

Taking this a little further, the ability to query CRM data allows you to extend the *data context* of a dialog process well beyond what can be done in a workflow. The data context of a workflow process is entirely determined by the relationships that exist between the workflow's primary entity and other entities in your Dynamics CRM. But because dialog processes can prompt a user with the results of a query against *any* record type, they don't have the same limitation.

For example, a workflow process might be automatically triggered to send an auto-responder e-mail to a new lead created from a form submitted from your web site. But the information included in the e-mail will be limited to entities with a relationship to lead. And since the lead entity does not have built-in relationships to other entities such as sales literature or product you would not be able to include information from those record types without customizing the system. But a dialog process can build queries for any of these record types, extending its data context beyond the lead entity's existing relationships and including virtually any information you need to include in a response.

Summary

This chapter introduced dialog processes, which run synchronously and with a wizard-like user experience. In contrast, workflow processes run asynchronously and in the background: that is, workflows do not *have* a user experience. The dialog UI consists of one or more *pages*, each of which can contain a series of *prompts* and *responses.* You can think of pages, prompts and responses are the fundamental building blocks of dialog processes, and as you build a dialog process you specify properties such as the prompt type (single or multiple lines of text, option set, lookup, etc.), the data type stored in the response and so forth.

We contrasted the actions and conditional logic available for dialog processes with those available for workflows. Unlike workflows, dialogs must have at least one page with a prompt and response. The other actions dialogs have that workflows do not include **Query CRM Data**, **Assign Value** and **Link Child Dialog**. One thing that workflows can do that dialogs cannot is wait: in the process designer this means that dialogs do not have the **Wait Condition** and **Parallel Wait Branch** options.

We reviewed several common uses of actions in dialog processes, such as creating and assigning records, sending email, changing record status and the like. Many of the actions performed by dialog processes are contained within conditional branches so your processes are flexible and can respond to user input.

One of the most important capabilities of dialog processes is their ability to query CRM data, and we conclude this chapter with a detailed discussion of the topic.

Chapter 5 - Advanced Topics in Dialog Processes

Calling a Child Dialog Process with *Link Child Dialog*

Dialogs, like workflows, can call child processes. The action you use to call a child dialog from a parent is **Link Child Dialog**, analogous to the **Start Child Workflow** action available for workflow processes.

And similarly to workflows, there are two main scenarios when you will want to call a child dialog process.

- **When you have a recursive process.** Suppose you have a dialog process that gathers information from a user and then uses that information to create a case record for an account. If you want to provide the option of creating several cases without requiring the user to select the account record and repeatedly start the dialog from the ribbon, this is a job for a recursive process, in which a dialog can repeatedly call *itself* as a child process.

- **When you have modular dialog processes you want to re-use**. For example, you may have a standard dialog process that allows a user to select one of several e-mail templates to construct and send a case acknowledgment e-mail to a customer after creating a case record. If several different case creation processes all use this standard process for sending the acknowledgment e-mail, breaking it out separately as a shared child process means you only have to change it in one place, if and when you need to make changes to it.

Recursive Dialog Processes

Let's examine a recursive dialog process, using the create-multiple-cases example just mentioned. The following figure shows how the properties for such a dialog, in this example named **Create Cases for Account**, might look.

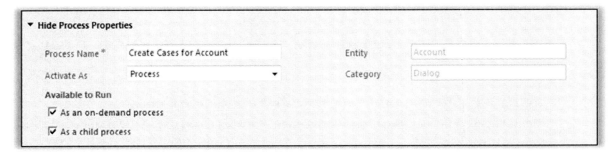

The most important point here is that both the **As an on-demand process** and **As a child process** options must be selected in the **Available to Run** section. If the first one isn't selected you'd have no way of kicking off the dialog in the first place; if the second isn't selected the dialog won't be able to call itself recursively.

Now let's take a look at the dialog logic, first in a Visio diagram.

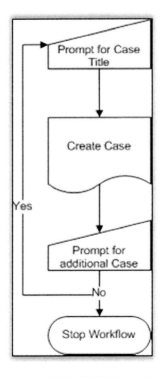

Now in the dialog designer.

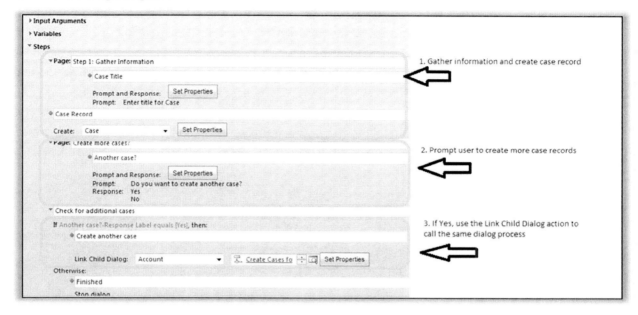

In the previous figure, clicking **Set Properties** on the **Link Child Dialog** step will allow you to browse and select the Create Cases for Account process. Again, you will only be able to select this process if **As a child process** is selected in the **Available to Run** section.

Tip: Select "As a child process", then click Save

In order to call a dialog process from itself – to recur, that is – it must be available to run as a child process. When you first create one of these, if you select **As a child process** and immediately attempt to add the **Link Child Dialog** step, you may notice that the dialog is not available. This is most likely because you haven't saved the dialog after selecting the **As a child process** option. So remember, after you select that option, save the dialog, and then you can browse to the process, calling it recursively with **Link Child Dialog**.

Reusable Dialog Processes

In the previous section we discussed calling a child dialog process to implement a recursive process. The other reason to use child dialogs is when you have several dialog steps *in common* across different dialog processes. If you break them out and put them into their own dialog process you can make your dialogs easier to understand, and easier to maintain.

For example, suppose you have several e-mail templates and you want to build a dialog process that prompts sales representatives with the templates, allowing them to select one and send the appropriate e-mail to a contact. While this might be a relatively simple dialog process, it also might be used in several different contexts: when a new contact is associated with an account, when a lead is converted to a contact or as a follow-up after a conversation with an existing contact. If each of *these* is implemented as a dialog process, it can be considerably easier to create a *separate* dialog for the e-mail selection, rather than replicating the same steps in each of the other processes. The following two diagrams provide a heuristic illustration of the difference:

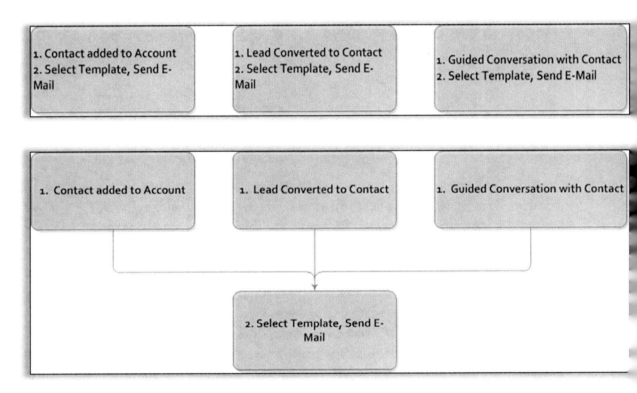

With the non-modular approach, if you want to change the logic of the second part of the processes, you have to modify three separate processes. With the modular approach you only have to modify one.

As with the recursive dialog example, remember to select the **Available as a child process** option in order to make a dialog "callable" from a parent process.

This dialog is divided into three stages, as the following figure shows. (The **Input Arguments** and **Variables** sections are not used in this dialog, so they're minimized to save space.)

Now let's see how this works, examining the main action in each of the three stages, respectively: the query properties, the prompt and response properties, and the send e-mail properties.

Query Properties

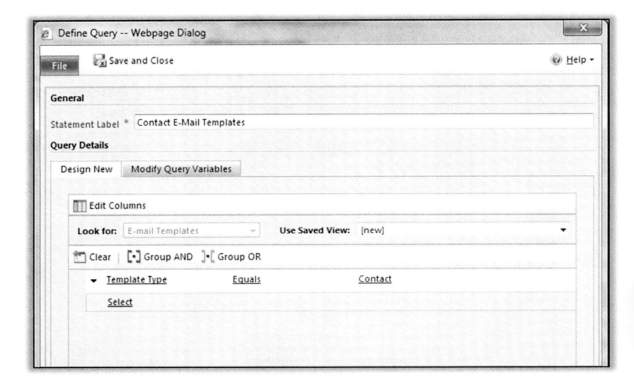

The Query properties are straightforward. In the current example, we simply query for all e-mail templates for contact records. As you will see below, I use the default templates, but in the real world you will likely delete those templates and create new ones for your business.

This is a "static" query, in the sense that we are not using the **Modify Query Variables** tab to dynamically filter the query. However, it would be possible to extend this, for example by making the filter dynamically select different template types depending on the context. What's the potential payoff for the added complexity? More re-use: imagine an *uber*-email template selection process that works whether for a contact, a lead, or any other record type you want to send e-mails to.

Prompt and Response Properties

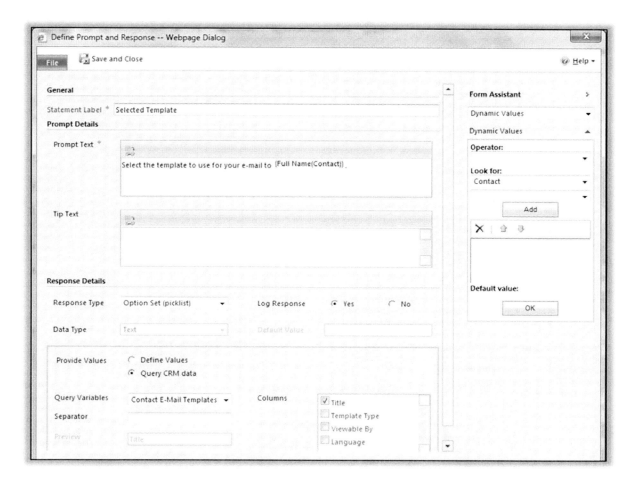

The Prompt and Response properties are similar to ones we've seen before, with **Provide Values** set to **Query CRM data**, and the **Query Variables** provided by the previously defined query, *Contact E-Mail Templates*. Perhaps the most interesting thing about this example is the use of dynamic values in the **Prompt Text** field. Both the **Prompt Text** and **Tip Text** fields can take advantage of dynamic values to make your dialog processes more...well, dynamic. We'll see more examples of this later in the book.

Send E-mail Properties

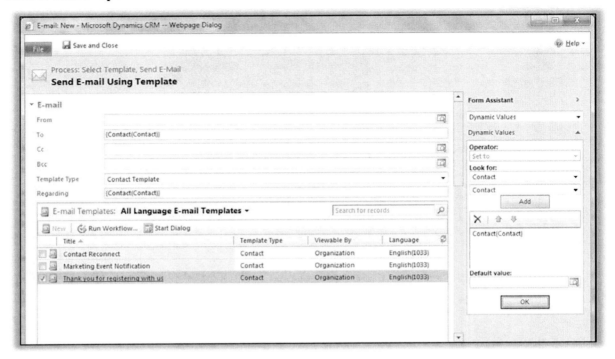

The Send E-Mail properties are where we specify the recipient on the **To** line (the contact), and select the appropriate template. Remember, this happens inside the conditional block, based on the value of the Selected Template (the response value from the prompt and response in stage 2).

Notice that in this example I left the **From** field empty. If you do this, the e-mail will be sent from the user running the dialog process. An alternative would be to fill this field with the owner of the contact record, but that would introduce the possibility of the e-mail being sent on behalf of another user. Depending on your business requirements, that may be the way to go, but it can also introduce unnecessary complexity.

After saving, closing and activating this process, it can be run on an on-demand basis, by selecting a contact record, clicking **Start Dialog** on the ribbon, and selecting the dialog process.

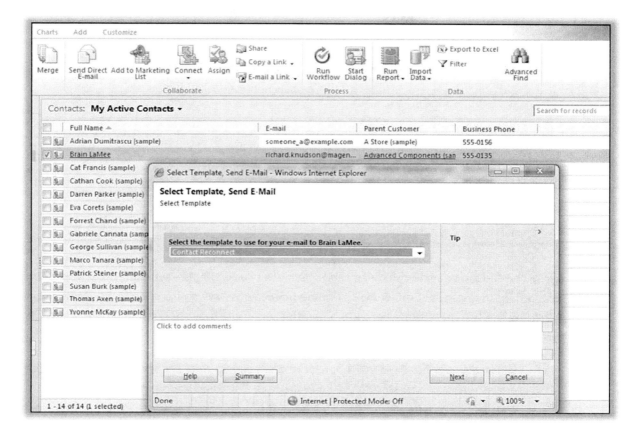

Once more, the reason this dialog is available to run from the UI like this is that the **As an on demand process** property is selected. Since the point of this exercise was to illustrate how to use child dialog processes, you can think of this as a bonus!

Here's what it looks like when you call this dialog, using the **Link Child Process** step, from another dialog.

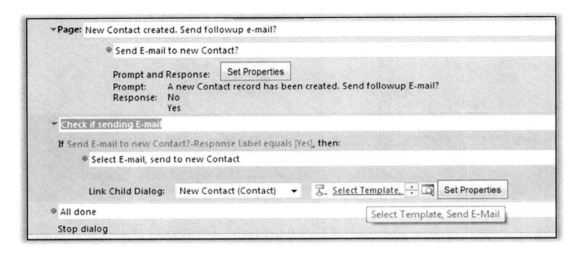

Again, the reason you can call it like this is because the **Available as a child process** property is selected. In the next section we will examine how to pass values from a parent dialog process to a child. But in the meantime, here are a few tips and hints that apply to all cross-dialog conversations initiated with **Link Child Dialog.**

- *When a Dynamics CRM 2011 parent process calls a child process, the context of the parent process is passed to the child process.* This is an important improvement compared to Dynamics CRM 4.0, where although a workflow could call a child workflow, the child knew nothing about the context of the parent.

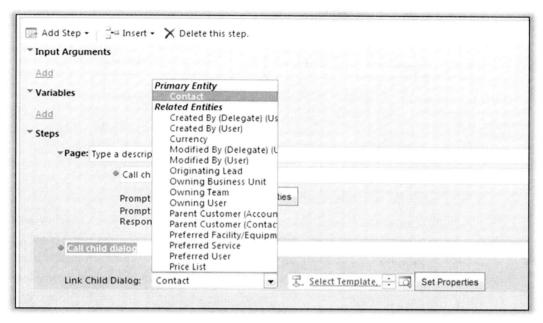

The process you're linking *to* (in this case, the **Select Template, Send E-Mail** example) knows which contact record you're on when you call it. Notice you can also call processes written for entities in the **Related Entities** section. And as you remember from our previous discussion in the workflows section of the book, these are all of the entities that are parent entities of the entity this process is written for. So for example, if you have a dialog process for the account entity and it's exposed as a child process, you can call it from here and the process engine will know to call the parent customer of the current contact record

- *Link Child Dialog can only be used as the last step in a dialog process!* That is, you cannot pass control to a child dialog and then pick up where you left off in the parent dialog when done. If you try to activate a dialog using Link Child Dialog where it is not the last step in the dialog, you get the following error.

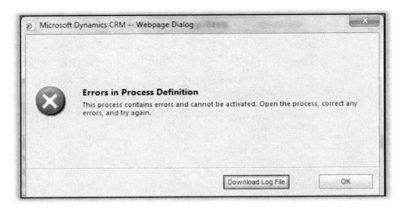

Interestingly, you can pass control to a child workflow (using the **Start Child Workflow** step) and then return to the parent process, picking up where you left off. This is because workflows run asynchronously and don't support user interaction. You must be careful with this, however. Because workflows are asynchronous, you cannot depend on them being completed when you return to the calling process! We will see an example of this later in the book; for now, file it in your "things to watch out for" category.

Using Variables in Dialog Processes

Variables are used for temporary data storage during the lifetime of a dialog. One of the most common reasons to use variables is to calculate a value based on other values. Here are a couple of examples where variables might be required.

- When a lead is converted to an opportunity, a sales representative might be prompted with several questions about the revenue potential, how supportive is the sponsor, what is the decision timeframe and so forth. Depending on the responses, an *Opportunity Score* variable could be calculated and used to update a custom field on the opportunity record.
- A satisfaction survey or a post-event evaluation could be implemented with a dialog process. Individual survey responses could be captured in fields in a custom entity, but you might want to calculate aggregate values (totals, or averages, say) as well. You could use variables to hold these calculated values.

You can create a new variable by clicking on the *Add* hyperlink in the **Variables** section of the process designer.

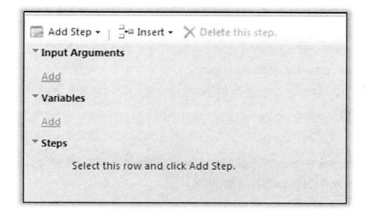

As you can see, variables have **Name, Data Type,** and **Default Value** properties.

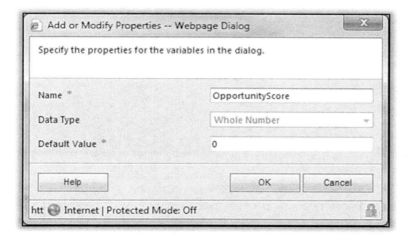

Notice in the previous figure that, just as when you specify the data type of the response in a prompt/response pair, the data type cannot be changed after saving. Some other important features to keep in mind include the following.

- The **Name** property cannot contain spaces or special characters, and must be unique within the dialog process.
- There are three options for the Data Type property:
    1. Use **Single Line of Text** for text values.
    2. Use **Whole Number** for integer values, in the range of -2 billion or so to +2 billion or thereabouts.

3. The **Floating Point** data type supports values in the range -100,000,000,000 and 100,000,000,000, and more precision to the right of the decimal point.
4. Use **Date and Time** when you want to capture both the date and the time.
5. Use **Date Only** when you only need the date.
6. Use **Lookup** if you need to store a value previously provided by the user as a Lookup response type.

You can see one of the differences between the **Whole Number** and **Floating Point** data types by comparing the **Default Value** field in the following two figures.

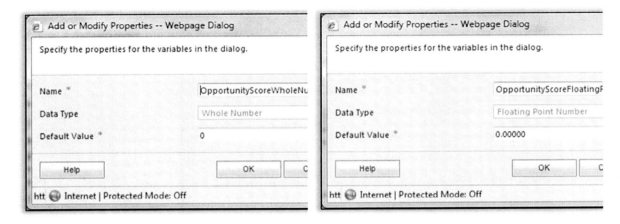

Example: Using Variables to Score Opportunity Records

Let's walk through the *Score Opportunity* dialog process example in detail. It's written for the Opportunity entity, and as in the previous example, is available to run both **As an on-demand process** and **As a child process**. The following figure shows **Properties** section, the **Variables** section expanded so you can see the **OpportunityScore** variable, and the three main stages of the dialog collapsed so you can see everything at once.

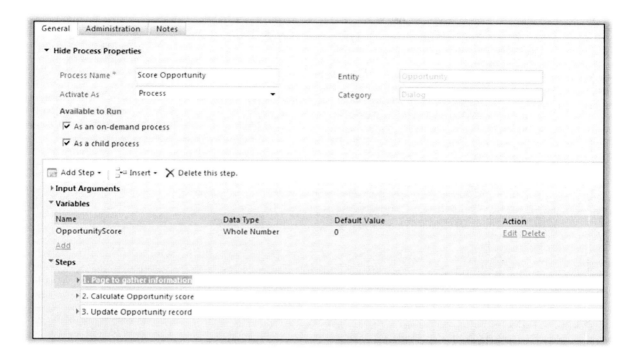

I'll drill down on each of the stages in succession.

Stage 1: Prompt and Collect Responses

The following figure shows stage 1 expanded.

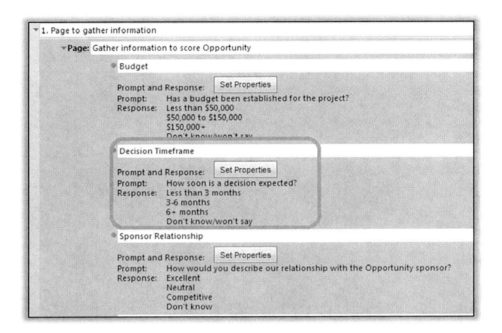

Stage 1 contains the single page of this dialog process, which exposes the prompt/response pairs. In the previous figure, the **Decision Timeframe** Prompt and Response is highlighted; clicking **Set Properties** opens the following **Define Prompt and Response** dialog.

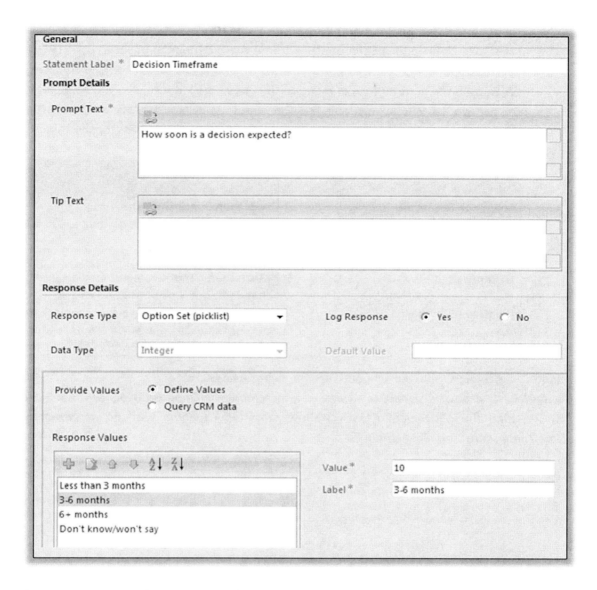

The most important things to notice here are:

- Notice the **Data Type** is set to **Integer**. We discussed this previously, but I want to emphasize the importance of getting this right the first time in. **Text** is the default, and I can't tell you how many times I've forgotten to change it in situations when I really need the **Integer** value. It can take a while to specify the several response values for an option set...and if you get the data type wrong the only way to fix it is to delete and start over!

- Next, notice that the 3-6 months Response Value is selected, and the values of the associated **Value** and **Label** properties. These really define the business rules behind the specific opportunity scoring algorithm being designed, and will of course vary from one organization to another (not to mention the questions!). But to give you a feel for how this can work, the following table lists the values for each of the four possible responses for the **Decision Timeframe** prompt, along with my thought process for the values.

Response Label	Response Value	Thought Process
Less than 3 months	0	Less than 3 months? Not enough time, and a possible indicator we're coming in too late in the process.
3-6 months	10	The sweet spot.
6+ months	5	More than 6 months might be a little better than less, but it's not as good as 3-6.
Don't know/won't say	-5	Either we haven't done our homework to find out, or the customer won't tell us. Either way it's bad, so we deduct points from the score.

Stage 2: Calculate OpportunityScore Variable using Assign Value

In stage 2, we use **Assign Value** to successively increment the *OpportunityScore* variable. You can see this in the following figure, which shows stage two expanded with the *Increment by Timeframe* score step highlighted.

Clicking on **Set Properties** for that step shows the following **Assign Value** dialog.

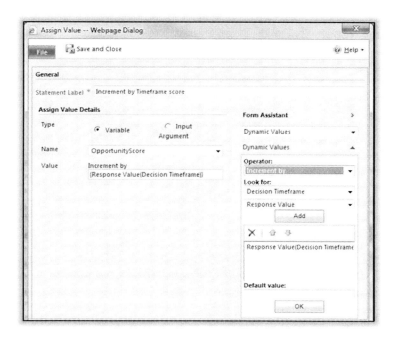

This ties back to the point I made in describing stage 1, about the importance of the **Integer** data value in this case. The value of the ***OpportunityScore*** variable is incremented here by the **Response Value** of the ***Decision Timeframe*** response. If I'd forgotten to specify **Integer** as the data type, the **Response Value** drop-down in the Dynamic Values section would be depressingly empty, reminding me too late that (once again!) I went too fast in the Prompt and Response dialog and got the wrong data type.

Another thing to watch out for here is the option selected for the **Operator**. For a cumulative score like the one calculated in this process, **Increment By** is the way to go. The first time I wrote a scoring dialog process like this one, I accidentally selected **Set to** on the very ast **Assign Value** step in the stage. When testing it, I kept wondering why no matter how good or bad I scored all the rest of the questions, the overall score never got much above or below zero. Don't let that happen to you!

For numeric fields, the operators you can use **Set to**, **Increment by**, **Decrement by**, **Multiply by**, and **Clear**. (No **Divide by**. Bummer!) You can see them all here.

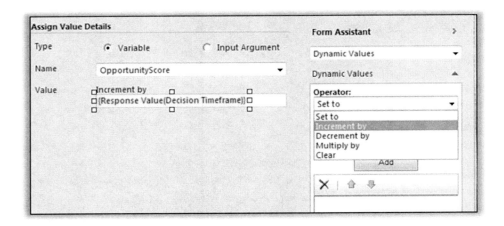

Stage 3: Update Custom Field on Opportunity with OpportunityScore Variable

Stage 3 is the easiest to understand, since all it does is use the calculated value of the **OpportunityScore** variable to update the opportunity record.

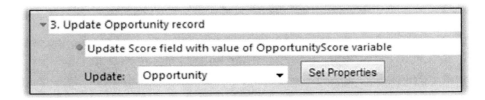

Click **Set Properties** to open the **Update Opportunity** dialog.

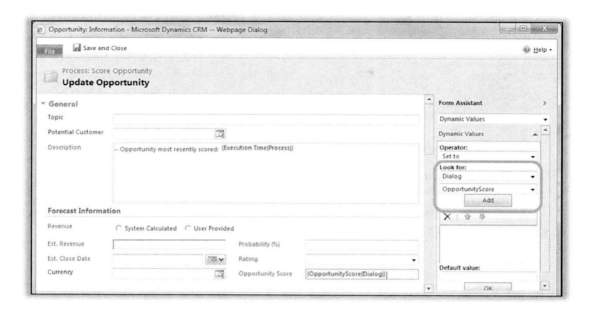

In this example, I added a custom field, ***Opportunity Score***, to the opportunity entity. I defined it as a **Whole Number** data type. This is important because it corresponds to the data type for the ***OpportunityScore*** variable in the dialog, which here is used to update the field value on the record.

Notice that **Dialog** is selected in the **Look for** drop-down. This is a special value that is used specifically to expose variables in dynamic values for dialog processes. You can verify this the next time you're in the dialog designer working on a dialog without any variables defined, in which case **Dialog** will not appear in the **Look for** drop-down.

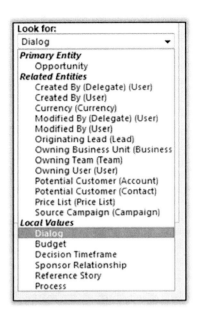

How it Works

Let's take a look at the user experience for the ***Score Opportunity*** dialog process. First, remember that it's written for the opportunity record type and it's available to run as an on-demand process. This means it can be run by clicking **Start Dialog** with an opportunity record selected on the data grid, or from the ribbon on the opportunity form.

From the data grid:

Or from the form:

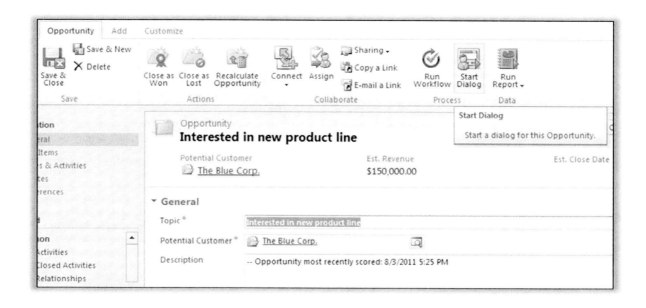

After selecting **Score Opportunity** and kicking it off, here's what the dialog process looks like.

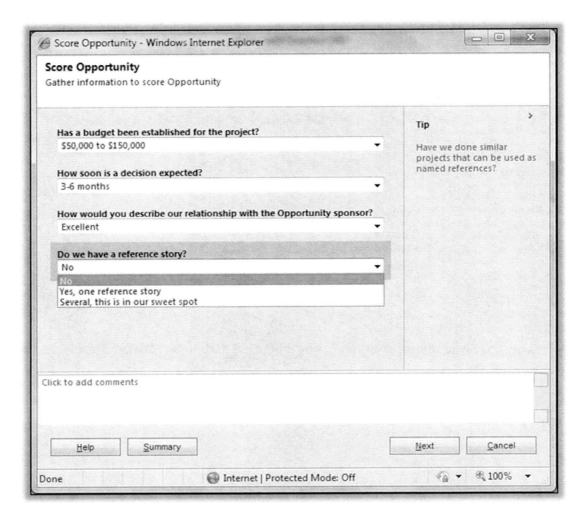

This dialog has a single page only, so after clicking **Next** and then **Finish**, the dialog gathers the responses, uses them to update the **OpportunityScore** variable, which in turn is used to update the opportunity record.

Here are a couple of observations on some of the business issues a process like this might raise.

- Notice that the implementation details of a process like this one impose some business rules. In this example, they mean that an opportunity can be scored more than once. This may be appropriate for some organizations, but you can also imagine imposing a "score once only" rule. Suppose instead of creating the dialog process for the opportunity record type and making it available for on-demand use, you only exposed it for use as a child process, and called it from a custom lead conversion process. This would effectively enforce the score once only rule...especially if you remember to take the ***Opportunity Score*** field off the opportunity form!

- The way I wrote this dialog process, the ***OpportunityScore*** field ranges from a maximum value of 50 to a minimum of -50. While there's nothing particularly scientific about the approach I used, I've known sales managers who claim to have a fool-proof lead qualification process consisting of a small number of simple questions a relatively inexperienced sales rep can ask a potential customer. If you're in that category, here's your chance to bake it into your CRM!

Passing Values to Child Dialogs with Input Arguments

Now we come to Input Arguments, which give you a way of passing values from a parent to a child dialog process. But given the previous discussion on the child process's awareness of the data context of the parent, you might wonder why this matters. The reason it matters is that while data context – the current record and all of its parent records – is important, it's not the *only* thing that's important.

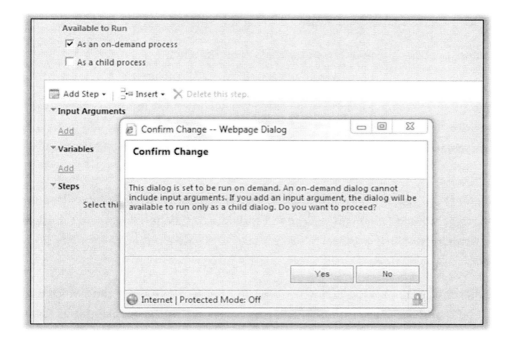

Calling Dialog Processes with a URL

The first time you read that in addition to starting a dialog manually from the ribbon in the usual way, you can also kick one off by referencing its URL you might wonder what that could be used for. This turns out to be a very important method of customizing the user experience, because it means that you can place custom buttons on the application ribbon or form ribbons in Dynamics CRM 2011, and give users one-click access to dialog processes.

In order to address this topic properly, we need to take a step back and discuss a couple of slightly more fundamental topics first.

Which Entity Should a Dialog be Written for?

Sometimes it's obvious which entity a dialog should be written for, but just as with workflow processes, sometimes it's not. Here are a couple examples of when it's an easy decision:

- If you want an interactive process where a user selects a record and then makes a copy of it, changing a few values in the process, the dialog should be written for the record type you want to copy. Case to case, opportunity to opportunity, and so forth.
- Suppose you want to create an alternative to the standard lead qualification process. Since you'd want to start the process from the context of a selected lead record, create this dialog process for the lead entity.

On the other hand, consider these different business requirements.

You have a process that creates a case record, but part of the process is to gather some information and use it to search for an existing customer record. If it's found, a case is created and associated with the customer. But if there is no existing customer record, you want to use the captured information to create one, and then associate the case record with the new customer.

If you want to create a dialog for that business process, which entity should it be written for? Not so obvious, right? Phone Call might be a good candidate, but depending on your business requirements, it might be a little artificial to force a user to create a phone call activity simply to start the dialog.

Scenarios like this one come up a lot, and when they do, the right answer to the "which entity?" question might be that there really *isn't* one. You might describe processes like this as "self-contained". That is, the process itself gathers all of the information required to take the appropriate action, and there's no need to start it from the context of a selected record.

Every process (workflow or dialog) requires an entity, however, so you have to select something! In situations like these the User entity is often the best choice.

Let's illustrate these issues with an example. Suppose a process gathers information to create an opportunity record, but you also want the process to check whether a customer record already exists, and if not, create a new customer record before creating the opportunity.

1. Gather basic contact information
2. Search for existing contact record
   a. If contact found
      i. Create new opportunity record, associate with existing contact record
   b. If contact not found
      i. Create new contact record
      ii. Create new opportunity record, associate with new contact record

This is a good example of requirements for a self-contained process: unless the process is kicked off with a phone call (or some other record type) 100% of the time, it's a forced fit to select one. What the user really wants in this situation is to "click a button and make it happen"! And while creating a dialog process against the User entity does not *automatically* provide this capability, it gets us pretty close.

We'll examine a dialog process – Opportunity Intake – that has the following properties.

For any reasonably complex process – and this one is in that category – you should follow some best practices.

- Structure it in logical stages in the Step Editor.
- Adopt a naming convention for process components like Response and Query labels, actions like Create Records and some others. This is an important topic and we will discuss it in detail elsewhere, but in this example you can see it in action.

The next figure shows Stage 1. We start with page that gathers first and last names, and a Yes/No radio button prompt for whether to create a new opportunity record. As you will see below, this last prompt isn't strictly necessary, but I included it in case we need to extend functionality later.

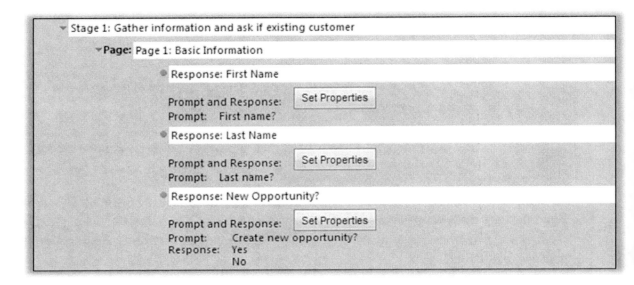

Next is Stage 2, where things start to get interesting. It starts out with a query, which uses the first and last name values entered in Stage 1, and constructs a dynamic query to search for that contact. Next, the query results are tested to see whether any potential matches were located. If so, they are presented in a prompt and response, and the selected one is stored in the "Response: Selected Contact" variable. If not, then a second set of prompt and response pairs are presented on a different version of Page 2, and the response are then used to create a new contact record.

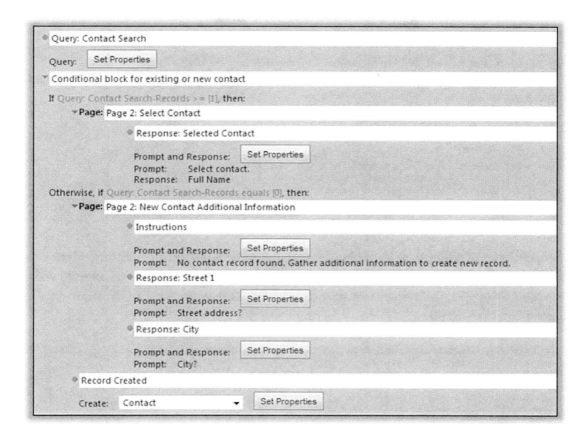

Perhaps the most interesting part of Stage 2 is the query that searches for existing contact records based on the first and last names gathered on Page 1. The query (shown in the next two figures, which you'd access by clicking **Set Properties** on the **Query** line) uses the trick discussed earlier in the book: on the Design New tab, enter placeholder values (e.g., "firstname" and "lastname") in the query designer for the First Name and Last Name fields.

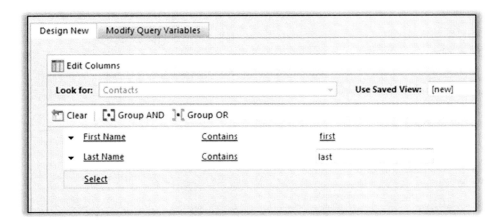

Then, click the **Modify Query Variables** tab and use Dynamic Values to substitute in the Response Text from the **Response: First Name** and **Response: Last Name** variables. (If you work through an example like this you will start to appreciate the importance of a naming convention like the one I use here!)

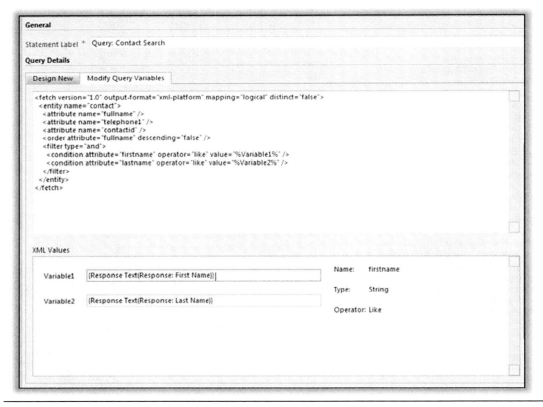

One more thing about the query: notice the **Operator** is set to **Like**, rather than **Equals**. Refer back to the previous figure and notice the use of **Contains** rather than **Equals**. In a query like this you will almost certainly want the more forgiving **Like** operator, which corresponds to **Contains** in the Advanced Find UI.

Finally we get to Stage 3. If we don't stop the dialog in the event the user responded No to the Create Opportunity? Prompt back in Stage 1, the Otherwise clause creates the new opportunity record. The only question is whether to attach it to an existing contact or to the new one created by the dialog, and we can apply the same checks here as before.

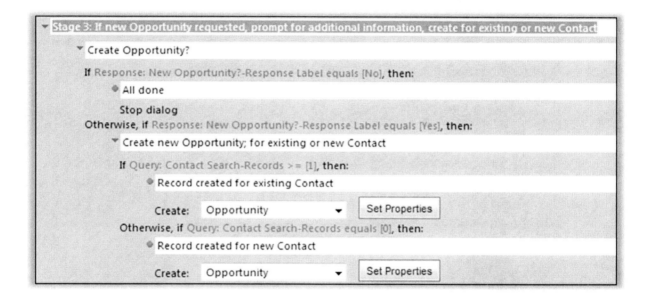

So, suppose you save and activate that dialog. Remember, it was created for the User entity, so you might think the only way to run it is to perform the following steps:

1. In the site map, click **Settings**, and then click **Administration**.
2. Click **Users**, select the user to associate the dialog with, and in the **Process** section of the ribbon, click **Start Dialog.**
3. Select the dialog and click **OK** to kick it off.

But if that's all we can do, why is User any better than any other record type? Excellent question. Please proceed to the next section!

URL-Addressable Forms

Run a dialog – any dialog – and on the first page, press the Ctrl+N key combination to open a new Internet Explorer window. The following figure illustrates this in the context of the Opportunity Intake dialog.

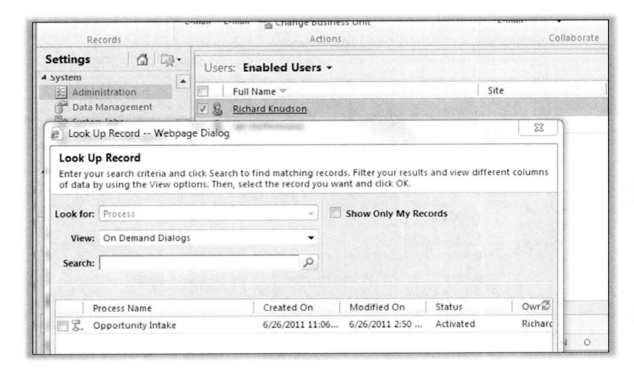

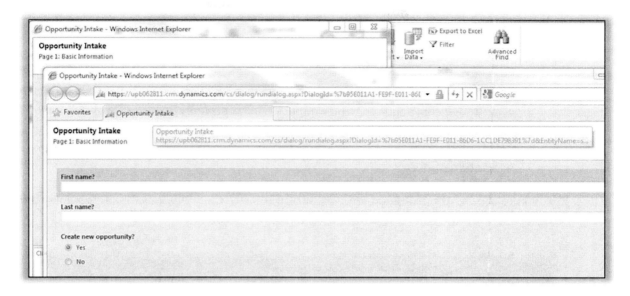

Notice that the URL is exposed in the new window's address box. If you select the URL, copy it with Ctrl+C and paste it with Ctrl+V, here's what it looks like:

https://upb062811.crm.dynamics.com/cs/dialog/rundialog.aspx?DialogId=%7b95E011A1-FE9F-E011-86D6-1CC1DE798391%7d&EntityName=systemuser&ObjectId=%7bE113A45E-218C-4027-921D-B8F0100564C0%7d

The format of this URL is important, as it's defined by a feature of Dynamics CRM referred to as "URL-addressable forms". This means that (almost) any form or window in Dynamics CRM can be accessed not only through the user-interface, but also directly, by its URL. To understand how you can exploit URL-addressable forms to customize the user experience, let's break down this initially nasty looking example:

URL Component	Purpose
`https://upb062811.crm.dynamics.com/cs/dialog/rundialog.aspx`	Includes the organization URL, plus instructions to CRM to run a dialog process.
`?DialogId=%7b95E011A1-FE9F-E011-86D6-1CC1DE798391%7d`	Includes the GUID of the dialog to run.
`&EntityName=systemuser`	Includes instructions that the dialog is written for the User (systemuser) entity.
`&ObjectId=%7bE113A45E-218C-4027-921D-B8F0100564C0%7d`	Includes the GUID of the user for which the dialog should be run.

Note: If you've ever wondered what those %7b and %7d things are in URLs like this, there's an excellent explanation at www.w3schools.com[14], specifically:

Basically, these are the URL-encoding characters for ASCII characters included in a URL. Since URLs often contain characters outside the ASCII set, these URL-encoding characters perform the conversion for us. Dynamics CRM commonly uses the "{" and "}" characters to enclose a GUID, so instead of {E113A45E-218C-4027-921D-B8F0100564C0}, a GUID inside a URL must be formatted like this: %7bE113A45E-218C-4027-921D-B8F0100564C0%7d

So…where are we, then? A good, easy way to appreciate the utility of URL-addressable forms is to drag and drop the URL to your desktop, to create a shortcut:

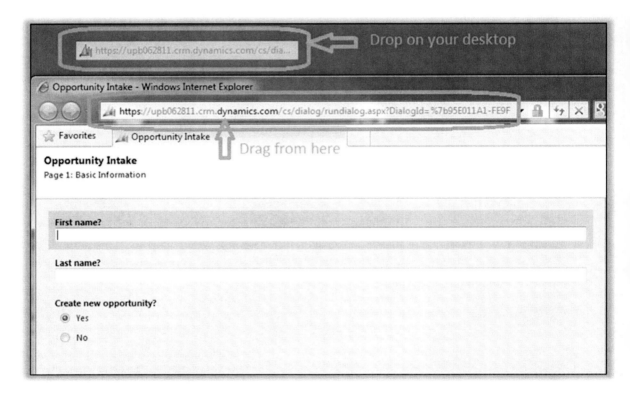

---

[14] http://www.w3schools.com/TAGS/ref_urlencode.asp

Finally, you can keep the shortcut in a folder with your other favorites.

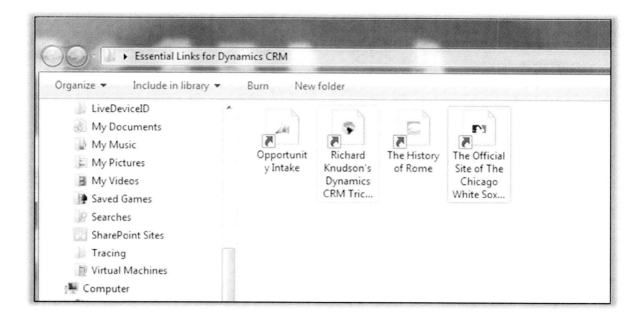

Now if you're thinking the approach I just described is a little bit hard-wired, you are correct. The URL just described will always run the dialog *for the user referenced in the URL*. That's fine for the do-it-yourself shortcut trick, but what you will probably want to do is create a way for any user to "click a button" and run a dialog process as themselves – that is, for the current user. That takes a little bit of Jscript, and two approaches – one easier, the other more complex – are described in the next two sections.

Calling a Dialog Process from an HTML Web Resource

As I mentioned previously, you will probably at some point want to call a dialog process with a custom button on one of the ribbons in Dynamics CRM 2011. While in some scenarios this will be the preferred approach, customizing the ribbons in CRM 2011 is a complex topic, and there *is* a simpler approach you can use.

Dynamics CRM 2011 introduces the concept of Web Resources. These include HTML pages, Jscript libraries, Silverlight applications, image files and a few others. What all web resources have in common is that they run entirely on the client (that is, in the browser). But just because they are client-only does not mean they cannot do a lot of interesting things!

If you have some experience with client-scripting in CRM 4.0, the most obvious "big win" with web resources is probably the ability to re-use centrally managed Jscript web resources from any form in your CRM 2011. But there are tons of other interesting applications of web resources, and the one I describe here is a specific example of an approach which can be used in many different contexts.

First, let's review the goal: we need a way to call a dialog process without requiring the user to navigate to a data grid, select a record and run the dialog from the ribbon. The example dialog I've been using is written for the User entity, so in order to run it the standard way, you would follow these steps.

1. On the site map, click **Settings**, and then click **Administration**.
2. Click **Users** on the Administration page.
3. On the Users tab of the ribbon, click **Start Dialog** in the Process section.
4. In the Look Up Record dialog, select the **Opportunity Intake** process and click **OK**:

What we really want is a button a user can click to kick off the dialog process. This will not only make it easier to run, but as you will see we can also use some simple Jscript code to make sure the dialog process runs for the current user.

From a technical standpoint, we need a web page with controls a user can interact with and that in turn can call Jscript functions. In Dynamics CRM 4.0, short of creating a server-based HTML or ASPX page, there really was no way to satisfy requirements like this, but in the current version we can, using two components.

1. An **HTML web resource** will provide the user experience (a single button for now) and will contain the Jscript we need to kick off the dialog process.
2. A **dashboard** can expose a web resource, so we can effectively use a dashboard as a "container" for the HTML page.

The following figure shows what this might look like.

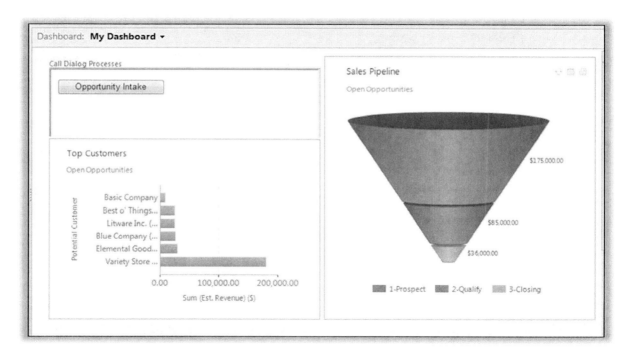

The component in the top left of this dashboard exposes the HTML web resource, and when a user clicks the Opportunity Intake button, the dialog kicks off just like it's supposed to. I sandwiched this in between a couple of other more traditional dashboard components, mainly to make the point that this really *is* a dashboard.

So with that as our near-term goal, let's walk through the process now of creating an HTML web resource to call a dialog like this.

Step by Step: Create an HTML Web Resource to Call a Dialog Process

1. Use a text editor to create an HTML file that you will upload into Dynamics CRM as an HTML web resource. Name it **CallDialog.html** and save it to disk. (The file listing is below, along with explanatory notes.)
2. In the site map, click **Settings** and then click **Customizations**.
3. On the Customization page, click **Customize the System**.
4. Click **Web Resources**, and then click **New**.
5. In the New Web Resource dialog, type */html/CallDialogs.html* in the **Name** field.
6. In the **Display Name** field, type *Call Dialogs*.
7. In the **Type** drop-down, select **Web Page (HTML)**.
8. Click the **Browse** button to locate and upload the file **CallDialog.html**.
9. Click Save, and the URL field should automatically fill with a URL. You can click it to test the HTML web resource.

CallDialog.HTML File Listing

```
<HTML>

<HEAD>

<SCRIPT LANGUAGE="JavaScript">

function callDialog() {
window.open("OrganizationURL/cs/dialog/rundialog.aspx?DialogId=%7bDialogGUID%7d&EntityName=systemuser&ObjectId=%7bUserGUID%7d", "",
"status=no,scrollbars=no,toolbars=no,menubar=no,location=no");

}

</SCRIPT>

</HEAD>

<BODY>

<FORM NAME="myForm">

<INPUT TYPE="button" NAME="Opportunity Intake" VALUE="Opportunity Intake"
onClick="callDialog();">

</HTML>
```

A couple of notes about this HTML web resource:

- If you read the previous section, you may recognize the somewhat stylized URL that is the first argument of the **window.open** method. If you're trying to do this yourself, this is the URL of the browser window you open using the Ctrl+N trick I mentioned above. Substitute in your values accordingly.

- Notice that I imported this file from disk to create the web resource, rather than edit it in the text editor provided in the Web Resource dialog. Here's what the Dynamics CRM 2011 SDK has to say on this topic.

   The text editor provided in the Web Resource Form is intended for use with very simple HTML editing. It is not suitable for more sophisticated HTML documents. For more sophisticated documents you should edit the code in an external editor and use the **Browse** *button to upload the contents of your file.*

- Most importantly, notice that the HTML is still hardwired, in that both the organization URL and the User GUID really *could* be generated dynamically by Jscript, giving you a function suitable for a System Dashboard that would kick off the dialog process for the current user. I presented the hardwired version first so you could focus on the mechanics of creating the web resource and isolate the **window.open** method that actually fires up the dialog process. The more flexible version of the HTML file is included next.

Calling a Dialog Process for the Current User

Customizing the ribbon to call a custom dialog process is somewhat complex and while I decided to make it out of scope for the book, it's actually not too bad, especially if you use a tool such as the ribbon editor available on codeplex.com[15]. However, what we'll examine in this section gets to the same essential functionality, which is to generalize the hardwired example from the previous section so that a dialog process written for the User entity can be called from a button on a dashboard, and always be called by the current user.

The key to generalizing a function like this is to use the **GetGlobalContext** function, which you can use when you include a reference to the ClientGlobalContext.js.aspx page located at the root

---

[15] http://ribboneditor.codeplex.com/

of the Web resources directory. You can reference it by including the following <SCRIPT> block inside the <HEAD> block at the top of your HTML file:

```
<SCRIPT src="../../ClientGlobalContext.js.aspx"></SCRIPT>
```

Then, you can include HTML like the following:

```
<A onclick=alert(GetGlobalContext().getUserId()) href="#">Current user id</A>
<A onclick=alert(GetGlobalContext().getServerUrl()) href="#">Current CRM organization URL</A>
```

The first uses the getUserID function to return the unique ID of the current user. The second uses the getServerUrl function to return the URL of the current Dynamics CRM organization. Referring back to the HTML code listing in the previous section, these are the two functions we need to generalize the code, generating the organization URL and the current user ID dynamically.

(For a complete listing of the functions made available by referring to the GetGlobalContext function, search the Dynamics CRM 2011 SDK for "GetGlobalContext".)

Taking it from the top, let's assume you want to build a dashboard that any user can navigate to and click a button to run a dialog process. You can expose as many dialogs in this way as you'd like, just remember that the scenario described here works for dialog processes created against the User entity.

Step by Step: Build a Dashboard to Allow Users to Run Dialog Processes
1. After creating a dialog process for the user entity, activate it.
2. Navigate to the users' grid, select a user and run the dialog process.
3. As soon as the dialog begins, press the key combination Ctrl+N. This opens a new window running the same dialog, exposing the URL so you can copy the GUID of the dialog to the clipboard. It should look something like the following figure, which has the dialog GUID highlighted.

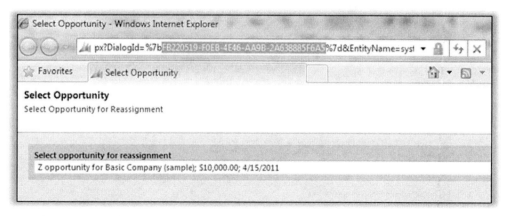

4. Copy that GUID to the Windows clipboard (for bonus points, save it into the Description field of the actual dialog process next time you get a chance). Then cancel the current dialog process, since the only reason we ran it here was to copy its GUID.
5. On the site map, click **Settings**, and then click **Customizations**.
6. Click **Customize the System**, and then click **Web Resources**.
7. Above the web resources grid, click the **New** button. The **New Web Resource** dialog will appear. Most organizations will want to create standardized naming conventions for web resources such as this one; using some relatively unobjectionable ones you could name it something like this figure illustrates.

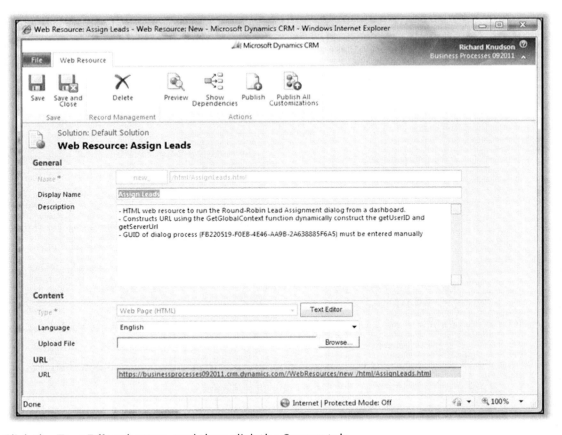

8. Click the **Text Editor** button, and then click the **Source** tab.

9. This example is as simple as possible to focus on the essential components. The reference to ClientGlobalContext.js.aspx must be added in order to use the GetGlobalContext functions. Put that inside the <HEAD></HEAD> block. Then, the single line of HTML code is as follows:

```
<A
onclick='window.navigate(GetGlobalContext().getServerUrl()+"cs/dialog/rundialog.aspx?Dialog
Id=%7bFB220519-F0EB-4E46-AA9B-2A638885F6A5%7d&amp;
EntityName=systemuser&amp;ObjectId="+GetGlobalContext().getUserId() )'
href="#">Round-Robin Lead Assignment</A>
```

Make sure it's inside the Body tag; the following figure shows what it looks like in the editor, with a few extra spaces added for readability.

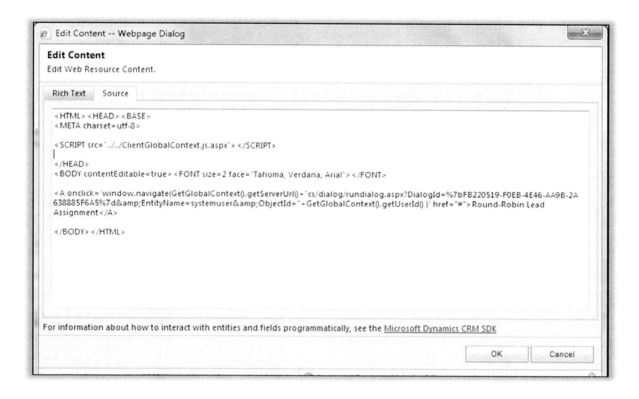

10. From here, click **OK**, then **Save & Close**, and then publish the web resource.
11. Then click **Workplace** on the site map, and then **Dashboards**.
12. Click **New**, to make a personal dashboard, and select the 2-Column Regular dashboard layout.
13. Click **Create**, and then remove all components except the one in the upper left. Give it an appropriate name and save it.
14. Click the single dashboard component, and then click **Web Resource** in the **Insert** section of the ribbon. Increase the height in the dashboard designer, since this approach will run the dialog inside the dashboard.
15. Browse to the HTML web resource created previously, and select it. Provide property settings like the following.

16. Click **OK**, and then **Save & Close** on the dashboard designer, and you should be ready to go.

In my example, here's what it looks like to the user, first before clicking the link and then as it is being run.

Calling a Dialog from a Dashboard   **Running a Dialog Inside a Dashboard**

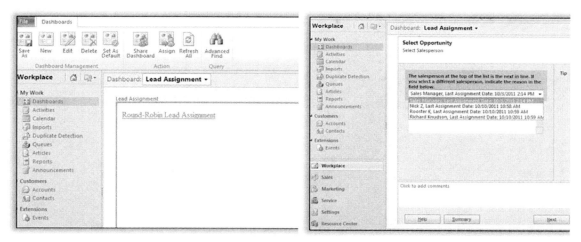

So there you have it. The UI is not elegant, and of course could be dressed up with custom buttons and so forth. But this book's about business processes. (The solution that comes along with the book does include a more polished dashboard so you can get some ideas on that part of the process.) The main thing is that this technique is generalizable, and can be used in many scenarios common with dialog processes, such as running dialog processes from a ribbon, the site map, external applications and so forth.

Summary

This chapter built upon Chapter 4's introduction to dialog processes, and covered several advanced techniques available in dialog processes.

First, we showed how to call child dialog processes, and covered the two most important reasons for doing so: to create recursive processes, and to re-use dialog process logic.

Next, we covered how to use variables within dialog processes. Variables can be used to store intermediate values, and can be updated as a process runs. We reviewed an example of this technique, in which a dialog process uses information gathered from the user to *score* an opportunity record. We also discussed how to use a special type of variable – an input argument – to pass values from a parent dialog to a child dialog it calls.

Finally, we discussed an important technique you can use to call dialogs by referring to their URLs. This is an example of a general Dynamics CRM technique referred to as URL-addressable forms, and we showed several of its applications for dialog processes.

Chapter 6 – Security and Solutions

So far we've focused on the fundamentals of building business processes in Dynamics CRM 2011. And with that focus on the fundamentals, we've implicitly made a couple of simplifying assumptions.

- Every process has been created, owned and run by a user with the System Administrator security role.
- Every process has worked.

However, since in the real world these assumptions are not always satisfied, it's time to relax them and drill down on two important topics, security and troubleshooting.

Security

In the business process context, you can generally think of *security* as determining which users can *create* dialog and workflow processes and which users can *run* them.

Troubleshooting

While the dialog and workflow processes we've discussed in this book do not require programming, they do require several of the disciplines associated with designing, developing and testing custom programs. *Troubleshooting* is one of the most important of these, and can be thought of as determining if your processes are working, and if (when!) they don't, how do you fix them?

Several other topics are covered in this chapter as well:

- Naming conventions for workflow and dialog processes.
- Comparing workflow and dialog processes to other Dynamics CRM 2011 customization techniques.
- An introduction to customization techniques commonly used in tandem with business process development.

Business Processes and Security

For Dynamics CRM 2011 business processes – workflow and dialog processes – the issue of security generally boils down to the following kinds of questions:

- Which users can run a workflow or dialog process?
- If a user can run a process, will it work correctly?
- Which users can create processes?

Before we dive into the deep end of the pool, let's examine a few scenarios in which issues like the ones we will review here are important.

- Suppose you're a system administrator and use utility workflows and dialogs to perform intelligent data updates, copy records and the like. Who else in your CRM organization will be able to run these processes? How can you lock processes down so that only you or selected users can run the processes?
- Suppose you have certain automatic workflow processes that should run whenever anybody in the organization creates a case or an opportunity record. How can you do that and how do you know that everybody has the privileges they need so that everything works?
- On the other hand, suppose some automatic processes should only run for certain groups of users. For example, suppose the West and East regions have different sales processes: how can a different workflow process on opportunity run, depending on where in the organization the user creating the opportunity lives?
- What if you want certain users to be able to run processes other users have created, but don't want them creating their own processes?

With scenarios like those in mind, let's divide this topic into two categories: how security works for automatic processes, and how it works for on-demand processes.

Security for Automatic Processes

We only need to discuss workflow processes here, since only workflows can run automatically in Dynamics CRM 2011. Two main questions need to be answered:

- Which users will trigger automatic workflows?
- When a user triggers an automatic workflow, will it run correctly?

We'll treat each of these in turn.

How do you know which users will trigger an automatic workflow?

This is determined by a user's security role(s), the scope of the workflow, and the position within the organization of a user who might trigger a workflow, *relative to the owner of the workflow.*

This can be pretty complex, so let's work through it in detail, keeping a specific scenario in mind:

- **User A** is the owner of an automatic workflow, such as one designed to run when an opportunity record is created.
- **User B** creates an opportunity record.

The question is; *under what conditions will the workflow be triggered when User B creates an opportunity record?*

The answer is determined by a combination of factors:

1. The first one is easy: User B must be assigned to a security role with **Organization** level privilege for **Execute Workflow Job**, in the **Miscellaneous Privileges** section of the security role definition. The only two possibilities for this privilege are **Organization** and **None**. If a security role's privilege to **Execute Workflow Job** is set to **None**, a user with only that security role will never trigger an automatic workflow. If the privilege is set to **Organization**, as in the following figure, it is *possible* for User B to trigger the workflow.

2. The second factor one is more complicated, since it depends both on the **Scope** specified for the workflow, and the business units both users are assigned to. Remember that the **Scope** property has four possible values: **User, Business Unit, Parent: Child Business Units**, and **Organization**. The following figure shows what the Properties section of the workflow designer will look like for the current example.

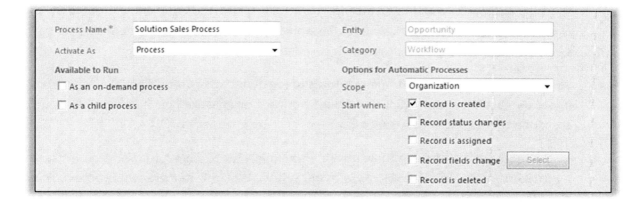

Since we've assumed that User B has **Organization** privilege on **Execute Workflow Job**, it's at least *possible* that the automatic workflow will run. But when *will* it run? Here are the various possibilities, when User B creates a new opportunity record:

Scope	When it will run
Organization	Always
Parent: Child Business Units	• User A is in same business unit as User B • User B is in a child business unit of User A's business unit
Business Unit	User A and User B are in the same business unit
User	Never

When a user triggers an automatic workflow, will it work correctly?

Now that we know when a user's action will *trigger* an automatic workflow, the question is whether it will work *correctly*. Another subtlety of workflow security is this important fact: **automatic workflows always run in the security context of the owner of the workflow**. This has several interesting implications.

When an automatic workflow creates a record, you may notice in the workflow designer that the **Owner** field is not required, even though no record can be saved without an owner. This is because automatic workflows, running in the security context as the owner of the workflow, will by default assign any created records to the owner of the workflow. So if you're the system administrator and the owner of lots of automatic workflows, make sure you apply the appropriate business logic when assigning records, otherwise you may wind up the owner of more records than you bargained for.

When an automatic workflow creates (or updates) a record, the value of the **Created By** (or **Modified By**) field will be the owner of the workflow. This can be initially confusing, since in one sense it's really the triggering user that *caused* the updates to happen.

The workflow runs with all of the privileges of the owner of the workflow. This is the most important factor in determining how things work out, so let's examine it in more detail, with scenarios at both ends of the spectrum.

- **Suppose User A (the workflow owner, remember) is a System Administrator.** If User B triggers the workflow, it will run with the System Administrator's security context. This doesn't guarantee it will work correctly, but it does guarantee that it will not fail due to insufficient privileges! For example, an automatic workflow might cause an infinite loop situation and fail for that reason, even if its owner has the System Administrator security role. But it will not fail because User B doesn't have privileges to assign a record from one user to another, because it's not running in User B's security context: it's running in the System Administrator security context.

- **Suppose User A has the Salesperson security role and is in a child business unit.** When User B triggers the workflow, it very well may fail because User A does not have a very generous security role. To see why this is a good thing, consider an example. User A creates an automatic workflow that runs whenever an account record is created and sets the **Scope** property to **Organization**. The workflow has a single action: it reassigns the account record to User A. When User B creates an account record, the workflow will be triggered, because its scope is set to organization. However, even if User B is a System Administrator the workflow will fail, because it's running as the Salesperson security role, which does not have privileges to reassign an account record away from a system admin.

Situations like the ones just described demand illustration, and I've included several in the examples at the end of the chapter.

Scenarios:

- User with **default Salesperson security role** creates an automatic workflow with **Scope** equal to **Organization**. Who else does it run for? Wow – does it really run for everybody in the organization, or does it depend on other user's role? It runs for:
    - System Administrator in root Business Unit (!). Is there no way to allow a user to create automatic workflows with User Scope only?
    - Will it run for a user in a different business unit? Yes, by default it runs for all users!
- Modify default Salesperson role, changing **Organization** to **None** for **Read** privilege on **Process** entity. Results:
    - User with role cannot create new dialogs or workflows (does not see Process Center)
    - User with role cannot run on-demand dialogs or workflows.
    - User with role will trigger automatic workflow owned by System Administrator at root BU!
    - Workflows previously written by this user (before Read on Process set to None) will continue to run.
- Modify default Salesperson role, changing **User** to **None** for **Create** privilege on **Process** entity. Results:

- o User with role cannot create new dialogs or workflows (does not see Process Center)
- o User with role can run on-demand dialogs or workflows.
- o User with role will trigger automatic workflow owned by System Administrator at root BU!
- o Workflows previously written by this user (before Read on Process set to None) will continue to run.

Moral of the story? If a user can create a process (Process Create privilege of at least User), the user can create an automatic process of organization scope! There does not appear to be a way to allow a user to create an automatic process but only create one with User scope. You can rely on their knowledge of how to and willingness to create one with User or Business Unit scope...but you can't prevent them from creating an Organization scoped workflow unless you prevent them from creating any workflow!

Security for On-Demand Processes

While only workflows can run as automatic processes, in Dynamics CRM 2011 both workflow and dialog processes can be run on an on-demand basis. The security *questions* for on-demand processes are similar to those for automatic ones:

- Which users will be able to see on-demand processes and attempt to run them?
- When a user runs an on-demand process, will it work?

But the *answers* are determined differently, mainly because of the following two points:

- Unlike automatic processes, **Scope** *does not matter for on-demand processes*.
- Unlike automatic processes, *on-demand processes run in the security context of the user running the process*.

We'll deal with each of the two questions in turn, employing the same scenario-based approach as in the previous section:

- User A is the owner of two on-demand processes. Both are utility processes to make copies of goal records, but one is a workflow and the other a dialog. The properties section of the process designer is shown in the following two figures.

- User B wants to run those on-demand processes.

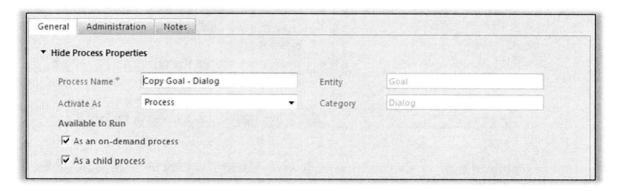

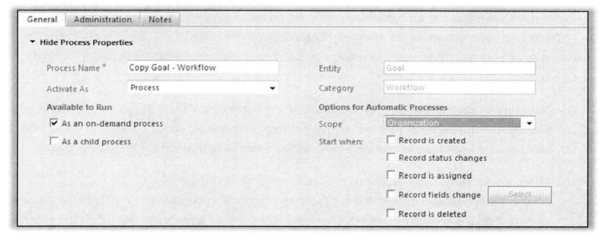

What determines if a user can run an on-demand process?
This is determined by a combination of factors.

1. User B's privilege on **Execute Workflow Job**. This works the same as for automatic processes. If a user's privilege on **Execute Workflow Job** is set to **Organization**, the user is eligible to run on-demand processes. The only alternative is **None**, and with that privilege a user will never be able to run an on-demand process.

2. User B's **Read** privilege for the **Process** entity, combined with the position in the organization relative to User A. The various possibilities can be summarized in a table similar to the one for automatic processes.

User B's Read Privilege on the Process Entity	When User B can Run an On-Demand Process
Organization	Always
Parent: Child Business Units	• User A is in same business unit as User B • User B is in a child business unit of User A's business unit • User A has shared the process with User B
Business Unit	• User A and User B are in the same business unit • User A has shared the process with User B
User	User A has shared the process with User B

Notice that security for on-demand processes works just like security for a "regular" entity, if you compare read privilege on the **Process** entity to read privilege on an entity such as account. If you have organization level read privileges on accounts and create an advanced find query on accounts, you can see all of them, no matter who owns them. If you have organization level read privilege on processes you can see and run any on-demand process regardless of who its owner is.

Also notice that the owner of an on-demand workflow can make it available to another user by sharing it. Just as with a "regular" entity, sharing provides access to something that a user's security role does not. We will present some scenarios to illustrate these points below.

When a user runs an on-demand process, will it work correctly?
On-demand processes, unlike automatic ones, run in the security context of the running user. So if an on-demand process is available for User B to run and it performs an action User B does not have sufficient privileges for, it will fail.

In practice, this means it's more likely that on-demand processes will not work correctly than automatic processes. This is because it tends to be system administrators who create and own most workflow and dialog processes. And since by default all security roles have organization read privilege on the process entity, all users can by default attempt to run any on-demand process owned by a system administrator. And since the system administrator role has privileges to do a lot more than any other roles, it's easy for a system administrator to create an on-demand workflow that will be available for another user to run...but will break when it runs!

Process Security Summary and Scenarios
I know this can seem like a bewildering array of possibilities, so here are some rules of thumb on the "will it work?" question.

- Automatic workflows created by a system administrator will usually work correctly when run, since they are run with system administrator security privileges.
- On-demand processes will usually work for the user who created them, since the process designer generally does not expose to you actions your security role does not give you privileges for.
- On-demand processes created by a system administrator are exposed to everybody, because by default all security roles have the read privilege for the process entity set to organization. These will often not work for many users, since they will have security roles with insufficient privileges for what the processes are trying to perform.

To hone your understanding of how security works for dialog and workflow processes, you should work through as many examples as you can, and it's especially important to have several different user accounts with different security roles. You can design a great workflow, but if the only way you test it is as a system administrator in the root business unit, it might not be so great when users run it in a complex production environment!

Let's walk through a few examples now. All of the ones presented here will be performed within a simple organizational structure: a root business unit and two child business units as the following figure illustrates.

Our example organization has three users, each assigned to one of the business units, and each named according to the single security role assigned to them.

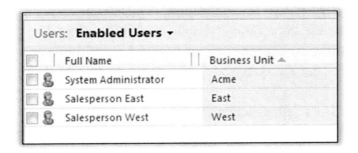

Let's start with Salesperson East and Salesperson West each assigned to the default Salesperson security role. The following figure shows the **Customization** tab for the Salesperson security role, with only the **Dialog Session** and **Process** entities shown, plus the **Miscellaneous Privileges** section so we can see the **Execute Workflow Job** privilege.

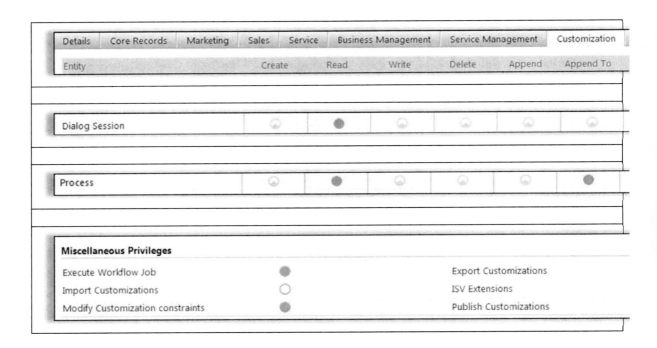

OK, let's roll up our sleeves and figure this stuff out! Scenarios 1-3 explore some commonly encountered scenarios with automatic workflows, when a combination of the workflow's scope and owner determines which users trigger it and what happens when it runs.

Scenario 1: System Administrator has created (and is the owner of) an automatic workflow on the opportunity entity to implement a version of the popular *Solution Selling* process. It runs when a new record is created and the **Scope** is set to **Organization**.

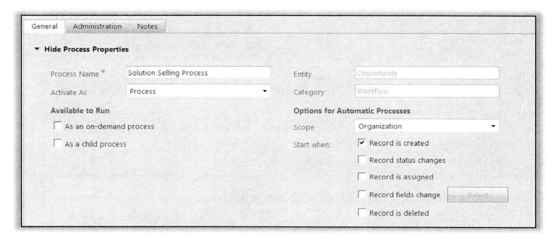

What happens when opportunity records are created?

Opportunity Created By	Results
Salesperson East	Workflow runs automatically, and correctly
Salesperson West	Workflow runs automatically, and correctly
System Administrator	Workflow runs automatically, and correctly

Scenario 2: System Administrator assigns the Solution Selling Process workflow to Salesperson East, and then re-activates the workflow. The workflow is organized into stages, and each stage creates an appropriate task.

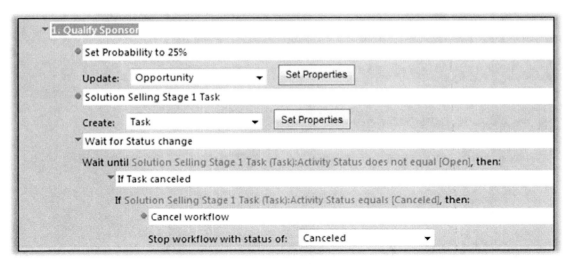

What happens when opportunity records are created?

Opportunity Created By	Results
Salesperson East	Workflow runs automatically, and correctly
Salesperson West	Workflow runs automatically, but not correctly
System Administrator	Workflow runs automatically, but not correctly

What happened in this case? Remember the workflow still has a scope of organization, so it will run for everybody. But since it is now owned by Salesperson East it runs with that user's privileges, and the default Salesperson role does not have (among other things) privileges to create activities such as tasks for other users. So the workflow hangs when it comes to the Create Task step, if it's running for anybody other than its current owner.

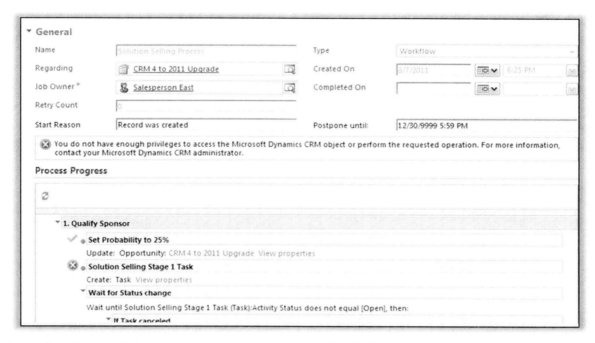

Scenario 3: System Administrator deactivates the Solution Selling Process workflow, changes the scope to Business Unit, and then reassigns it to Salesperson East. Salesperson East then activates it.

What happens when opportunity records are created?

Opportunity Created By	Results
Salesperson East	Workflow runs automatically, and correctly
Salesperson West	Workflow does not run
System Administrator	Workflow does not run

These results are due to the change of scope to Business Unit: here, the only users that will trigger the workflow are users in the same business unit as Salesperson East. If different departments within a single organization have different sales processes, that's a good reason to create business units for each department.

Scenarios 4-6 explore these issues from a different angle: what happens when you modify the default security roles? Scenario 4 *starts* in the same place Scenario 1 did: with the default security roles, and the Solution Selling Process workflow assigned to System Administrator with a scope of organization.

Scenario 4: System Administrator modifies the Salesperson security role, changing the Read privilege for the Process entity from Organization to User.

What happens when opportunity records are created?

Opportunity Created By	Results
Salesperson East	Workflow runs automatically, and correctly
Salesperson West	Workflow runs automatically, and correctly
System Administrator	Workflow runs automatically, and correctly

This is because only Scope matters for automatic workflow processes. Provided a user has the Execute Workflow Job miscellaneous privilege and anything other than **None** on the Read privilege for the Process entity, an automatic workflow scoped to organization will run.

Scenario 5: With the same modifications to the default Salesperson security role in effect, System Administrator creates an on-demand dialog process for the opportunity entity.

Who can run the on-demand dialog process?

- Salesperson East navigates to the opportunity data grid and selects a record and clicks Start Dialog. The process does not appear in the Look Up Record dialog.
- Salesperson East navigates to the opportunity data grid and selects a record and clicks Start Dialog. The process does not appear in the Look Up Record dialog.
- System Administrator navigates to the opportunity data grid and selects a record and clicks Start Dialog. The process does appear in the Look Up Record dialog.

This is because unlike automatic processes, it's not scope but a user's privileges on the process entity that determine which on-demand processes can be run. In this scenario the salespersons only have User level Read privilege on process, so they will only see on-demand processes they own (or ones that have been shared with them).

Scenario 6: System Administrator restores the original settings for the Salesperson security role, changing the Read privilege for the Process entity from User back to Organization.

Who can run the on-demand dialog process?

System Administrator, Salesperson East and Salesperson West can all run the on-demand dialog process.

Which Users can *Create* Processes?

The previous two sections addressed the security questions about who can run processes and what results to expect when processes are run. There's another important question, however, that should also be taken into account: who can *create* processes?

A user's ability to create both workflow and dialog processes is determined by the privileges they have on the **Process** entity. This is highlighted in the following figure, which displays the Customization tab for the default Salesperson security role:

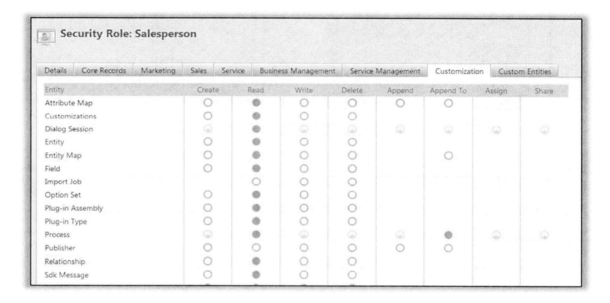

Notice that this security role, not a particularly generous one, has user-level **Create** privilege for the **Process** entity. In fact, *every one* of the default security roles has a minimum of user-level create privileges for the process entity. This means that unless you customize the default roles or create custom roles, every user can create workflow or dialog processes.

There *may* be organizations where it would be appropriate for all users to have privileges to create business processes...but in my experience, there aren't very many! To understand why, consider the following automatic workflow process, created and owned by a user with the default **Customer Service Representative** security role. The following figure shows the **General** tab in the workflow designer:

And the next figure shows the **Administration** tab for the same workflow process:

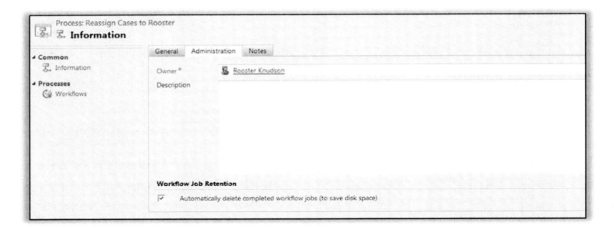

You can probably see the potential problem here: once activated, this workflow runs automatically, and with a Scope value set to Organization, it reassigns every case record to the user that created and owns the workflow. Worse yet, the **Automatically delete completed workflow jobs** option is selected, so it might not be obvious at first why every new case is getting assigned to Rooster.

Of course, most users wouldn't create automatic workflows to increase their case load. And in the real world, most users are doing their best just trying to remember what happened to their completed activities and how to qualify leads, and so probably don't spend a lot of time creating automatic workflows with a scope of organization.

But the point is, with the default security roles, they *can*, and for most of the enterprise system administrators I know, this is reason enough to customize the default security roles. Assuming you're in this category, here are two solutions to consider and adapt to your requirements:

1. **Customize security roles to set the access level to None for the Create privilege on the Process entity.** If users' security role(s) are set this way, they simply will not be able to create dialog or workflow processes. This is probably the easiest approach. The only potential problem with it is that some users really might *need* the ability to create dialogs or workflows.
2. **Customize security roles to fine-tune the actions users can perform.** Remember: automatic workflows run in the security context of the user that owns the workflow. So in the previous example, the potential problem could be solved by customizing the Customer Service Representative role, changing the Assign privilege from Organization (its default for that role) to User, for example.

On balance, I prefer the first solution over the second. To prevent most users from creating processes while accommodating users that really do have that requirement, you could implement a solution like the following:

1. Set the create privilege to none for the process entity in every "user" security role. (You can't change the System Administrator role, and you probably don't need to change a security role such as System Customizer.)
2. Create a custom security role, Process Designer. Create it "from scratch" (that is, without copying an existing role). The Core Records tab will look like the following figure:

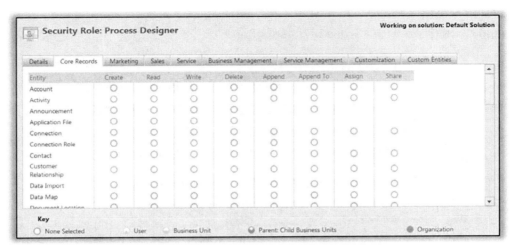

3. On the Customization tab, change the Create privilege for the Process entity to user-level, as the following figure illustrates. This is the only change you need to make to this security role:

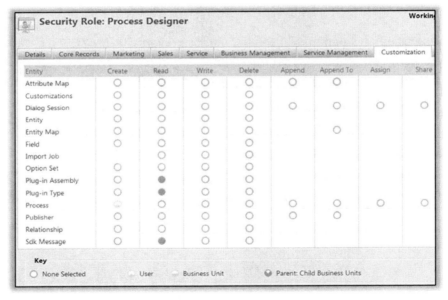

4. Create a team called Process Designers, and assign the Process Designer security role to the team.

Now, any user needing to create processes can be added as a member of the Process Designers team. Because a team member inherits any privileges of the team, this single-purpose security role, assigned to the team, will allow members to create processes...and allow you, as the system administrator, an easy way to keep track of who can create them.

Automatic Workflow Example

In Chapter three we examined several automatic workflow processes, including workflows to automate sales processes and to manage the routing and escalation of service cases. In most of the previous examples the workflow processes were scoped at the organization level; that is, the value of the **Scope** property was set to **Organization** as in the following figure.

And as you've seen in the previous section, that would mean that any user that *can* create an opportunity record (referring to the previous figure) *will* trigger the Solution Sales Process when a new record is saved.

In my experience this can be confusing at first, so I wanted to work through an example that illustrates in detail what is actually the more common real-world scenario: when you need an automatic process to be triggered only for *some* users within the Dynamics CRM organization.

To illustrate, let's walk through a sales process scenario with the following business requirements:

- An organization has two business units, sales and service, each of which is a child of the root business unit.
- Any user in the organization can create an opportunity record.
- An automatic workflow should be applied to new opportunity records to implement the organization's sales process, but only if the opportunity is owned by a user in the sales business unit.

The following figure shows an organizational structure we can use, in terms of users and the Dynamics CRM business units they are assigned to:

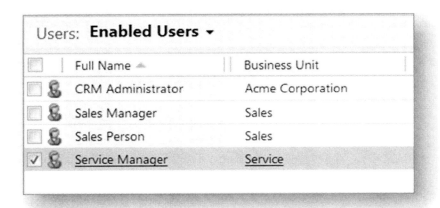

Translating the business requirements just reviewed, what we want is for opportunities owned by a user in the Sales business unit to trigger the sales process workflow; opportunities owned by users outside of that business unit should not trigger the sales process workflow.

To accomplish that, the sales process workflow should have a scope value of organization, and it should be owned by a user in the Sales business unit. For our example, Sales Manager is probably the appropriate user to own the workflow, and the following two figures show how a workflow process satisfying these requirements will look. (For the points being illustrated here, the logic of the workflow isn't that important, so we will focus just on the process properties.)

First, you can see from the following figure that the **Scope** is set to **Business Unit**, and the **Record is created** trigger is selected.

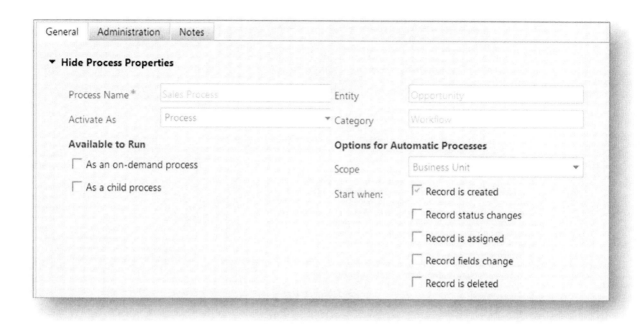

The following figure shows the **Administration** tab, where you can see that Sales Manager is the owner of the process:

Testing and Troubleshooting Automatic Workflow Scope

Let's suppose that a process such as this one is activated, and opportunities are being created. How can you tell if the process is running automatically for the users in the Sales business unit, and not running for everybody else? Well, when I said above that the actual process logic isn't *that* important for this discussion, I didn't mean it was *entirely* unimportant, so let's take a quick look at it in the following figure:

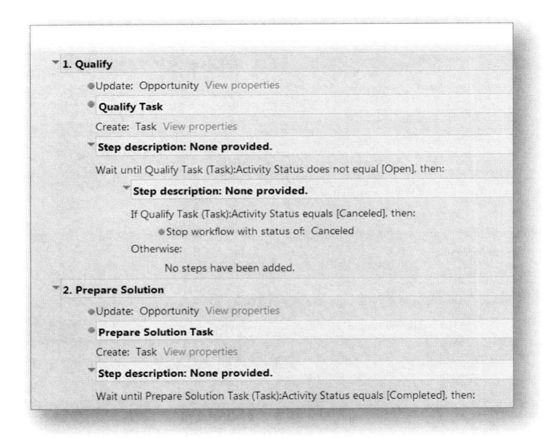

This is similar to some of the sales process workflows we examined in Chapter 3. For the current discussion, the most important point is that the sales process is broken out into stages: stage 1 is *Qualify*, stage 2 *Prepare Solution*, and so forth. Also, notice the Update step in each stage. As in some of the sales process examples seen previously, the Update step sets field values appropriate for the stage; in this process, the Pipeline Phase field is filled in with the name of each stage.

So the value of the Pipeline Phase field gives us one indicator of which records the process is being applied to. For example, the following figure is an advanced find view filtered to show only the opportunity records created since the automatic process was activated. Notice that only

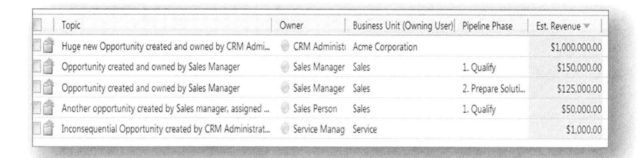

	Topic	Owner	Business Unit (Owning User)	Pipeline Phase	Est. Revenue ▾
	Huge new Opportunity created and owned by CRM Admi...	CRM Administi	Acme Corporation		$1,000,000.00
	Opportunity created and owned by Sales Manager	Sales Manager	Sales	1. Qualify	$150,000.00
	Opportunity created and owned by Sales Manager	Sales Manager	Sales	2. Prepare Soluti...	$125,000.00
	Another opportunity created by Sales manager, assigned ...	Sales Person	Sales	1. Qualify	$50,000.00
	Inconsequential Opportunity created by CRM Administrat...	Service Manag	Service		$1,000.00

three of the five records have a value in the Pipeline Phase field:

You can see that only the records owned by users in the Sales business unit have values for the Pipeline Phase field, so that's an indication the automatic process is only being triggered by the appropriate users.

But because this sales process workflow uses stages, we have an easy, visually obvious, and more precise way of examining which opportunity records the process is being applied to, in the form of the default **Sales Pipeline** report. The following figure shows what it looks like when run against the same data set displayed in the previous advanced find view:

The most important items of note here are the **Group By Sales Process** and **Group By** drop-down lists, highlighted in the figure. Remember from the discussion in Chapter three that the **Group By Sales Process** drop-down presents a list of staged workflows written for the opportunity record type, and that **Group By** allows you to select several different ways of applying a secondary grouping to the report. In the figure, I've selected Sales Process in the first one and Sales Stage in the second, and if you compare the Total Opportunities and Total Estimated Revenue numbers (also highlighted) with the advanced find view, you can see that the Group By Sales Process parameter actually *filters* the report data set! (I've never found this particularly intuitive, and I still have to remind myself sometimes that the Sales Pipeline report works like this!).

To sharpen your understanding further, examine the following figure:

Here, you can see the same filter is applied (opportunities for which the Sales Process workflow is running), but the Group By value is now Sales User (owner). This is probably the best way to see that the Sales Process workflow, since it's owned by a user in the Sales business unit and is scoped to the business unit level, will only run for opportunity records owned by users within that business unit.

Incidentally, you can demonstrate to yourself the filtering function of the Group By Sales Process parameter by selecting a value of None, as illustrated in the following figure:

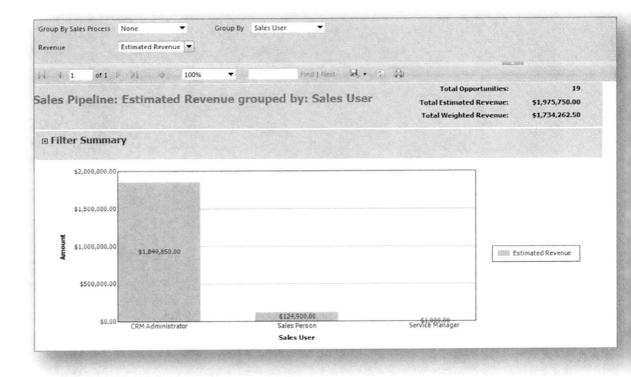

Here, notice that 19 opportunity records are included, rather than just the three records for which the Sales Process workflow is currently running.

Assigning and Activating Automatic Workflow Processes

Continuing our example, suppose the sales process workflow is created by the CRM Administrator user, who you will recall is assigned to the root business unit of this CRM organization. In my experience, this is a common scenario, and the smaller the organization the more likely it is that the user building workflow processes will be a user in the root business unit with the System Administrator security role.

So CRM Admin has created the sales process workflow and tested it to make sure that it only gets triggered by users in the root business unit (remember, that's where CRM Admin is, so during testing that's how it will work.) Then it comes time to put it into product so CRM Admin goes to assign the process to Sales Manager, and he sees the following:

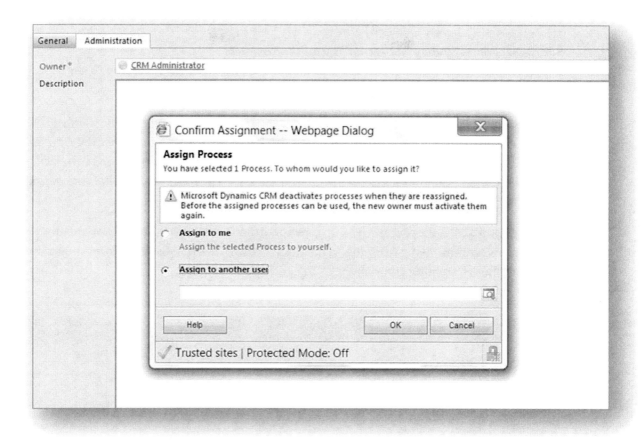

This **Assign Process** dialog can be taken literally: unless the process is owned by Sales Manager, or another user in the sales business unit, it won't run for the right users. And it can't be assigned to Sales Manager without deactivating it. Now it's not that big of a deal to activate a process, and most of the sales managers I know can follow directions well enough to accomplish it, but it's not exactly intuitive, and again, you must remember to instruct the new owner to activate the process or it won't ever run for *any* users.

Solutions and Business Processes

Solutions, and Why they Matter for Business Processes

Dynamics CRM 2011 introduced the concept of a "solution", which according to the SDK (http://msdn.microsoft.com/en-us/library/gg334576.aspx[16]) are

> ...how customizers and developers author, package, and maintain units of software that extend Microsoft Dynamics CRM 2011 and Microsoft Dynamics CRM Online. Customizers and developers distribute solutions so that organizations can use Microsoft Dynamics CRM to install and uninstall the business functionality defined by the solution.

Workflow and dialog processes make up one important category of the components that can be included in solutions. Again from the Dynamics CRM SDK, the following diagram shows the different types of solution components.

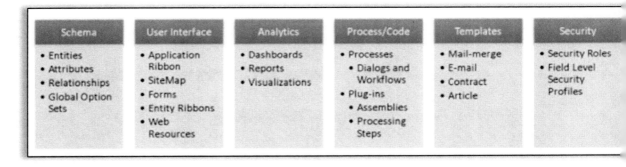

Depending on your organization and your role in the overall management of your CRM, there are several scenarios supported by Dynamics CRM 2011 solutions. Here are some of the most important:

- **Enterprise developers** typically perform customizations for a single company. In an on-premise deployment, several Dynamics CRM organizations are often used for different purposes: for example, many development teams use one for development, one for testing, and one for production. In this scenario the question is how to most efficiently

---

[16] http://msdn.microsoft.com/en-us/library/gg334576.aspx

use solutions to move processes and other customizations from the development to the test and finally to the production organization.

- **Independent software developers/vendors** (ISVs) typically develop commercial add-ons. In Dynamics CRM 2011 these are usually developed in the form of a *managed solution*.
- **Consultants** develop customizations for one or more clients, but unlike ISVs, consultants generally develop custom solutions for each client.

Basically, solutions allow you to package customizations in Dynamics CRM, and move them from one CRM organization (the source) to another (the target). In the context of Dynamics CRM business processes, there are several important issues you will need to consider.

- In order to move processes from one CRM organization to another, what components apart from the workflow and dialog processes need to be included within the solution?
- Assuming you create a solution package and you can import it successfully, will the processes work, or will you need to make changes to them to get them to work?
- How do you create a self-contained solution – that is, one that can easily be moved from one organization to another, and everything "just works."

Next we'll examine several frequently encountered scenarios in which you can create self-contained solutions.

Scenario 1: Process for Un-customized System Entities

This is the simplest case. Suppose you've written a workflow or dialog process for an un-customized system entity, such as account, contact or opportunity. Further, suppose the process does not refer to any custom fields. As you add business processes like these to a solution, you will receive a warning in the form of the **Missing Required Components** dialog. For example, if you add a process written for a default version of the opportunity entity, you will see the following dialog.

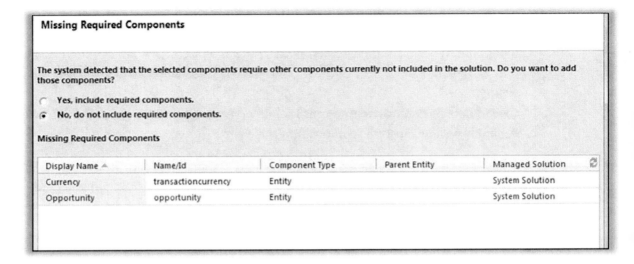

However, in this case you can ignore the warning, because:

- System entities cannot be deleted, so the target organization will have the opportunity entity.
- The process only refers to system fields, which cannot be deleted either.

Scenario 2: Process for Customized System Entities

Suppose you've written a workflow for the opportunity entity, but the workflow depends on a customization of the entity. This scenario has at least two important variations:

2.1 – Custom values for system fields

For example, suppose you have a workflow for the opportunity entity that updates the system field **Pipeline Phase** based on the value selected by the user for the system field **Process Code**. The pipeline phase field is a text field used by the default sales pipeline charts, and is not displayed on the default opportunity form. The process code field is an option set field but by default has no values and is not displayed on the opportunity form, so if you want users to be able to select values from it, you must first add some values to it and then place it on the form.

Suppose I've added three values – Stage 1, Stage 2 and Stage 3 – to the process code field. The following figure shows a simple version of a workflow that updates the pipeline phase field based on the selected value of the process code field.

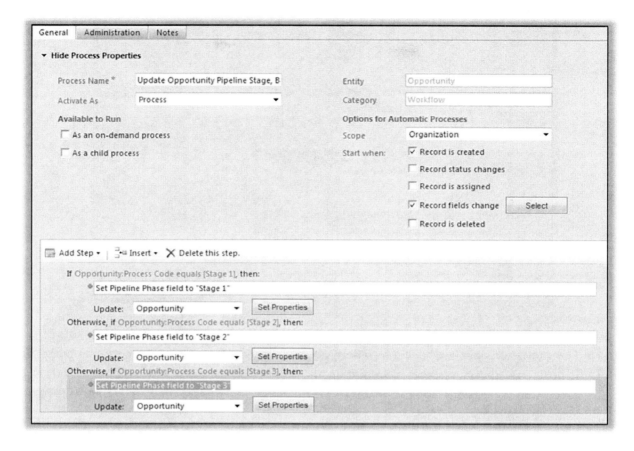

If you add this process to a solution, export that solution from the source organization and then import it into the target organization, the export/import experience will be the same as in the previous example: you will see the Missing Required Components warning dialog, but the import will still work fine.

However, when you open the process in the target organization, it will look a little different.

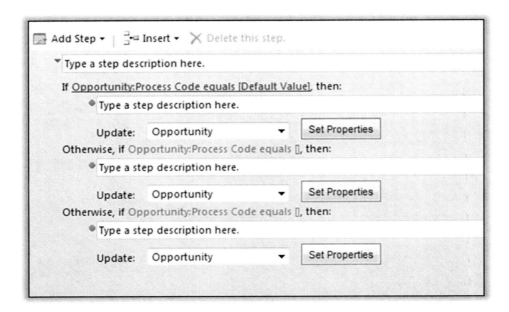

Notice that the **If** and **Otherwise** conditions aren't quite right. This is because the target organization does not have the custom values – Stages 1 through 3 – added to the process code field. The process designer picks that up and displays Opportunity:Process Code equals []. In this scenario you need to add the values to the field and then update the If and Otherwise conditions in the workflow.

2.2 – Custom fields

In the previous scenario, we might say that although the opportunity entity was customized, it wasn't customized very much! Suppose instead that the workflow process referred to one or more *custom fields*, rather than simply custom values of system fields. For example, suppose a custom option set field, Sales Stage, is added to the opportunity entity and that's what is used to drive the sales process. The step editor for a workflow that uses this custom field might look like the following figure.

Step description: None provided.

If Opportunity:Sales Stage equals [1. Qualify], then:
    ●Update: Opportunity View properties
Otherwise, if Opportunity:Sales Stage equals [2. Define Solution], then:
    ●Update: Opportunity View properties
Otherwise, if Opportunity:Sales Stage equals [3. Negotiate and Close], then:
    ●Update: Opportunity View properties

If you add a process like that to a solution and do not add the opportunity entity, here's the
Missing Required Components dialog you will see when you try to export the solution:

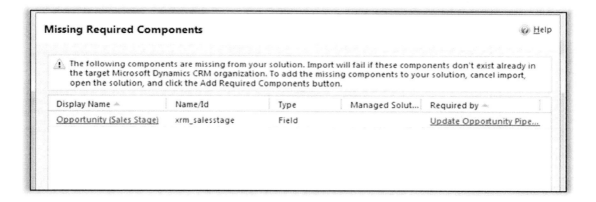

If you happen to already have that custom field in the target organization you can ignore the
warning, export the solution and successfully import it to the target. But if that field does not
exist in the target, the import will indeed fail.

Scenario 3: Processes for Custom Entities

This scenario may raise a more obvious potential problem, but it's worth reviewing it since it
comes up a lot. Suppose a process refers to a custom entity, such as the configurable SLA
process discussed previously. If you create a solution and start by adding such a process to the
solution, you will see a version of the **Missing Required Components** dialog.

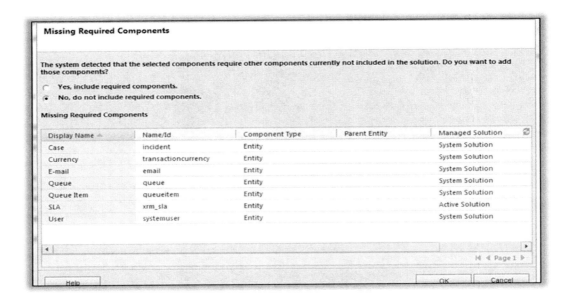

In this example, the custom entity SLA is referred to by the workflow, and as I mentioned, it's probably obvious that it either needs to be added to the solution or already exist in the target organization for the solution import to work. If you ignore the warnings and attempt to import it anyway, you will see something like the following figure.

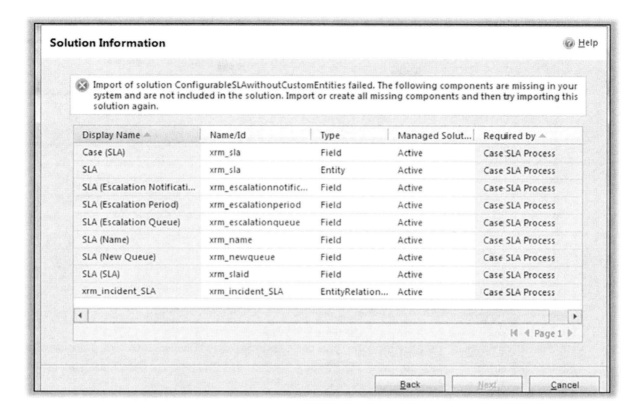

Scenario 4: Processes and Child Processes

Suppose you've created a workflow or dialog process that calls a child process. For example, a simplified version of a dialog we discussed earlier might look like this.

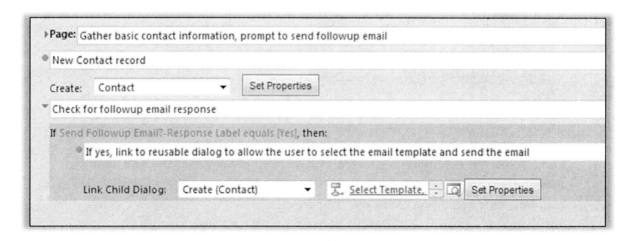

Suppose you add a process like that one to a solution and forget to add the child process. When you export the solution you will see the by now familiar **Missing Required Components** dialog, which will pick up the dependency of the parent process on the child process.

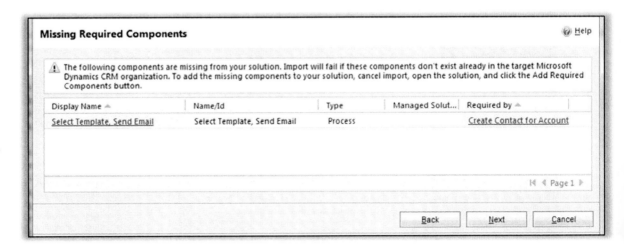

In this scenario as in the previous one, you cannot import the solution into a target organization unless the solution either contains the missing component (in this case the child process) or it already exists in the target organization.

Let's play this example out a little further. Suppose you'd created a solution and added only the parent dialog to it.

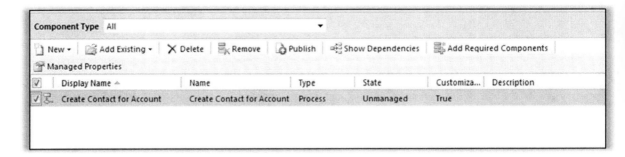

Then, you select the Create Contact for Account component, click the **Add Required Components** button and click OK to confirm. The system adds several components to the solution, most notably including the child process.

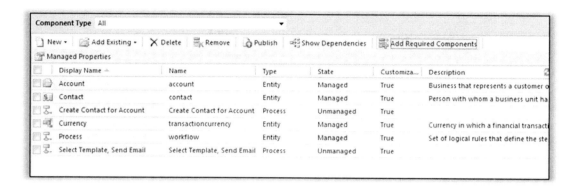

Now that you've added the required components you can export the solution, and import it successfully to a target organization. However…it won't necessarily work, as the following scenario illustrates!

Scenario 5: Processes and Templates

In the previous discussion of dialog processes, we reviewed an example that used a Query CRM Data step to build a query of e-mail templates, and then prompted a user to select one to use for an e-mail generated by the dialog process. Let's take a closer look at a similar dialog process, and examine some of the issues that arise if you attempt to move such a process from one CRM organization to another in the form of a solution package. The following figure illustrates how you might build the query for a dialog process.

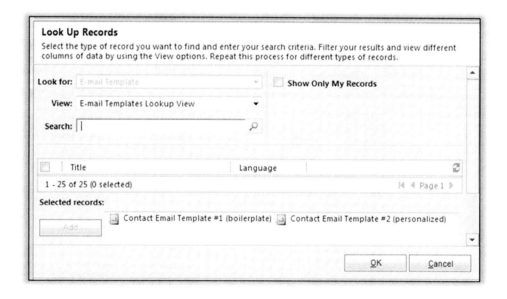

The most important thing to note here is that *specific templates* are being selected in the query. This is generally the approach you use, since you only want the user to be able to select one of the templates appropriate for the purpose of the dialog process.

In this example, the dialog is written for the contact entity, and all it does is build the query, prompt the user to select the e-mail template, and then send the e-mail.

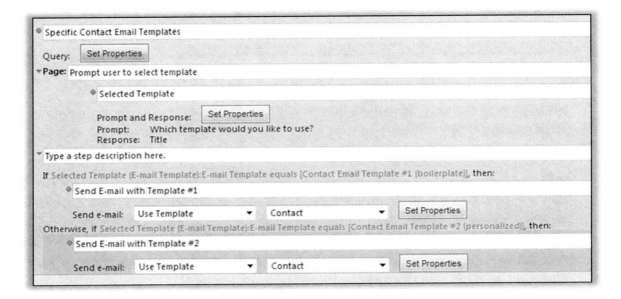

Suppose you follow these steps to create a solution and add this dialog process to it:

1. Click **Settings** and then click **Solutions**.
2. On the solutions toolbar, click **New**.
3. Provide an appropriate name, select the publisher and enter a version number, such as the following figure illustrates.

4. In the solution explorer, click **Processes**, click **Add Existing**, and then select the dialog process and click **OK**. In this scenario, the **Missing Required Components** dialog prompts you to include several components

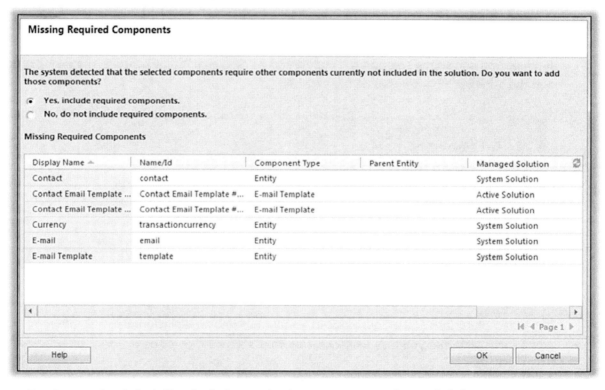

5. Accept the default **Yes, include required components** option and click **OK**.

If you then export the solution as an unmanaged solution and import that solution into a different CRM organization, you will get the following results:

- The solution will import successfully.
- After the dialog process is activated, it will work the same way it did in the source organization.

This example illustrates an important point about Dynamics CRM 2011 solutions, and one that might not be obvious if you're new to working with solutions: templates – such as the e-mail templates used in this example – can be included as solution components, and if they are, they will be imported into the target organization along with the rest of the solution components.

A good way to appreciate the importance of this fact is to walk through the previous step-by-step example, but on step 5, select the **No, do not include required components** option. If you do this, what you will find is that the exported solution will not be able to be imported successfully: in this example, the two e-mail templates used by the process really *are* required, and the solution won't import without them. The other "missing required components" are not really required in the same sense: as system components, they all will exist in the target organization and so the solution will import and work even if it only contains the dialog process and the e-mail templates used by the process.

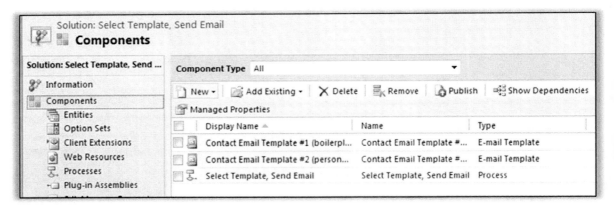

E-mail templates are one of four kinds of templates that can be included as a solution component, and that you may have occasion to use in workflows and dialogs.

Solution Dependencies, Required Components and Data

The previous scenarios have illustrated an important aspect of how solution components interact with each other in the overall context of a solution. A common thread in these scenarios was the **Missing Components** dialog, which will always remind you of *dependencies* you've created within your solution. You can think of *dependencies* and *required components* as two sides of the same coin: if component A requires component B in order to run correctly, component A has a *dependency* on B, and B is a *required component* for A.

Business processes are similar to other solution components in that they can be both required by other components and can be dependent on them. As we've seen, the presence of dependencies within a solution does not necessarily mean you should add every required component to a solution. To review, the scenarios we've discussed feature some of the most commonly encountered issues.

- Business processes typically have numerous references to system entities. We've seen examples of workflows and dialogs with many different system entities – account, contact, user, opportunity, case, and so on -- as their primary entity, and we've seen examples of processes creating and updating other entities, both related and unrelated ones. These situations create dependencies, but that does not mean you need to add every required component to a solution in order to export a process from a source organization and import it to a target. In general, if the missing required components are un-customized system entities, you do not need to add those components to your solution.
- But if a process refers to custom attributes – such as a custom field – of a system entity, then the required components will either need to already exist in the target organization or included in the solution in order for the solution to import successfully.
- We've also seen that solutions can create dependencies for components such as templates. This is very convenient, since it means that you can create a self-contained solution with business processes that make extensive use of custom e-mail templates, for example. The solution will pick up those requirements and allow you to bundle up the required templates into your solution, which can then be imported into a target organization and run as-is.

But unfortunately there are plenty of scenarios in which a business process can have a practical dependence on other pieces of a Dynamics CRM application that cannot be included as solution components. The basic problem can be illustrated with a look at the following figure, which includes everything that is currently considered a solution component.

For the most part, solution components consist of schema and UI customizations, custom code and processes, and security configurations. What's missing? *Data!* That is, while solutions can include the entire definition of customized system entities and custom entities, they cannot include an entity's data records.

At first this might not seem like a very binding constraint. After all, if you want to perform a data migration you can use the native data import wizard or a third-party application such as Scribe, right? But the more you work with workflow and dialog processes, and the more you try to move them from one CRM organization to another, the more you wish certain types of data could be included as components of solutions. What *certain types* of data do I mean? Here's my short list of the entities whose data are most frequently referred to in workflows and dialogs, and – as you will shortly see – without which solutions cannot be used to make business processes truly portable from one organization to another:

- Queues
- Business Units
- Teams

- Sites
- Sales Territories
- Products

These are some of the trickier situations you will encounter, and at present there's no real solution to the kinds of problems you will encounter, other than your awareness of them and a little manual labor required to fix the problems as they arise. The following scenarios will help to illustrate the problem and show you the kinds of things you will need to watch out for.

Scenario 6: Processes and Queues

We've seen several examples throughout the book of how workflow and dialog processes can be used to route items to queues. For example, a commonly encountered requirement in the area of service processes is to route a service case to a specific queue, depending on various characteristics of the case (case type, priority level, etc.) and the customer (industry, whether they have a contract or SLA, and so forth). Given how common a reliance on queue routing is for service processes, and how well dialogs and workflows perform this task, you'd think you could build a process to take advantage of queues, and easily move it from one organization to another. Unfortunately, while queues can be added to a solution as solution components, it's only schema customizations to those entities that are included – not the actual queues themselves.

Consider the following simplified version of a case routing workflow.

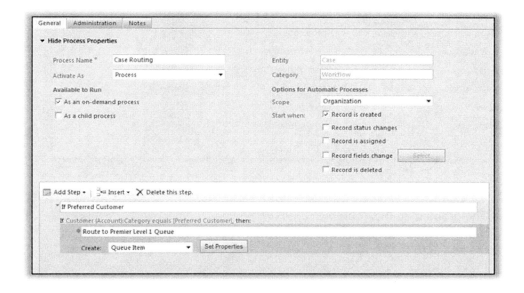

If the account a new case is created for is a preferred customer, the case is routed to an appropriate queue. The following figure illustrates setting up the properties for the **Create Queue Item** step.

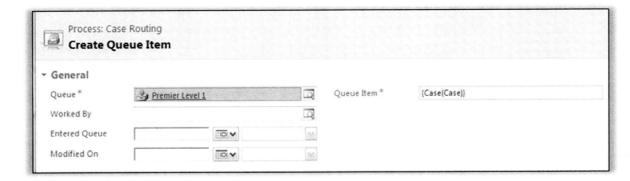

If you create a solution, and add that solution to it, you will be prompted to add several other required components, including both the queue and queue item entities. If you work through an example like this one, and add all required components as instructed, the solution will contain the components shown here.

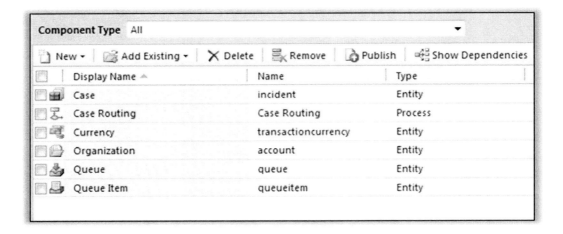

You can export this solution as an unmanaged solution and import it successfully into a target organization. The problem in this example comes when you try to activate the workflow, when you will receive the **Errors in Process Definition** dialog.

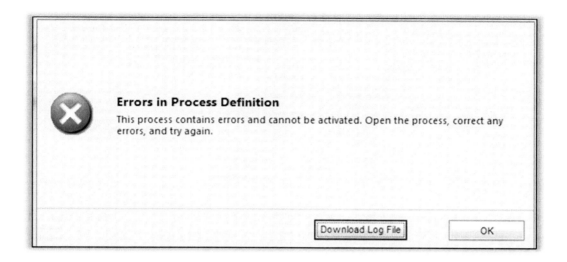

If you open the workflow in the designer, you will see something like the following figure.

And drilling into the properties dialog for the Create Queue Item step.

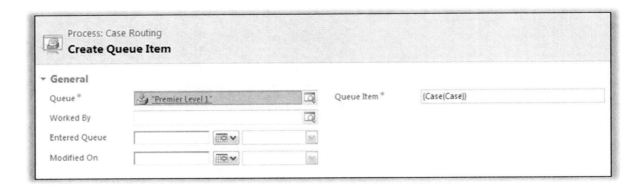

Although at first it looks ok, the clue to the error is the quotation marks around the queue name. What's happening here is that a specific record is being referred to in the workflow; in this sense the workflow is "hardwired". Behind the scenes, even though the process designer displays the name of the queue (Premier Level 1) it actually uses the GUID to perform the lookup. (This is the same as everywhere else in Dynamics CRM.) So it does not matter if the target CRM organization already has a queue called Premier Level 1 or not: either way, the GUID will not be the same, the lookup won't resolve, and you'll get these errors. The only way to fix them is to manually select them within the design environment.

There's nothing wrong with the way the workflow is written: in this context the *logic* is correct, since the workflow really does need to route the case to a specific queue based on the account category.

Scenario 7: Processes, Territories and Business Units

A similar limitation exists when it comes to the interaction within a solution of business processes and record types such as users, teams and business units. For example, consider the following simple workflow that assigns account records based on a specified value of the **Territory** field.

> *If you haven't worked with territories, you can add and maintain them on the **Business Management** page, where they are referred to as **Sales Territories**. They are available on the default account form, in the Details section, where they can be selected with the **Territories** lookup field.*

The logic in this example is simple: if an account record has East or Central specified in its territory field, it gets assigned to the default team for the appropriate business unit. Here's what the workflow looks like, correctly configured in its source organization.

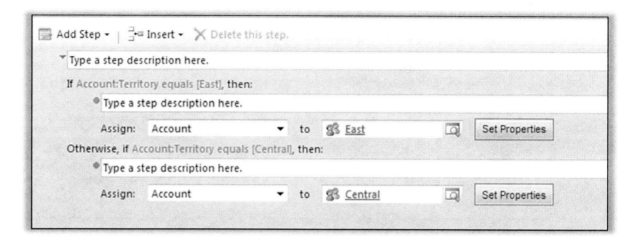

Suppose you want to move the workflow to another organization. When you add the workflow to a solution, the solution manager will pick up its dependence on the account, team, and territory entities, and you can add them to the solution.

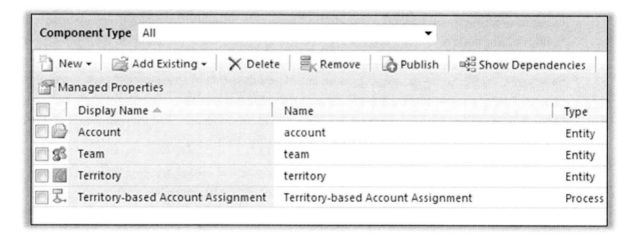

Then, you can export the solution and import it into the target organization. It will import successfully, but as in the previous scenario, if you attempt to activate the workflow you will get the **Errors in Process Definition** dialog.

If you open the process then in the target organization, you will see something like the following figure.

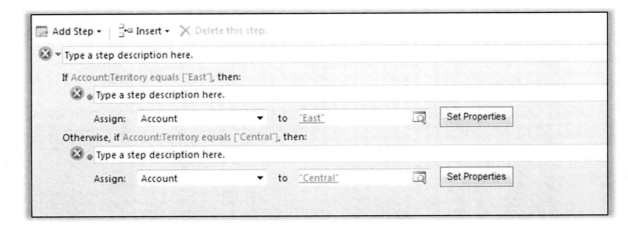

As in the previous scenario, it does not matter if the East and Central values for the territory entity already exist, or if the East or Central business units exist. The problem is that the records are looked up by their GUIDs, and those will be different between the source and target organizations.

In the examples shown here, the workflows are simple enough that fixing them up doesn't take that long. But believe me, you won't add too many options before having to fix them all every time you move a process from one organization to the other becomes pretty tedious! You can have what appear to be exactly the same set of values for all of these record types (users, business units, teams, territories, etc.) in different CRM organizations, but if a business process refer to them other than by dynamic values, you will need to perform this manual fix-up process any time you move the process from one organization to the other.

But remember in the previous section I included a scenario where a dialog process created a query for e-mail templates a user could select from within the process. In *that* scenario not just the schema definition of e-mail templates, but specific templates themselves, were included as solution components. Evidently there's something special about *templates* that allows us to include them as bona-fide solution components, both the definition and specific records, in order to create a works-as-is solution that relies on them.

My guess is, in a service-update in the not-too-distant future, a similar functionality will be made available for record types such as queues, territories, teams and the other ones discussed here, so that solutions with processes that require those components can be made fully portable across CRM organizations.

Summary

This chapter covered two topics you will need a solid understanding of to build, deploy and troubleshoot Dynamics CRM business processes: security and solutions.

We began the security topic with a discussion of which users can run business processes and the related question of what happens when they do. For the first question, the most important distinction to make is between automatic and on-demand processes:

- Whether a user triggers an **automatic** workflow is determined by a combination of the user's business unit, the process owner's business unit, and the scope of the workflow.
- **On-demand** processes are different: a user's access to these is determined by a combination of their privilege on **Execute Workflow Job** (a miscellaneous task privilege located on the security role Customization tab); their privilege on the **Process** entity, and their place in the organization relative to the owner of the process.

For the second question ("will it work?") the distinction between automatic and on-demand processes is also the key thing:

- Automatic workflows run in the security context of the owner of the workflow.
- On-demand processes take place in the security context of the user running the process.

An important point, and one that's easy to forget, is that an automatic workflow owned by a system administrator still might not work! You can demonstrate this with the following experiment:

1. Sign in to a Dynamics CRM organization as a user with the System Administrator security role.
2. Select a record, and attempt to assign it to a user whose security role has no privileges on that record type.

The error message you get when you do this interactively makes it obvious: users without privileges to own certain record types cannot have those records assigned to them, regardless of who's trying to do the assigning!

Next, we discussed which users can *create* business processes. Here, the most important point is that for most system administrators, the default security roles are probably too generous, in that all users can create business processes. After discussing the potential problems of the overly generous default roles, we reviewed potential solutions.

Solutions, introduced in Dynamics CRM 2011, are the mechanism you use to package customizations, and business processes are one of the important components you can package within a solution. After a brief introduction to solutions, we discussed several of the process-specific issues you will encounter.

In particular, we pointed out that business processes will often have dependencies on data – such as business units, territories, queues and the like – which cannot be part of a solution.

Chapter 7- Tips, Tricks and Traps

Workflows and Dialogs *Can* Update Closed Records

This is something I have to frequently remind myself of: the fact that forms are read only after a record is closed is enforced at the form level, *not* by the system. What this means is that while you cannot open a closed or inactive record through its form and make any changes, a workflow *can* make changes. For example, suppose you wanted to make some changes to closed opportunity records. One scenario might be that you want all probability values set to 100% when an opportunity is closed as won. (There are any number of other changes you might want to make to closed opportunity records, but this simple one will serve for the present purpose).

If you didn't know you could accomplish that with a workflow you might re-open them and perform a bulk edit. However, once you realize that you can only *close* opportunity records one at a time, you'll probably wish there were a better way!

But while a user may not interactively edit closed records – such as opportunities with status values of Won or Lost – a workflow or a dialog process sometimes can. And provided you remember this, the workflow itself is pretty straightforward.

The following figure shows one I find useful.

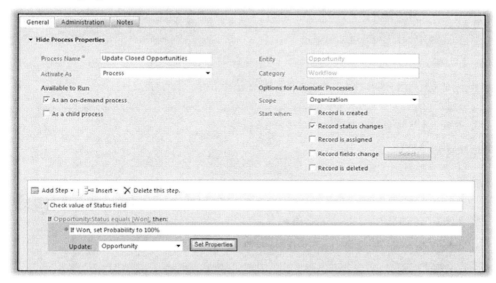

Here are a few things to keep in mind on this topic:

- A workflow like this can be triggered by **Record status changes**. Then if the first step is a conditional check for a status value of Won, the Probability field can be updated only if the condition is met.

- The way I've written this example, exposing it as an **on-demand process** can be helpful in updating any opportunities closed before the automatic version of the workflow was around. In any event, this is not one of those situations where running a workflow on demand can cause problems, so there's no harm in exposing it for potential on demand use.

- While workflow and dialog processes can update closed records like accounts, contacts, opportunities and the like, they cannot update closed activity records (hence my *sometimes* qualification above). Suppose you made a workflow similar to the one shown above on opportunity, only you substituted Phone Call for Opportunity. After clicking Mark Complete to close a phone call, if you monitored the workflow's progress you'd see that the system job had a Status Reason value of Waiting.

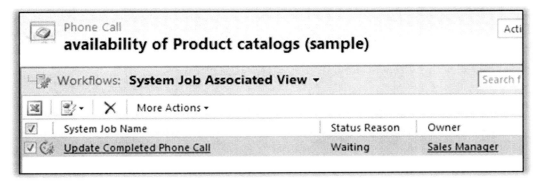

And then if you opened the system job for more information.

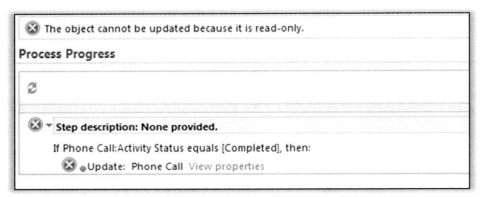

While they cannot update a closed activity record, they can do something else that gives us the same eventual result, so please read on.

Workflows and Dialogs *Can* Re-Open Closed Activities

As you've just seen, processes can update inactive or closed records that cannot be updated interactively by a user, but only for non-activity record types. This is yet another example of how activity record types are different from other record types.

One more example is that in contrast to records like leads, contacts, accounts, cases or opportunities, when a record like an appointment or a phone call is completed, a user cannot interactively "un-complete" it. That doesn't mean you can't do it – just that you can't do it through the UI. Fortunately, you can accomplish this through a workflow or dialog process.

The following two figures show two of the simplest workflows you'll ever see, specifically designed for this purpose. The first one is for re-opening a closed e-mail.

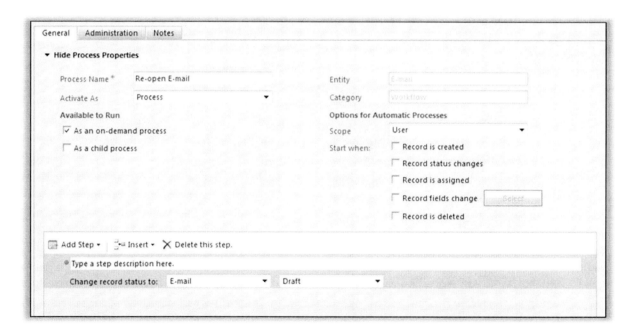

The next one handles closed appointments.

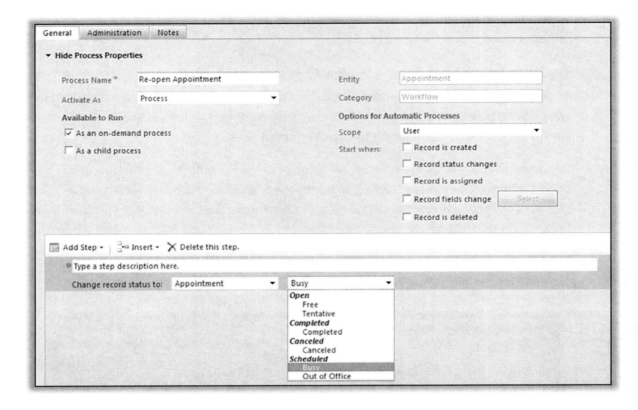

When would you need to re-open activity records?

In my experience a requirement like this often surfaces in the context of "fixing" accidentally closed records. For example, I recently performed a large data migration for a customer, with the instructions that all activity records were to be migrated as completed activities. After migrating the data I noticed that several hundred "completed" phone calls and appointments were already recorded for the coming year. It turned out that the instructions were incorrect and that these in fact were scheduled activities and should have been migrated with the appropriate open status values. If the fixes needed to be applied to several thousand records, it would probably be quicker to re-migrate the data; for the several hundred records I needed to deal with, it was much quicker to fix the data, by re-opening the activities with workflows like the ones shown here.

Another use-case scenario has to do with a subtlety of using the Outlook client, but that's a big enough topic to deserve its very own section, so please read on.

Workflows and Synchronized Outlook Records

My views on the Dynamics CRM Client for Microsoft Office Outlook (a.k.a. the Outlook client) have changed over the years, partly because it has become more stable, and partly because I've learned to use it more effectively. I believe that if it's deployed and maintained properly and users get the training they need, it can provide huge productivity improvements for organizations with users of Outlook.

But nothing's perfect, and there are a few problems you may run into, which fortunately can be solved with a workflow technique I'll discuss here.

The issues I want to address here have to do with records that are synchronized between Outlook and CRM. Appointment activities and contact records are both in this category and are usually where I run into problems, although similar issues might arise for tasks, phone calls and e-mails.

The problem arises because CRM and Outlook have different forms for each of these record types. In particular, organizations often customize the CRM appointment and contact forms in several ways, such as adding custom fields and custom business logic in the form of JScript functions that run when a CRM form is loaded.

Suppose you create an appointment in Outlook and use the **Set Regarding** button to promote it to CRM. Or suppose you create a contact in Outlook and use Set Parent to create a synchronized contact record in CRM. When records are created in Outlook and pushed up to CRM, here's what happens with reference to the two kinds of customizations just mentioned.

Customization	What happens?
Custom fields on appointment or contact forms in CRM	Appointment or contact record is created in Dynamics CRM, custom CRM fields are not populated, and records are saved even if required fields do not contain data.
JScript functions run when CRM form is loaded	JScript functions do not run.

The reason those customizations are not applied is that they are enforced at the form level, and when you create a record in Outlook and then push it up to CRM, the CRM form is never loaded. Earlier in the book, we examined some of the differences between workflows and JScript, so while you may be familiar with the general topic, let's take a look now at examples of two specific problems that can arise and how you can use workflows to solve them.

Problem #1: When promoting contacts from Outlook, how can you automatically add them to marketing lists?

I wouldn't say I'm lazy, but I'd sure rather not type any more than I need to. And using the Outlook client as I do, this means I rarely need to create a Dynamics CRM contact record from scratch. I'd much rather right-click an email address, select **Add to Outlook contacts**, update whatever I need to on the contact record and then click **Set Parent** to promote to CRM.

My specific problem with this approach has to do with marketing. I maintain a marketing list of contacts in CRM for monthly email newsletters and related activities. And it's a combination of various field values on the contact record – some of which are custom and therefore not on the Outlook form – that determines inclusion in my marketing list.

So, consider the following figure.

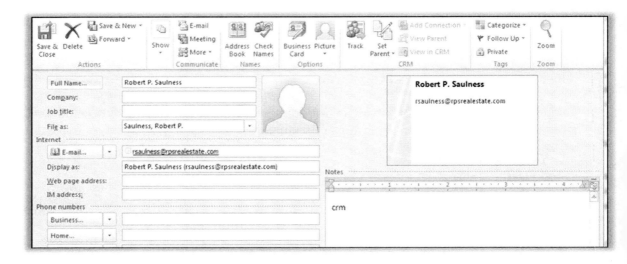

Notice that the Notes field contains the single word "crm". Then consider the following figure, which shows an automatic workflow that runs when a contact record is created in my CRM.

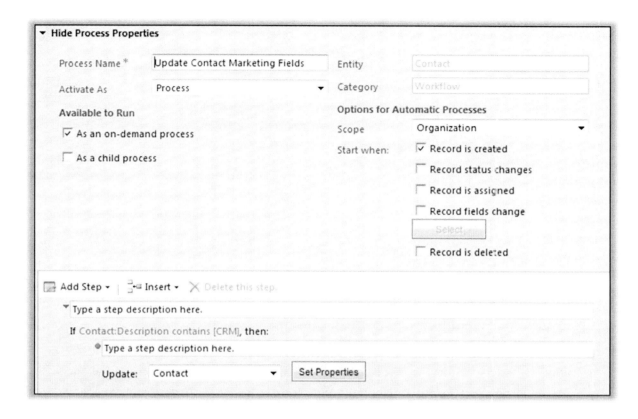

Set Properties for the Update step simply selects a checkbox field for inclusion in my marketing list, so I won't bother showing that. The important thing here is that the **Notes** field from Outlook maps to the **Description** field in Dynamics CRM. So even though you cannot update a custom field directly in CRM, you can sometimes use automatic workflow logic to do so. Obviously you would not want to require users to type long complex text strings, or require them to remember too much...but for me, remembering to type CRM (or crm) is a small price to pay.

This little workflow is my business process version of the Energizer Bunny, it just keeps on going and going and ...

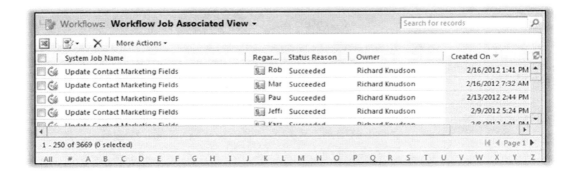

Problem #2: When promoting appointments from Outlook, how can you make sure that required fields are filled in?

Problems of the Problem #1 variety are easily solved, but Problem #2 problems are a little trickier. I see versions of this problem all the time, probably because adding custom fields to the CRM appointment form is such a common requirement.

For example, recently I worked with a client for whom activity reporting – specifically on appointments – was a critical success factor in their selling process. They needed one little custom drop-down field on the appointment form, which you can see from the following figure, is a required field:

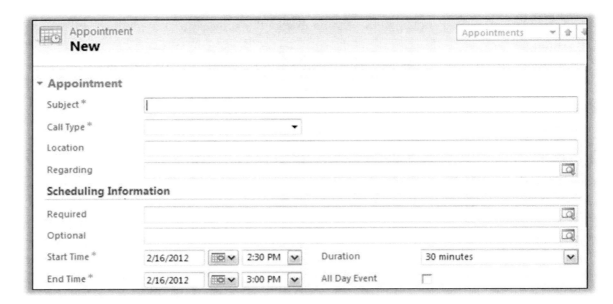

The first time you encounter this it's easy to forget that there's no **Call Type** field on the Outlook version of the appointment form, and to subsequently be surprised when you find out there are so many appointment records saved in your CRM with no value in the **Call Type** field! But that's how it works, and again, it's because constraints like this is applied at the CRM form level, and unless a user opens the appointment in CRM they can easily miss it.

The problem gets a little worse, however, when you realize that not only can you *create* a new appointment without opening the form, but you can also *complete* one. And sure enough, since form logic and constraints are not applied unless the form is open, you may well end up with plenty of completed appointment records lacking good data for fields like the one I have shown here.

The solutions to problems like this one are a little more complex, and of course they will be dependent on the specific constraints you need to enforce and the logic you need to apply. But let me show you the solution I implemented for my client in this instance, and then you can adapt the approach to your requirements.

And this (finally!) brings me back to the discussion from the previous topic about working with inactive records or completed activities. Let's summarize the differences between regular and activity record types, regarding what you can and cannot do with inactive/completed records:

- **Inactive regular record types** (accounts, contacts...) are read only; user must reactivate to modify. However, they can be modified directly by a workflow or dialog process without being reactivated.
- **Completed Activities** (appointments, phone calls...) are read only; users cannot re-open them through the UI. Processes cannot modify them directly, but can re-open then and then re-close them.

Why does this matter? My client with the required custom field on the appointment form only does reporting on *completed* appointments, and has business rules that can be used to determine the value of the call type field. They prefer it to be supplied by the user on the form, but if it's not we can apply workflow logic when the appointment is completed.

For these requirements, an automatic workflow that runs on the Record status changes trigger will do the trick. Just in case there are existing records that need to be fixed up, I might make this workflow available for on-demand use as well. In any case, there's (usually) no harm in exposing it for on-demand use. Here are the workflow properties.

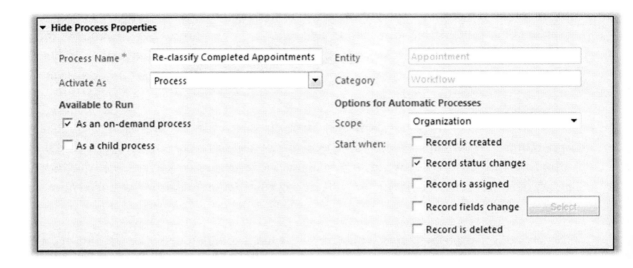

You can see here the basic structure of the workflow in the step editor.

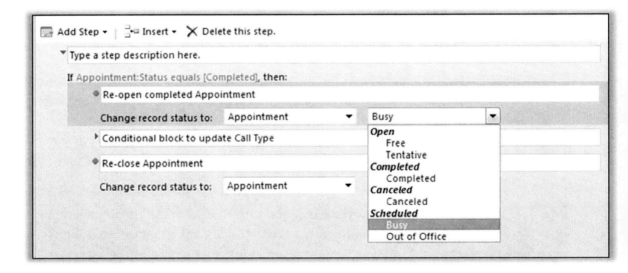

It starts with a Check Condition, and only runs the rest of the logic if the appointment record's status is completed. If it is, we need to re-open it, and as we've seen elsewhere, you set the status indirectly, by selecting one of the status reason values. Since the only goal of this first step is to open the record for editing, it doesn't matter whether an **Open** or **Scheduled** status reason is selected.

At that point the workflow process can perform a conditional update of the **Call Type** field, and I've collapsed the conditional block to save space and since that's not really the important point of this exercise.

Finally, the last step needs to re-set the status to **Completed**. (And this time it does matter!)

Troubleshooting Tip: Modifying Running Workflows

Generally speaking, there are two main reasons you might need to modify a process:

a. It's broken and needs to be fixed.
b. A change to your business process needs to be reflected in its CRM workflow implementation.

The issue I want to discuss here arises when a workflow is running on several records, and either is broken and needs to be fixed, or simply needs to be modified. When you make whatever change you need to make, what happens to any running instances of the workflow?

When troubleshooting workflows, I find it helpful to make the following distinction between *run-time* errors and *process* errors.

Run-time Errors

Run-time errors are ones that can be fixed by changing something *other than the process itself*, such as a user's business unit or security roles. One commonly encountered example of this is when a workflow attempts to assign a record to a user whose security role does not have sufficient privileges to the record being assigned. For these kinds of errors, you can generally fix the problem and then resume the process.

Suppose a workflow runs automatically when a case record is created, and for certain conditions routes cases to users' queues or assigns case records to specific users. For example, the following simple case routing workflow first checks the value of the **Case Type** field, and for Request case types, performs two actions: routes to the personal queue of User B and then assigns the case to User B.

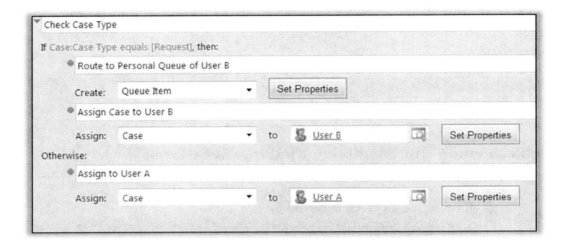

In order for this to work, User B must at a minimum have user-level access on the Read privilege for cases. If this user's security role does not have at least that level of privilege on cases, the workflow will be triggered but it will not run all the way through. For example, if you opened the form for a case with request selected as the case type and clicked Workflows on left navigation; you'd see something like the following figure.

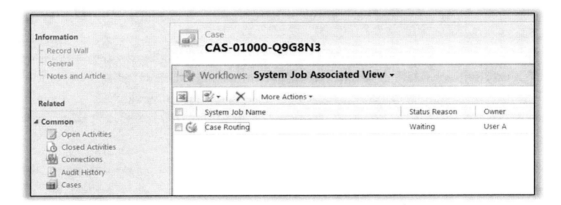

The Case Routing workflow is running but its Status Reason is **Waiting**. The fact that there's no wait condition in the workflow should be a clue that something is not right! You can get more detail on the running workflow job by clicking the system job name to open the System Job form.

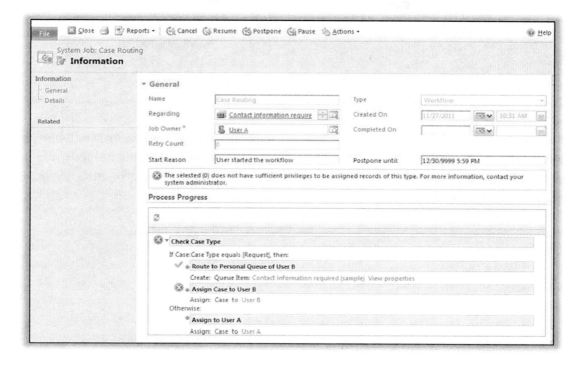

In situations such as this one, the error message is usually descriptive enough for you to understand the problem. Notice in particular that the **Create Queue Item** step worked fine, because you don't need privileges on a record (here, case) in order to have a queue item created for it. But the next step – the **Assign Case** step – failed because of the security role.

One way to fix a problem like this is to change the security role. A security role such as the one shown in the next figure would definitely account for the error message we just saw.

Suppose you changed it by setting the Read privilege on case to user-level, as is illustrated here.

Next, all you need to do is return to the System Job form and click **Resume** on the ribbon (you can also do this by selecting the system job record on the grid and selecting Resume from the More Actions menu). After clicking Resume you will see the Resume Confirmation dialog as shown in the following figure.

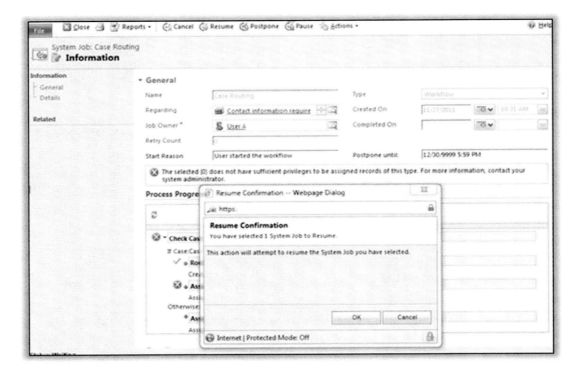

Finally, after clicking OK and waiting a few seconds, you can refresh the System Job form and verify that now the workflow runs all the way through to completion.

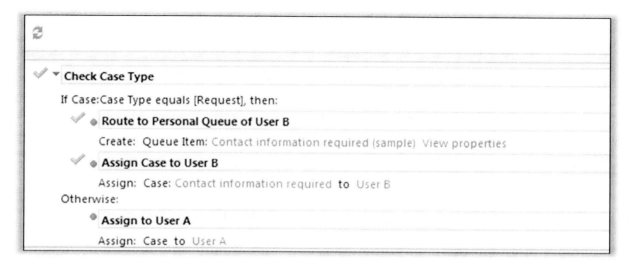

So the distinguishing characteristic of run-time errors is that you can fix whatever is causing the process to not run correctly, without making any changes to the process itself. An important point to keep in mind regarding these kinds of errors is that problems can arise from either the security role of the user *running* the process or the security role of the *owner* of the process. One common misconception is that automatic workflows owned by a user with the System Administrator role will "always work". After all, we know that automatic workflows run in the security context of the owner of the workflow, so if the owner is a system administrator, what can go wrong? The answer, it turns out, is plenty. Even system administrators cannot assign records to users without sufficient privileges on those record types. The example we just ran through is of this kind of problem: it doesn't matter who owns the workflow in these situations, since a workflow can never assign a record to a user without sufficient privileges on that record type.

From my experience, here are a few of the situations where I frequently see run-time errors in workflows and dialogs.

- **Sending e-mails.** By default, only the System Administrator security role has privileges to **Send E-mail as Another User**. However, users with security roles such as CEO/Business Manager, or the Marketing Manager or Sales Manager roles might need to create workflow with that capability. They do have privileges to create such a workflow...but it won't work unless their security roles are customized.
- **Custom entities.** Remember that when you create a custom entity, no security roles have access to it by default. So any workflows you create that assign, update,

append or append to custom entities will generally *not* work for any user with un-customized default security roles.

- **Assigning records to teams.** This can be confusing at first, since teams work so much differently in CRM 2011 than they did in previous versions. In particular, you should familiarize yourself with the *default teams for business units*. These exist for every business unit, and have several properties that are different from those of other teams. For example, they cannot be deleted, and they contain every user in the business unit they're associated with. This is essentially the purpose of these default teams, and every user in a business *must* be a member of the business unit's default team. In many situations you may want to assign records to teams, but remember: teams don't have security roles by default, and default teams are no exception to this rule. So before you assign records to teams – whether interactively or through a process – remember to assign security roles first.

Process Errors

Process errors are – as they sound—errors that require a *change to the process itself*. I demonstrated an example of a process error above, in the discussion of updating closed activity records. To review, the following figure shows what you would see if you were troubleshooting a workflow trying to update a completed Phone Call.

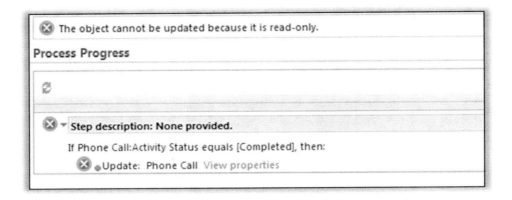

As we saw, the logic of the workflow is wrong, so we needed to change it. And in situations like these, unlike run-time errors, you must deactivate the process, fix the logic, and reactivate it. When I first encountered this, I figured I could fix the logic, reactivate the workflow, open the system job form for the running process and use the **Resume** button.

But no matter how many times I clicked **Resume** it just never worked! It's probably more obvious to you than it was to me, but it's because the running process is the old process with the error in it. Going forward all new system jobs will be running the new process, but any existing ones are all running the old one.

So if you want to fix them, the only way to do it is to cancel all of the existing running processes and apply the new one. In situations like this, you'll be glad if you've stayed on top of your running system processes, and in the section below on **Queries, Reports and Dashboards**, I give you some tips about how to do that.

Working with Read-only Form Fields

Suppose you have a form field that you want to update with a workflow, and you do not want users to be able to update it interactively on the form. This is a frequently encountered requirement; here are just a few examples.

- You have a gated sales process, and the sales stage field on the opportunity form should only advance to the next stage after the tasks for the current stage are complete. The sales stage field should be read-only on the form, and only updated by the sales process workflow.
- You've added a custom field, Last Activity Date, to the account entity, and a workflow automatically updates it when certain kinds of activities are closed for an account. (An example of this was discussed in Chapter 3.)
- You've created a custom entity, **Marketing Event**, and added a field to it called **Revenue Generated by Event**. Whenever an opportunity, tied back to a marketing event, closes as won, a workflow increments the revenue field.

To make this concrete, let's implement the marketing event example just mentioned.

And suppose further that you've already specified the field as read-only on the form, and published the opportunity entity. You open the workflow designer and modify the properties for the **Update Opportunity** step, locate the sales stage field and try to click inside it. Oops: no can do! You cannot select the field.

If you have not seen this before it's a definite head-scratcher. What's happening is that since the field is on the form as read-only and it's published, you cannot modify it the way you normally would in the workflow designer – it's read-only there also! This seems a little odd at first, but as of this writing, that's how it works. The solution is simple: modify the form, uncheck the read-only option, and publish opportunity. Then when you open the workflow designer, you can update the field with dynamic values as usual. And when you're finished modifying the process, you can open up the opportunity form again, re-set the field to read-only, and everything works fine.

Working with Required Fields

A similar issue arises with required fields as with read-only fields. For example, suppose you create a workflow to copy an opportunity record, and that when you create the workflow you do not have it copy the value of the Probability field. Then, suppose you change the **Requirement Level** for probability from its default, to Business Required:

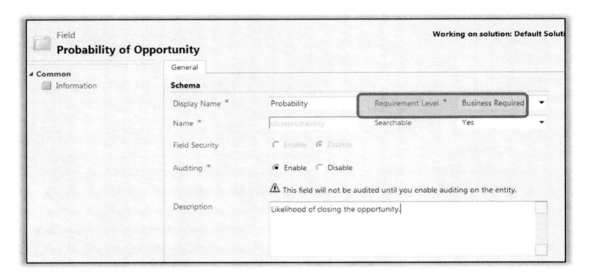

After publishing customizations, the field will be required and users will not be able to save opportunity records without supplying a value for probability. However, if you run the Copy Opportunity workflow it will still work, successfully creating a new opportunity record even though there's no value in the required probability field. Another head-scratcher the first time you see it.

What's happening in this case is that it's the *form* that enforces settings like Requirement Level. So, if records are created non-interactively (such as by a workflow, or by importing records), the form is bypassed and form constraints are not applied.

And as in the previous discussion about read-only forms, the *order* in which you do things matters. To continue the opportunity probability example, suppose that after changing the Requirement Level, you deactivate the Copy Opportunity workflow to make some changes to it.

In particular, if you click Set Properties on the Create Record step, you will notice that the required field indicator (the red asterisk) shows up on the probability field. And if you try to save your changes, you will discover that the process designer enforces requirement settings just as the user form does:

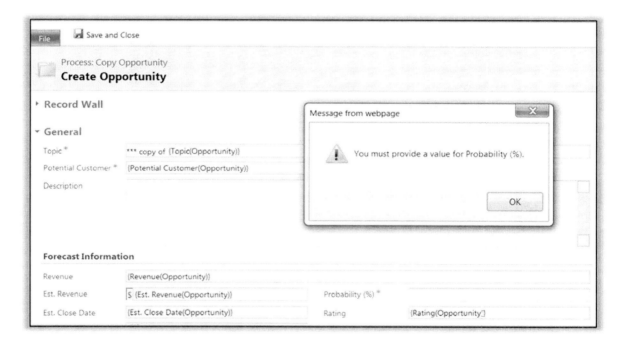

Again, the first time you encounter this scenario it seems odd that the process will continue to work, creating records without required fields, but that you cannot modify it in the process designer and save it without filling in the newly required field.

In fact, you cannot even activate a process that creates records without providing values for required fields. So, suppose you try the following little experiment:

1. Create the Copy Opportunity workflow, without providing a value for probability.

2. Activate the workflow.
3. Change the requirement level on probability to Business Required and publish customizations.
4. Copy an opportunity with the workflow to verify that it still works fine.
5. Deactivate the workflow, and without making any changes, attempt to reactivate it. You should see the following dialog:

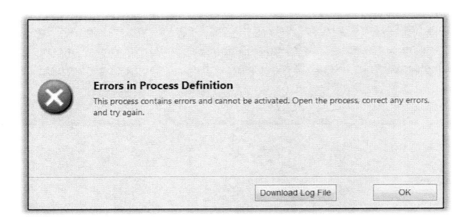

Strange but true.

Workflows, Importing Records, and Bulk Updates

Here's something that's important to remember and easy to forget: automatic workflows triggered by the "Record is created" event run any time a new record is created, even if it's created by Dynamics CRM's Data Management/Import feature. Here's a common business scenario where this might be important.

Suppose you have a number of processes that happen in the normal course of business when new Lead records are created. And suppose "in the normal course of business" means when leads are created in the following ways:

- Someone visits your web site and fills out a request information form.
- Someone calls on the phone in response to a magazine ad.
- Your marketing manager returns from a tradeshow with a big stack of business cards.

Contrast those with purchasing a list of hundreds or thousands of names and importing them all as Lead records. Probably because the Lead record is a nice, flexible, general-purpose entity that can be used for lots of different kinds of "leads", it tends to be used for records that might really require significantly different kinds of follow up.

If you have a characteristic lead qualification process that is implemented as an automatic workflow on the Lead record's create trigger, you might consider temporarily turning it off (unpublishing it) before you import those thousands of Jigsaw leads...otherwise it will run for all of them!

Besides imports, there are plenty of other situations when automatic workflows can be triggered that you need to be aware of. Bulk edits are an example of this. Suppose you've written a workflow that runs automatically on the Fields change trigger, and it sends an email notifying a user if they've been selected as the **Preferred User** on the account form. If you select multiple account records, click the Edit button on the ribbon, and update the Preferred User for the selected accounts, the workflow will run. Probably a good thing, on balance, but you should be aware of it.

Queries, Reports, and Dashboards

In Chapter 2 we saw how an advanced find query on System Jobs can be used to monitor running workflow processes. Now I want to examine this topic in more detail. This is more important the larger your CRM deployment. I won't attempt to quantify the word *large* in this context, but the challenge of managing automatic workflows increases faster than you might think.

For example, suppose you manage a CRM organization with fifty salespeople and twenty customer service representatives (CSR), and that you've implemented automatic workflows for your sales and case routing/escalation processes. Further, suppose that the average salesperson has thirty open opportunities at any given time and the average CSR opens five cases daily. A little workflow math tells us that at a point in time you would have 1,500 sales process workflows running, and that each month 2,000 new case routing workflows are triggered.

No matter how well your processes are designed and tested, with large numbers like those you can count on the unexpected, and techniques like the ones described here can help you identify and troubleshoot problems.

Advanced Find Queries for System Jobs

To review, advanced find can be used to query the **System Jobs** entity. This contains a **System Job Type** field, and **Workflow** is one of the many system job types you can filter for. You can further filter on the **Status Reason** field, and status reason values of **Waiting** and **Waiting for Resources are** the most interesting for monitoring running workflow jobs.

The following figure shows the **Query** view of Advanced Find for a query like this.

Clicking the **Results** button will show you the default view of the qualifying system jobs.

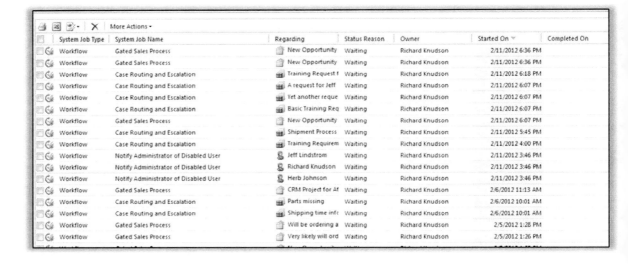

As I said, that's the *default* view for system jobs, but here is a much more interesting view.

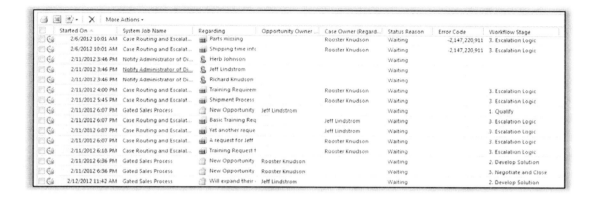

This view includes several columns not found in the default view, such as the owners of the underlying records the workflows are running on, and System Jobs fields **Error Code** and **Workflow Stage**. To understand how to construct a query like this, follow these steps:

1. Open an Advanced Find window, select **System Jobs** in the **Look For** drop-down, and construct a query like the one in the first figure in this section.
2. Click **Edit Columns**, and in the Edit Columns dialog, click **Add Columns**.
3. In the Add Columns dialog select the **Error Code**, **Message**, **Message Name** and **Workflow Stage** fields, as illustrated in the following figure.

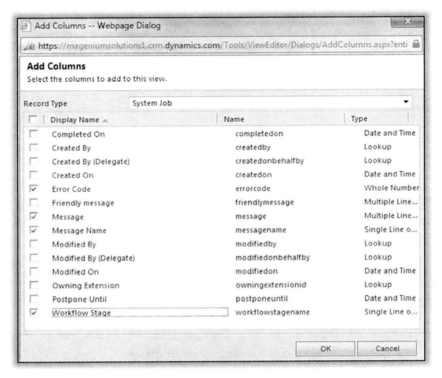

4. Click **OK** to add those columns to your view.

At this point you'd have a more interesting view, but it can be even more interesting by adding columns for the owners of the records workflows are running against, such as case and opportunity. Remember that advanced find can add columns from any parent record, and as it turns out, any entity you can run a system job against has a parent-child relationship to the system job entity. To see how you can exploit this in advanced find, pick up where we left off and follow these steps:

5. Click **Add Columns** again, and then click the Record Type drop-down and select **Regarding (Case),** as the following figure illustrates.

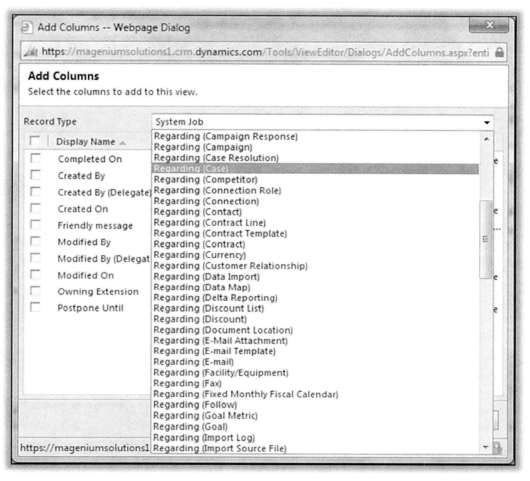

6. Once **Regarding (Case)** is selected, you can select any of the fields from the case entity. For this example, select the **Owner** field.

7. Then repeat steps 5 and 6 to select the **Owner** field from the **Regarding (Opportunity)** record type. At this point the Add Columns dialog will look something like the following figure, and all you need to do is move and size the columns to your liking.

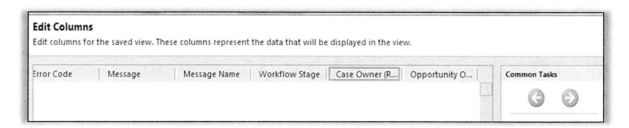

When you create a query like this you can click **Save As** to make a copy of the query and save it. This creates a Personal View that will by default only be visible to you, but can be shared out to other users. In the examples that follow I will make use of three personal views of system jobs, each of which has the same basic columns, but slightly different filters.

- Waiting Workflow System Jobs. This is the one just created.
- Waiting Workflow System Jobs with Errors.

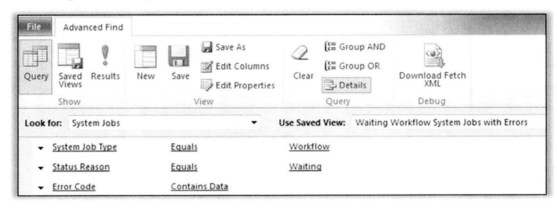

- All Workflow System Jobs with Errors.

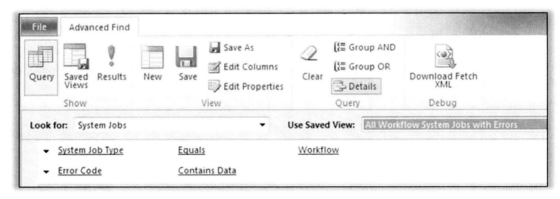

Some Limitations on Customizing and Reporting on the System Jobs Entity
You might have wondered why in the previous examples I saved those custom views as personal views rather than customizing the System Jobs entity and creating new system views. The reason is, because you can't customize the System Jobs entity.

This seems surprising at first, since in many ways System Jobs is treated as a standard entity: you select it in the Look for drop-down just like other record types, you can query it in advanced find, write reports for it, and so forth.

But you cannot customize it, which imposes several constraints, one of which we just encountered. Another one is that you cannot create charts for system jobs the way you might for other entities.

Another limitation is that you cannot even export system jobs records to Excel. From an advanced find query you *can* export the FetchXML, however, and then you could use that as the basis for custom reports. In the following two sections we will examine how to use reports and dashboards – using the core CRM feature set – to monitor running workflows.

Reports

You can use the Report Wizard to build custom reports for workflow system jobs. For example, the following figure shows a report format I've sometimes found helpful.

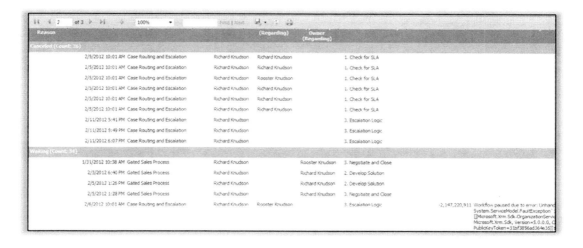

This report contains many of the same fields in the advanced find queries we just looked at. In fact, when I create a report like this one I usually base it on one of the saved personal views. Here's what this one looks like in the report designer.

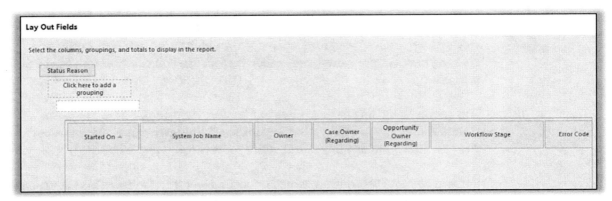

Notice that it's grouped on Status Reason. In the version of the report I'm showing here, I include all workflow jobs, regardless of status reason, so it's reasonable to group on that field.

A slightly different version of this report might filter out everything except Waiting workflows. And in this version I'd drop the grouping on Status Reason and perhaps replace it with a grouping on System Job Name, as the following figure illustrates:

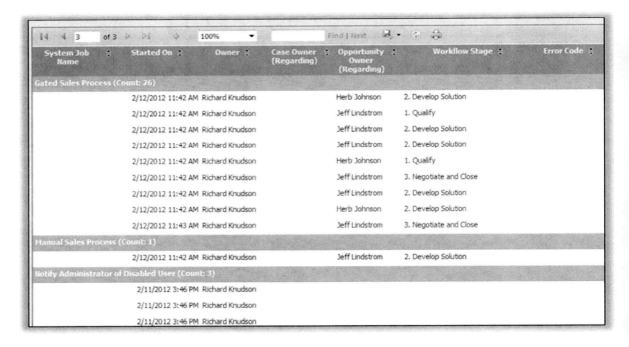

Dashboards

Even though we cannot create custom charts for the System Jobs entity, dashboards can expose more than charts, and can still be a useful technique for monitoring workflow processes.

Dashboard components can contain charts, lists, Iframes and Web resources. I'll show an example here of how you can take advantage of lists to create a dashboard like the one illustrated in the following figure.

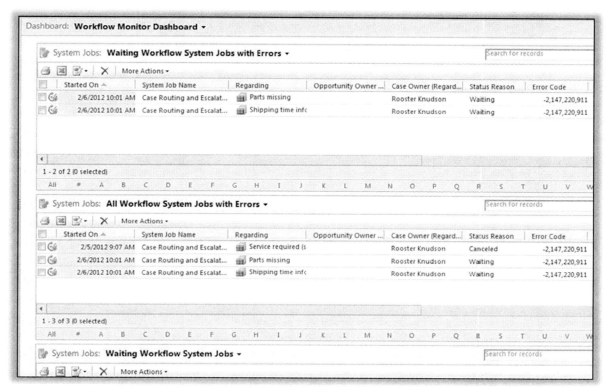

This dashboard consists of three components, each of which contains a list. As you can see from the figure, each list is based on system jobs, and simply uses the three saved personal views we walked through earlier. Once you understand the basic technique of creating saved views for system jobs, exposing them on a dashboard like this is straightforward.

1. On the site map, click **Workplace**, then click **Dashboards**.
2. Click **New**, select the **Three-Column Overview Dashboard** layout, and click **Create**.
3. Name the dashboard *Workflow Monitor*, and then delete all three components on the first row.
4. Double click the first Tab and de-select the **Visible by Default** option.
5. Then select the second tab and double-click it to set its Tab Properties. De-select **Show the label of this tab on the dashboard**, then click **OK**.
6. Click **List** on the **Insert** tab.

7. In the **Record Type** drop-down, select **System Jobs**, then in the **View** drop-down, select one of the saved views.

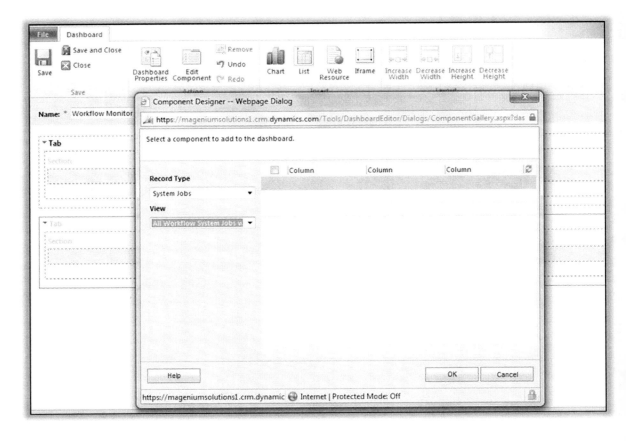

8. Click OK, and then click Increase Width twice to make the list take up all three columns.
9. Then repeat steps 6-8 for as many other views as you'd like to expose on the dashboard.

User Management

One of the examples at the end of Chapter 2 was of what I refer to as a user configuration workflow. The main point of that example was that that the user entity is different in some ways from other entities. In particular, since bulk edit is not supported for user records, the easiest way to update multiple records is usually with a workflow process.

A different aspect of user management has to do with managing disabled users. To understand why this is important, consider again the scenario described in the previous section, where you manage a CRM organization with fifty salespeople and twenty CSR's, and you've implemented automatic workflows for your sales and case routing/escalation processes.

Workflows of course often refer to users, sending them notification emails, assigning them tasks, assigning records to them and so forth. Sometimes a user might be referred to in a general way. For example, a workflow might assign a new case to the user specified as the **Preferred User** in the **Service Preferences** section of the default account form. Other times a user might be referred to specifically. For example, a specific CSR might be assigned as the owner for certain kinds of case records.

You can probably guess that problems may arise if sales, service or other business processes continue to send notification emails, and assign tasks and records to users who are no longer with your organization or using CRM! What kinds of problems?

Well, the *business* problems are the ones you'd expect: leads and cases are unlikely to be followed up on as promptly as they should be if they're assigned to somebody who's no longer with your organization!

However, the Dynamics CRM-specific *technical* problems are different than you might expect: in particular, disabling a user often has *no* impact on business processes that refer to that user. One of the main reasons for this is that in Dynamics CRM records can still be assigned to a disabled user. So, if a user is disabled in Dynamics CRM after leaving your organization, most business processes referring to that user will still run as they did before. This is a situation where you'd probably *want* those workflows to break. If they did, for example, the dashboards we examined in the previous section would be very valuable since you'd never be more than one click away from a view you could use to find and fix those broken business processes.

And it's important to note that this behavior is different in Dynamics CRM 2011 than it was in the 4.0 version, in which a workflow process would "break" if it tried to assign a record to a disabled user.

So, while disabling a user does not in itself cause processes referring to that user to fail, removing all security roles from a user will get the job done. That's the good news. The bad news is that workflows cannot manage security roles: there's no way in the process designer to associated users with security roles.

Building the Disabled User Process Workflow

With that as background information, let's see what we *can* do to manage the process of disabling users. What we want is an automatic workflow written for the user record type. When a user is disabled, it should send an email to a special queue for User Management, and it can cc a system administrator user. The email message should provide a link to the user's record and a reminder that all security roles should be removed.

However, as soon as you create the **Disabled User Process** workflow on the user entity and try to configure its properties, you notice another anomaly of the user record type: of the five **Start when** triggers available for most record types, only the **Record is created** and **Record fields change** triggers are available. As we've seen previously, there are no status records available in the **Record fields change** options, so our only option is the **Record is created** trigger.

At first that might not sound too promising, but there is an approach we can use: the first step of the workflow can be a **Wait Condition**, with the condition being **User:Status equals Disabled**. The following figure illustrates this workflow in the designer.

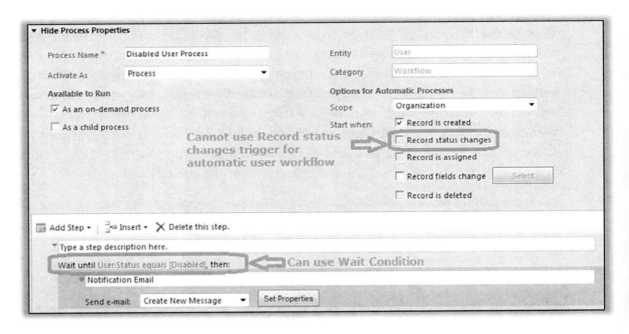

For this example, I configured the notification e-mail properties as illustrated in the following figure.

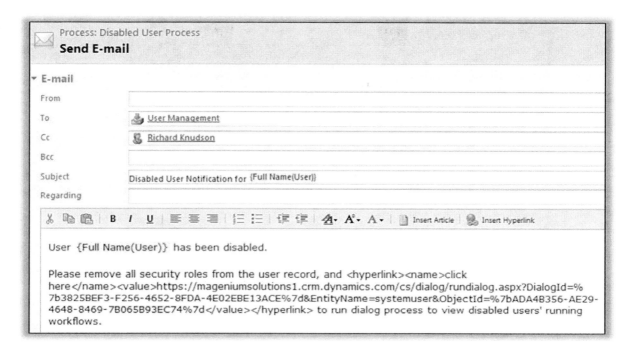

Notice that the workflow runs automatically when a user record is created. I also might expose a workflow like this for on-demand use, especially if you create the workflow process after having added users to your Dynamics CRM.

To understand how this works, let's walk through the user experience, step by step.

1. I'll start by selecting all users and running the workflow on an on-demand basis.

2. After clicking OK and waiting a few seconds, open a user record and click Workflows in left navigation. You'll see that it's running, with a Status Reason of **Waiting** as expected:

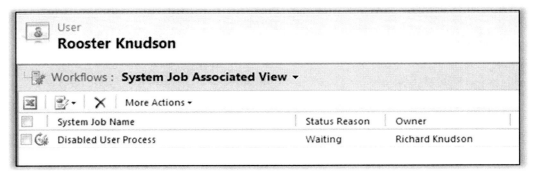

3. Then I'll disable that user, select the **Disabled Users** view, open the user's record and verify that the workflow now has a status reason of **Succeeded**.

4. I modified the Workflow Monitor Dashboard discussed in the previous section, by placing a list of **Disabled User Notification** emails on the top row.

5.   Finally, here's what the received email looks like.

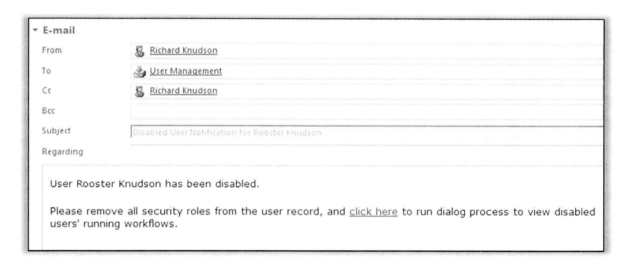

In case you wondered about the gnarly-looking content in the body of the email, now you might recognize it as yet another application of URL-addressable forms to launch a dialog process by its URL. To review, remember that the three components a dialog URL needs are the organization URL, the dialog GUID, and the GUID of the user calling the dialog. If you look closely, you can see these all in the following figure.

User {Full Name(User)} has been disabled.

Please remove all security roles from the user record, and <hyperlink><name>click here</name><value>https://mageniumsolutions1.crm.dynamics.com/cs/dialog/rundialog.aspx?DialogId=%7b3825BEF3-F256-4652-8FDA-4E02EBE13ACE%7d&EntityName=systemuser&ObjectId=%7bADA4B356-AE29-4648-8469-7B065B93EC74%7d</value></hyperlink> to run dialog process to view disabled users' running workflows.

I took advantage of the **Insert Hyperlink** feature, available in the workflow designer only when editing an e-mail activity record. Basically, everything between the <hyperlink> and </hyperlink> tags is inserted like this, after clicking the **Insert Hyperlink** button.

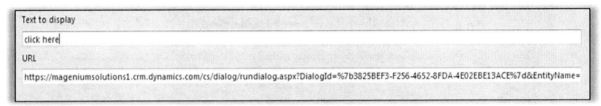

Text to display

click here

URL

https://mageniumsolutions1.crm.dynamics.com/cs/dialog/rundialog.aspx?DialogId=%7b3825BEF3-F256-8FDA-4E02EBE13ACE%7d&EntityName=

Building a Dialog Process to Check for a Disabled User's Processes

The dialog process itself is an interesting application of a number of techniques we've previously discussed, so let's have a quick look at what it does and how it works. The dialog process is written for the user entity, and is divided into four stages in the designer. The first two stages are shown here.

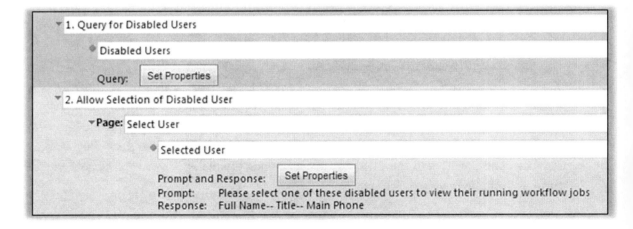

Stage 1 builds a query for all disabled users, and stage 2 uses a **Prompt and Response** to allow the user to select one of them.

The following figure show stages 3 and 4:

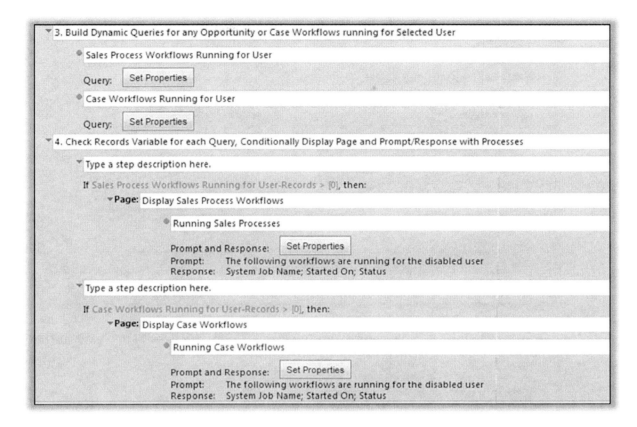

Stage 3 constructs two dynamic queries, using the Selected User from stage 2. Let's examine the first one of these to establish the pattern. When creating the new query, select System Jobs in the Look for drop-down, and filter for the familiar status reason values. Here, however, we only want to see running workflow processes that are regarding opportunity records.

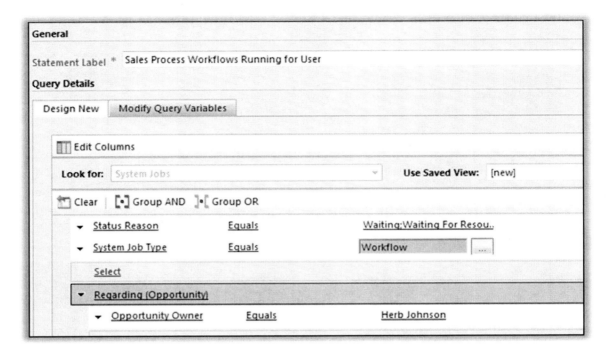

As we've seen before, we now need to use the Modify Query Variables UI to create custom FetchXML, as the following figure illustrates.

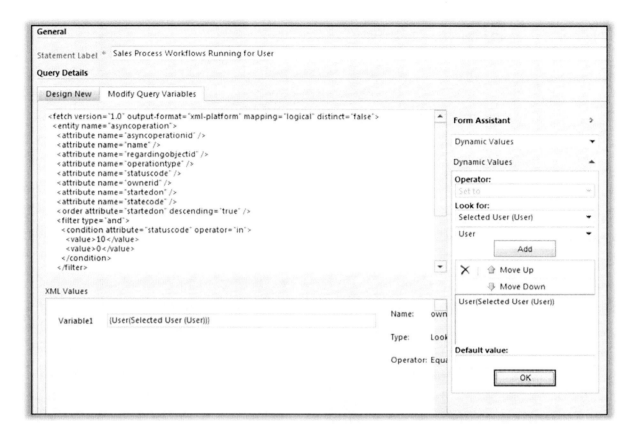

Remember what this is doing: a specific user must be supplied in the **Design New** tab, but in the **Modify Query Variables** tab you can use dynamic values to replace it with the **Selected User** variable created within the process.

The following two figures show the dialog process as it runs. The first one is Prompt and Response in stage 2, allowing the selection of a user from all disabled users.

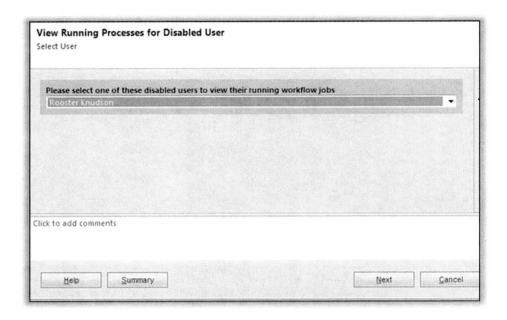

The next figure shows the dialog's Prompt and Response for running case workflows.

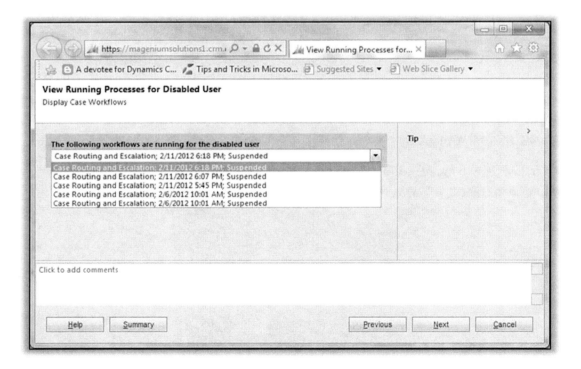

Remember that both the case and opportunity pages will appear only if there are running processes. So in this process, no news really *is* good news, since it means the disabled user has no running processes you need to worry about.

And unlike most of the other dialog processes we've seen, this one is purely informational. We don't do anything with the results other than to inform the system administrator whether the disabled user has some running processes or not.

Removing a Disabled User's Security Roles
Whatever else you do when a user is disabled, don't forget to do this. Again, the problem is that simply disabling a user does *not* mean that records cannot be assigned. So any processes that assign records to them will still work just fine, and in this situation that's not a good thing!

After removing my disabled user's security roles, suppose a case is created that would normally be assigned to that user. For example, in the service-level agreement workflow example in Chapter 6, a case created for an account with an SLA will be assigned to the service representative specified in the SLA.

A quick check of the **Workflow Monitor Dashboard** draws my attention to a single record.

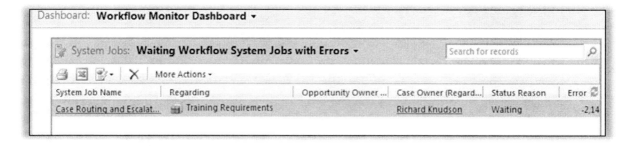

Clicking on the link in the **System Job Name** column reminds me what the problem is.

Now all I need to do is fix the Case Routing and Escalation workflow, and the fate of western civilization will be saved.

Summary

This chapter is something of a catch-all: topics I thought were too important not to include, but that didn't fit neatly anywhere else. The first two topics are techniques for using workflows to update otherwise read-only records. Most record types – accounts, contacts, leads, opportunities and so forth – can be updated by a workflow process even after they are closed. Activity records – appointments, tasks and so forth – cannot be updated even by a workflow in their closed state. But, they *can* be re-opened by a workflow, modified, and then closed out again.

Next we discussed some problems that often arise when users synch records from the Outlook client to Dynamics CRM, and how workflow processes can be used to solve them.

And no matter how careful you are in designing processes, you will inevitably encounter situations where things don't quite work as expected. This is the province of troubleshooting, and we discussed two of the most frequently encountered situations you will have to troubleshoot: when you need to change something external to the process, and when you need to change the process itself.

Two related topics – working with read-only and required fields – were reviewed next. We showed that under certain conditions, processes can update read-only fields and can create records without providing values for required fields. An important point in this regard is that process designer forms enforce the same restrictions as user forms. For example, after a read-only field is published, it's read-only both to interactive users and to the process designer. But running processes bypass forms when creating or modifying records, so they can be used to provide values in read-only fields (often desirable) as well as to create records with no values in required fields (usually not!).

Next we discussed two additional scenarios in which records can be created or modified without using interactive forms: data imports and bulk edits. Since automatic workflow triggers are applied at the database level, data imports and bulk edits can trigger automatic workflows, and it's important for the process designer to be aware of this.

The next section provided a detailed discussion of an important topic for administrators of large Dynamics CRM organizations with extensive use of business processes. The detailed discussion was about how to use advanced find queries, reports and dashboards to monitor workflow system jobs. The general point is to think of system jobs as "regular records". Then it's natural to apply the same querying, reporting and visualization tools to the challenge of monitoring workflows as you would to monitoring your sales pipeline.

The final section discussed the topic of user management, beginning with a review of some of the important differences – from the standpoint of workflows and dialogs – between user records and other record types. The rest of this section illustrated a specific issue in this area, the "disabled user scenario."

INDEX

CPSIA information can be obtained at www.ICGtesting.com
Printed in the USA
BVOW060648021112

304411BV00004B/3/P

9 780981 511849